AF784926

DIGITAL STRATEGIES IN THE PHARMACEUTICAL INDUSTRY

Digital Strategies

IN THE PHARMACEUTICAL INDUSTRY

Leonard Lerer

and

Mike Piper

palgrave
macmillan

© Leonard Lerer and Mike Piper 2003

All rights reserved. No reproduction, copy or transmission of this publication may be made without written permission.

No paragraph of this publication may be reproduced, copied or transmitted save with written permission or in accordance with the provisions of the Copyright, Designs and Patents Act 1988, or under the terms of any licence permitting limited copying issued by the Copyright Licensing Agency, 90 Tottenham Court Road, London W1T 4LP.

Any person who does any unauthorised act in relation to this publication may be liable to criminal prosecution and civil claims for damages.

The authors have asserted their right to be identified as the authors of this work in accordance with the Copyright, Designs and Patents Act 1988.

First published 2003 by
PALGRAVE MACMILLAN
Houndmills, Basingstoke, Hampshire RG21 6XS and
175 Fifth Avenue, New York, N.Y. 10010
Companies and representatives throughout the world

PALGRAVE MACMILLAN is the global academic imprint of the Palgrave Macmillan division of St. Martin's Press, LLC and of Palgrave Macmillan Ltd. Macmillan® is a registered trademark in the United States, United Kingdom and other countries. Palgrave is a registered trademark in the European Union and other countries.

ISBN 1–4039–0379–4 hardback

This book is printed on paper suitable for recycling and made from fully managed and sustained forest sources.

A catalogue record for this book is available from the British Library.

A catalog record for this book is available from the Library of Congress.

Editing and origination by Aardvark Editorial, Mendham, Suffolk

10 9 8 7 6 5 4 3 2 1
12 11 10 09 08 07 06 05 04 03

Printed and bound in Great Britain by
Creative Print & Design (Wales), Ebbw Vale

Contents

Part III
Digital Strategies: Manufacturing, Supply Chain and Distribution

Part IV
Digital Strategies: Marketing and Sales

List of figures

List of tables

Acknowledgements

The success of this endeavour is directly attributable to the pharmaceutical, medical device and biotechnology senior managers who have freely shared their experiences with us. Similarly, we thank all the vendors and consultants in the burgeoning field of 'e-pharma' for allowing us access to a wide range of materials.

Leonard Lerer wishes to recognize INSEAD, where he worked as a researcher and teacher. INSEAD eLab is thanked for providing a grant for research travel. Cap Gemini Ernst & Young supported research projects into life sciences e-business and customer relationship management and is thanked for an excellent collaboration.

We would like to thank Stephen Rutt of Palgrave Macmillan for his immediate enthusiasm and support for this project.

LEONARD LERER
leonard.lerer@lbsegment.com
MIKE PIPER
mike.piper@lbsegment.com

The authors and publishers wish to thank the following for their permission to use figures and tables: Advanstar Communications for Table 6.1; Boston Consulting Group for Figures 5.4 and 10.5; Cap Gemini Ernst & Young for Table 9.2 and Figures 4.1, 9.1, 9.7 and 12.1; Forrester Research for Table 6.2 and Figures 5.6, 5.7, 7.2, 9.3, 9.4, 10.2, 10.4 and 11.1; Harris Interactive for Table 11.1; IDC for Figure 5.2; Jupiter Media Metrix for Figure 10.3; the Medical Broadcasting Company for Table 10.3; PricewaterhouseCoopers for Figure 5.9; S. Rangan and R. Adner (INSEAD Working Papers) for Figure 12.4; Red Herring for Table 3.1; Rosetta Marketing Strategies for Figure 9.2; Brian Smith, Managing Editor and the *International Journal of Medical*

Marketing for sections of an article published by Leonard Lerer; and ZS Associates for Figures 9.5 and 10.6.

We have attempted to acknowledge all sources and trace the copyright holders when required, but in the rapidly evolving world of life sciences digital strategy we may have inadvertently overlooked some sources. Please inform us and we will attempt to make the required arrangements as soon as possible.

List of abbreviations

AMA	American Medical Association
API	application programming interface
B2B	business-to-business
B2C	business-to-consumer
CAD/CAM	computer-aided design/computer-aided manufacture
CAGR	compound annual growth rate
CME	continuing medical education
CRM	customer relationship management
CRO	contract research organization
CSC	customer service centre
CTM	clinical trial management
DTC	direct-to-consumer
DTP	direct-to-physician
EBM	evidence-based medicine
EC	European Commission
EDC	electronic data capture
EDI	electronic data interchange
EMR	electronic medical record
EPA	Environmental Protection Agency (US)
ERP	enterprise resource planning
ETMS	electronic territory management systems
FDA	Food and Drug Administration (US)
GDP	gross domestic product
GMP	good manufacturing practice
GPO	group purchasing organization
IP	intellectual property

MCO	managed care organization
NIH	National Institutes of Health (US)
OTC	over-the-counter
PRM	patient relationship management
P2P	peer-to-peer
PDA	personal digital assistant
R&D	research & development
ROI	return on investment
SFA	sales force automation
XML	eXtensible Markup Language

PART I

An Introduction to Pharmaceutical Digital Strategies

CHAPTER

1 Introduction

In less than a decade, it has been possible to witness digital technology[1] in the pharmaceutical industry traverse almost a full circle from the first tentative steps with sophisticated computing, websites and portals, the fears of competition and powerful intermediaries, the dotcom hype, the disillusionment of the dashed Internet dream and, more recently, the cautious exploration of new approaches and technologies such as e-R&D, e-detailing and CRM (customer relationship management). The astute observer will see many parallels between the pharmaceutical industry's relationship with digital technologies and its approach to biotechnology. In the early 1980s, when biotechnology began to show great promise, many pharmaceutical companies adopted a wait-and-see position. At that time, some experts predicted that biotechnology start-ups signalled the beginning of the end of the multinational pharmaceutical company. At the start of the twenty-first century, we find the global pharmaceutical industry still flourishing, some biotechnology giants and a myriad of smaller companies still dependent on mainstream pharmaceutical companies for financial support and the ultimate commercialization of their innovative products. During the dotcom boom, most pharmaceutical companies made tentative investments in establishing e-business structures, but no single organization committed itself to complete transformation into a virtual or e-driven company. For an industry as profitable and large as pharma-

1 For the purposes of this book, we use the term digital technology to describe the application of computing (both hardware and software) and Internet/intranet-related communications activity in health and healthcare. Our focus is largely on e-health; the interface between all the players in the health value chain (consumers, patients, physicians, payers, governments, insurers and providers of health-related products and services) and digital technologies (mainly the Internet).

ceuticals, even the limited interest in the Internet has been more than sufficient to fuel the growth of a burgeoning e-health industry, as technology providers, service companies, consultancies and a host of start-ups seek their slice of a multi-billion dollar research, development, sales and marketing pie. While the diffusion of Internet innovation into the pharmaceutical industry may have been patchy, literally thousands of conferences, publications, reports, magazines and even some empirical research have accompanied it.

Compared with other industries, pharmaceuticals (and healthcare as a whole) have been relatively slow to embrace the Internet. The reasons for this reticence are manifold, including the imperative to be cautious or conservative in an area as important as health and the absence of many of the drivers that contributed to the flowering of e-business in other sectors. Pharmaceutical companies entered the dotcom era with record profits and no tangible evidence that not embracing the Internet would constitute either a real threat or an important loss of competitive advantage. From a research and development viewpoint, the industry had already invested considerably in computing power. And pharmaceutical marketers remained confident that the Internet could never seriously undermine their key tool and major barrier to market entry, the legions of sales representatives and their personal relationships with physicians. Communicating with patients or consumers was touted as the next frontier in e-health and a limitless area of opportunity for pharmaceutical marketing. The reality was a modest Internet penetration in many countries and little opportunity to convert a near-insatiable demand for health information into sustainable selling relationships. The pharmaceutical industry has spent recent years critically appraising its first forays into the Internet. Many companies have closed down or are decentralizing their e-business units and writing off considerable investments in health portals and other initiatives. Clearly, new paradigms are required for an industry where there is a complexity of transactions (for example the customer of the pharmaceutical company is a physician, yet it is not the physician who actually purchases the prescribed drug) and it is against this backdrop that we explore the utility of developing and implementing a digital strategy. We hope to demonstrate a solid business case for investment in the Internet and avenues for optimal implementation and the generation of excellent return on investment.

In order to explore why a pharmaceutical company should invest in digital technologies, we need to develop a simple model of those attributes that are attractive and useful in the discovery and marketing of drugs. The Internet permits rapid personal (or preferably one-to-one) communication – this can either be very simple, as in the case of email or highly complex, as in the case of web-based interactive communication. The Internet, as a communications channel, facilitates a wide range of transactions ranging from information sharing to commercial exchange. At the most simplistic level, pharmaceutical companies already use the Internet for internal and external communications, promotion of products and a cornucopia of transactions. However, a combination of forces will, in the near future, cause companies to prioritize the Internet. These forces ostensibly lie well outside the scope of e-business and include unspectacular pipelines, critical media coverage, social and political pressures, patent expiries, new therapeutic technologies and changes in the economics of health and healthcare. There is a growing dissatisfaction with the cost and quality of service amongst the industry's customers, in particular payers and patients (or, as we should perhaps refer to them, consumers) [1]. The industry is faced with a need to both improve service and cut costs. Digital technology and the Internet are seen as the most likely enablers of this and, as a result, the pharmaceutical industry is belatedly entering the e-age.

No introduction to digital strategy in the pharmaceutical industry would be complete without some discussion of the economics of healthcare in the industrialized world. Irrespective of the reimbursement system used, there is widespread concern about the explosion in health-related expenditure, and economic, demographic and political pressures have complicated the healthcare resource allocation debate (see Figure 1.1). Healthcare is the largest sector of the US economy with annual spending of over $1 trillion. The industry accounts for one in every seven dollars spent in the US. Analysts believe that up to 25 per cent of this is wasted through inefficiency [2]. A

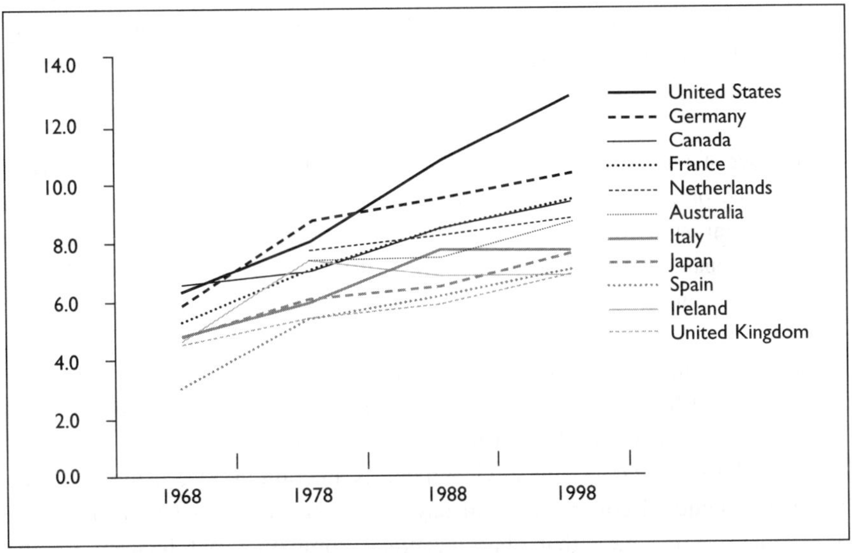

Figure 1.1 Expenditure on health as a percentage of GDP

Source: OECD Health Data

number of e-health enterprises, notably a company called WebMD, were premised upon the application of the Internet to facilitate rapid transaction processing in health cost reimbursement, thereby reducing some of this waste. The population of the industrialized world is steadily aging and, at the same time, medical treatment is becoming increasingly expensive. In the US, average prescription prices rose 10.5 per cent from 1999 to 2000 [3]. Although price controls in Europe are more rigorous, consumers are demanding innovative (and expensive) treatments. The role of the Internet in fuelling increasing prescription drug costs is controversial. Web-based information on new drugs does, to a limited extent, influence consumers, who then 'demand' these products from their physicians. In the US, concerns about healthcare costs have manifested in the rise of the managed care model. The role of managed care organizations (MCOs) is to control healthcare costs by limiting treatment choice to certain approved products and providers. MCOs have gone from providing less than 30 per cent of US drug payments in 1990 to about 60 per cent by 2000 [4]. Once again, the Internet is seen as a good way of managing the healthcare transaction, for example in informing physicians and pharmacists of the availability of lower cost generic drugs or better processing and analysing of reimbursement claims. For the burgeoning employment-based health insurance industry in the USA, the Internet has become an essential tool for allowing customers to manage their accounts and choose service packages. In Europe, cost concerns have led to the formation of additional regulatory bodies, such as the UK's National Institute for Clinical Excellence (NICE), which are primarily concerned with the cost-effectiveness of reimbursed treatments. Among the objectives of NICE is to

> improve standards of patient care … by establishing a process which will enable evidence of clinical and cost effectiveness to be brought together to inform a judgement on the value of the treatment relative to alternative uses of resources in the National Health Service [and] result in the issue of guidance on whether the treatment can be recommended for routine use in the NHS. – www.nice.org.uk

However, the latest evidence suggests that NICE is responsible for a net rise in government health spending, by giving the best innovative treatments a seal of approval that leads to their faster adoption in the clinic.

The pharmaco-economic environment is becoming increasingly hostile for pharmaceutical companies, and payers, be they insurers or governments, are critical of the case that pharmaceutical companies put forward for the reimbursement of expensive treatments that are often only marginally better than products currently on the market. The Internet offers new avenues for mobilizing patient interest groups and disseminating supporting evidence for pharmaceutical marketing.

The Internet, as a channel for communication with individuals, be they patients, their families or consumers interested in a lifestyle or 'wellness' product, permits pharmaceutical companies to interact with purchasing decision-makers more consistently and on a virtual face-to-face basis. A wealth of opportunities exists for Internet health, wellness and disease management programmes to build sustainable, trust-based relationships.

The penetration of such programmes is often limited by the fact that most people only wish to interact with health providers when they have a problem or a pressing concern. While some success has been achieved in establishing e-communities of chronic disease sufferers (such as diabetics or asthmatics), pharmaceutical companies have had mixed results with their dissemination of health and product information via sophisticated websites and portals. Traditionally, the pharmaceutical industry has been largely physician and product focused and has not devoted more than a small percentage of the total marketing budget to experiment with and implement large-scale marketing programmes aimed at individual consumers. Prescription drug marketing, heavily weighted towards the sales representative, remains the cornerstone of pharmaceutical companies' activities and while we have seen substantial advances in areas such as sales force automation (SFA), we are still far from fully Internet-based interactions.

However, in the medium term, technology (both digital and biotechnology) will change the way that physicians, consumers and payers interact, and pharmaceutical companies must actively shape their offerings or value propositions if they want to be in a position to take advantage of technological advances and changes in the way that healthcare will be delivered. A convergence of biology and digital technology will force healthcare to change from an industry that delivers largely the same service to every patient (notwithstanding differences in health coverage or the ability to pay) to an industry that provides an increasingly personalized service to each consumer, based on their preferences, needs and desires. Satisfying our needs, influenced by our individual genetic susceptibility to disease and response to treatments, will lead to what has been termed 'individualized medicine'. We contend that the delivery of this data-intensive personalized service will only be practical with, and will drive, the widespread adoption of digital technologies. We are on the threshold of major advances in medicine. Remote diagnostics, artificial intelligence and biomonitoring devices will allow us to manage many aspects of our health without the direct intervention of physicians. In our opinion, this is the real digital technology revolution, which offers the first tangible opportunity for a pharmaceutical company to deal directly with the end-consumer, the patient, and opens the door to innovative collaboration with physicians to ensure that customized therapeutic solutions can be created and delivered. Internet-based disease management packages will increasingly be bundled with specific treatment regimes to lock physicians and patients into a long-term relationship with a drug.

A digital technology strategy is simply not an area that any pharmaceutical company can afford to leave to others. Embracing the digital age requires extensive reflection on how the Internet can be used to support the pharmaceutical industry across the value chain and prepare for the inevitable opportunities in therapeutics and technology.

CHAPTER

2 Principles of pharmaceutical digital strategy

Information technology in pharmaceutical companies

Introduction

> The biotechnology and pharmaceutical industry is going through a significant change, and information technology (IT) will play a prominent role in supporting this transition. – Bruce Fadem, CIO and VP of American Home Products, 2001 [5]

The head of R&D of a large European pharmaceutical company described his first exposure to email, almost 20 years ago, as an 'incredible surprise'. He immediately saw the opportunities to run efficient, rapid, global clinical trials, for scientific information to be widely and easily disseminated and for truly collaborative research endeavours. Now, at the end of his distinguished career, he confided that he was astonished that he was seen as technologically backward, just because, when presented with the latest in web technology or e-R&D, he found it impossible to demonstrate the same excitement that he did when he saw the first electronic communication on a flickering monochrome screen. Maybe he did not, as his young collaborators kept saying, 'get it'. But his true belief in the role of digital technologies in the pharmaceutical industry was demonstrated when, following the dotcom crash, his enthusiasm and investment in Internet applications for R&D increased substantially.

Pharmaceutical companies have always been heavy users of digital technologies. The pharmaceutical value chain demands technological solutions for R&D, supply chain and enterprise resource planning, customer relationship management, financial control and knowledge sharing. The sheer size of a global pharmaceutical giant, having a huge headquarters and affiliates or market companies spread across the globe, makes it a fertile area for developing innovative information technology solutions. Being both resource rich and conservative has driven pharmaceutical companies to develop many of their systems in-house, a distinctly mixed blessing. Few open or industry standards allow proprietary applications to communicate with each other, a problem that becomes all too evident after each pharmaceutical mega-merger. Other factors slowing the adoption of innovative solutions are the need for strict regulatory compliance and a lack of vendor systems tailored for the industry. With some exceptions, mainly in the area of heavyweight computing power for research, pharmaceutical companies have not been a priority market for software and IT service vendors. The reasons for this include the fact that the pharmaceutical 'transaction' is fairly specialized and specific and has characteristics in terms of volume and stakeholders that require a complex service offering. According to a study conducted by the consultants at KPMG, pharmaceutical companies have moved into e-commerce more slowly than other industries, because they are less willing to take on increased profit volatility, create lower short-term revenues or alienate existing customers [6]. These are indeed realistic concerns. We will, for example, explore in depth the implications of e-marketing for the intensely personal relationship between sales representatives and physicians; pharmaceutical companies, unlike banks, cannot virtually overnight move their customer interactions onto the Internet.

It is estimated that large pharmaceutical companies are currently spending between 0.5 per cent and 1 per cent of sales on e-business initiatives [7]. In a forecast analysis, the research house Gartner predicts that US pharmaceutical companies' IT spending will increase at a CAGR (compound annual growth rate) of 12.8 per cent from $3 billion in 2000 to more than $5.5 billion by

Genentech was one of the first biotechnology companies to create human pharmaceuticals using recombinant DNA technology. Information technology is a vital component in most of the company's operations. Genentech makes IT investments at every major step in the value chain:

- Clinical trial and patient records (data management). Particularly important is the automation of medical record systems. 'It's a gigantic paper system now, both for the healthcare or reimbursement side and for companies like ours with clinical trials,' says Polly Moore, Vice President of

continued from previous page

Information Resources. 'Lots of different parties would find life much easier if there were a standard and if it moved from paper to automation. It's a huge undertaking, but over probably the next ten years, it's going to be solved.'

- Manufacturing and supply chain. This is also undergoing a move from paper-based to automated management of production documentation. 'We have a large project going on right now to put in new systems in manufacturing that will enable us eventually to do what are called "electronic batch records",' Ms Moore says. 'This is an area of the company that is traditionally fairly conservative because, of course, it's highly regulated.'
- Global partnering for research development, marketing and sales. Collaborative R&D and marketing on a worldwide basis have been dramatically improved through the use of IT. 'Many of our projects now are done with partner companies all over the world, and by far the best way to stay in touch is electronically,' Ms Moore says. 'You find yourself developing tools that will enable that kind of global, co-ordinated product development in a safe and secure way.'
- Sales and marketing. Some of the most immediate returns on IT investment have been in sales and marketing applications. The company has a sales force of about 400 in the US. To support it, the company has replaced a system of ad hoc emails and Federal Express deliveries with an intranet that has reduced shipping and printing costs [9].

2005. Gartner forecasts that spending on software and external services will outpace spending for hardware, network equipment and internal services [8].

Pharmaceutical companies spend up to about 5 per cent of annual revenues on IT products and services. An approximately $15 billion budget across the industry is large enough to warrant a place for an information technology VP on most boards who manages a large number of employees across the world (Table 2.1). Companies spend their IT budgets on new product and technology purchases (18 per cent), consulting and outsourcing (18 per cent), research and development (4 per cent), salaries and benefits (36 per cent), applications (10 per cent) and other expenses (14 per cent) [5]. The sheer size of IT infrastructure in pharmaceutical giants makes post-merger integration a major challenge. GlaxoSmithKline (GSK) spent nearly £3 million linking up its

TABLE 2.1

IT employees by pharmaceutical company (2001)

Company	Number of IT employees	Total number of employees	% of employees in IT
Abbott Laboratories	5,000	71,000	7
American Home Products	2,475	48,000	5
AstraZeneca	3,380	55,000	6
Bristol-Myers Squibb	2,010	44,000	5
Eli Lilly	2,589	36,000	7
GlaxoSmithKline	6,000	100,000	6
Pfizer	3,182	90,000	4

Source: [5], Hoovers.com

IT systems in the 100 days after the merger of GlaxoWellcome and SmithKlineBeecham. However, it will take almost four years before basic systems such as email are standardized across its 100,000 staff. A GSK spokesman claimed that for such a knowledge-intensive business, the potential losses could have been as high as £1 million per day if, for example, the email system had failed. The key concern in those first 100 days was the integration of research and development applications [10].

The Internet age has brought with it a speed and transparency that challenges current regulatory paradigms and results in increased scrutiny from the US Food and Drug Administration (FDA), medical authorities and consumers. It is estimated that biotechnology and pharmaceutical companies spend as much as 40 per cent of their IT budgets to manage compliance among their various IT systems, run by manufacturing, research and development and retail business units. Many companies are wrestling with new FDA guidelines for electronic records. FDA Regulation 21 CFR Part 11, for example, calls for the management of digital signatures and traceability of electronic records. While the law has been on the books since 1997, the FDA has increased attention on it now that the industry no longer has to worry about Y2K compliance work. A 2001 report estimated that biotechnology and pharmaceutical companies would spend $100 million to $250 million to make sure their electronic records were properly secured in compliance with that single regulation [5].

Leading the IT transformation

Pharmaceutical manufacturers are certainly prioritizing IT decision-making in terms of both the level at which corporate decisions are being taken and the speed of implementation, as they seek ways whereby information systems can add to operational effectiveness throughout the company [11]. Companies are now aware of the need for integrated IT and e-business solutions across the value chain. In e-commerce, the difficulty lies in determining whether to partner with a specialist provider or to do the implementation internally. For example, some pharmaceutical companies are partnering with existing health information providers on the web to reach consumers, while some rely on company web pages. Another example is the increase in the number of Internet companies that offer e-clinical trial services and end-to-end integration of the supply chain. If a company decides to partner with an existing online company, there is then the question: with whom to partner? Most are attempting to develop new systems and integrate them with legacy systems using a mix of reputable vendors:

- AstraZeneca Pharmaceuticals faced the task of integrating its IT operations, and building systems that would let its 40,000 worldwide employees operate as a single, global company. Depending on their location, systems ran on Windows 95, 98, or NT 4.x Workstations, and networks ran on various Novell NetWare versions or Windows NT Servers. The Swiss operation used SAP R/3 as its enterprise resource planning (ERP) system. The UK and US operations ran a custom-built ERP system and two versions of PeopleSoft applications, as well as a range of custom and package specialty applications designed for the pharmaceutical industry. AstraZeneca has standardized on SAP R/3 for finance, human resources, legal and manufacturing operations. The company also provided its sales personnel with sales force automation and customer relationship management (CRM) tools custom-built to run on the Oracle database [11].
- AstraZeneca outsourced its information technology services to IBM on a seven-year contract worth $1.7 billion in a drive to cut costs and improve performance. The move enabled AstraZeneca to sharpen its focus on strategic opportunities such as e-business and informatics in R&D. IBM works with other drug companies, such as Aventis, in the same area [12].
- Bristol-Myers Squibb deployed SAP R/3 worldwide in 2001, except in Asia and South America. The company also consolidated strategic purchasing at the business level using Ariba Inc. procurement tools integrated with SAP, resulting in millions of dollars worth of savings. The CIO stated that when the company wanted to order new PCs, instead of each

department of each division ordering their own, the company consolidated the purchase. The company demanded deep discounts on the large purchase and got them. For basic supplies, most of the company's 25,000 US and 55,000 worldwide employees order from their desktop via a portal based on Plumtree Software Inc.'s enterprise portal product and Ariba procurement. Orders are handled centrally and routed to the contract source for each item. Plumtree's portal also lets the company put its human resources operation online, permitting employees to track and modify their benefits and retirement plans [11].

Promoting digital innovation in the pharmaceutical industry

Faced with the rapid evolution of e-business, pharmaceutical companies have grappled with how to diffuse digital innovation into an industry that has a reputation for being extremely conservative and slow to change. As we discussed in the introductory chapter, the technology boom occurred at a time when the pharmaceutical manufacturers were earning record profits and many executives saw little point in changing a winning business model. On the other hand, senior managers were keen to leverage the Internet as a channel for communicating with and selling to physicians and consumers and did not want to be left behind on the e-wave. Following a fashion that started in the then well-capitalized technology industry, some pharmaceutical giants set up venture capital arms to invest in e-business and digital technologies, while others set aside small budgets for pilot projects:

- Merck & Co., Inc. formed a new subsidiary, Merck Capital Ventures, to invest up to $100 million in capital in private Internet and other emerging businesses focused in areas related to the commercialization, distribution and delivery of pharmaceuticals and related healthcare services. The goal was to build a venture capital portfolio of promising emerging companies that could bring added capabilities to Merck's and Merck-Medco's core businesses and provide attractive long-term investment returns [13, 14].
- Eli Lilly formed the e-Lilly venture fund, which uses Lilly's pharmaceutical expertise and financing capabilities to transform novel business ideas into successful companies. The initial investment fund was $50 million. The investments were selected on their ability to help Lilly reduce the risk and increase the productivity of research and development, reduce the cost and increase the speed of clinical trials and increase sales of Lilly brands through more intimate customer relationships [15].

The jury is still out as to whether the venture capital approach is the best avenue for diffusing innovation into a pharma behemoth. We also need to consider the message that the venture capital approach sends to internal IT stakeholders, namely that innovation is not nurtured within and has to be bought at a high premium.

Conclusions – 'the take home messages'

Pharmaceutical companies have delivered excellent investment returns and senior managers operate within a resource-rich environment. In some senses, this is the 'curse of plenty' where it is difficult to imagine, plan and implement for a far harsher and cruelly competitive future. Today's pharmaceutical giants are structured to develop and deliver blockbuster products to a largely homogeneous customer population. It is arguable whether mega-mergers, where the primary aims are scale in R&D and cost cutting, will give birth to the companies best adapted to the changing healthcare environment. Large companies have an enormous inertia that makes them resistant to change. Success demands best-of-breed competencies at all stages in an increasingly complex value chain. Some would claim that the future will see the competitive advantage passing from monolithic pharma giants (who may control their value chain, but lack agility) to alliances of smaller, more agile, best-of-breed partners (such as a target identification and validation boutique, a combinatorial chemistry boutique, a contract research organization (CRO), a contract manufacturer and a contract sales organization (CSO)). Here, the individual partners would self-select on the basis of their ability to develop the best service for a particular customer segment. This model is fraught with pitfalls, as each component may be prone to the very problems of inertia and loss of market sensitivity that 'unbundling' was supposed to overcome.

Perhaps, in the near future, we will see pharmaceutical companies looking not much different from today, but a lot 'leaner' in terms of personnel head-counts [1]. We foresee a far greater place for the digital strategy, e-business and the Internet in the pharmaceutical company of the near future. While many applications are specific to components of the pharmaceutical value chain, such as e-clinical trials in drug development and e-CRM in sales and marketing, it is more than reasonable to expect that digital technologies, in the light of the speed, efficiency and transparency which they offer, will be increasingly applied to save money and improve customer service, be those customers internal or external.

- Despite the vagaries of the technology sector in the financial markets, pharmaceutical and biotechnology companies are committed to substantial investment in digital technologies.
- Pharmaceutical companies no longer have the luxury of being able to build expensive, customized IT solutions. Open and global standards are now mandatory.
- IT innovation must be nurtured internally; thinking and strategy cannot be outsourced. However, external service providers can indeed better manage many of the operational aspects of digital technology.
- Digital technologies can be applied as a cost-saving tool, and this will increase in importance as the pharmaceutical industry faces pressure to cut product prices. From drug discovery, to clinical trials, to physician detailing, the Internet will begin to play a pivotal role in day-to-day business.

The dynamics of the health sector – implications for digital strategy

Introduction

The healthcare industry is highly fragmented and, as it has few common data standards, remains paper intensive. The US healthcare industry (that is, providers and payers) allocates about two to three per cent of its budget to IT, as compared with five to ten per cent for other industries such as retail and financial services [2]. The healthcare industry has been a slow adopter of IT for several reasons, amongst them a conservative culture, a shortage of resources, few open standards and privacy concerns. In the US, physicians are directly or indirectly involved in about 80 per cent of all healthcare spending [2]. Nearly half of the 600,000 physicians in the US work in practices of one or two doctors, and many of these practices have neither the resources nor the expertise to form a seamless IT network with laboratories, drug manufacturers, insurers and hospitals. Hospitals are more likely to spend their limited budget on medical equipment than on IT systems where the return on investment may not be immediately apparent. In the absence of any economic drivers for IT innovation, physicians are perfectly happy to let other staff perform low-level administration such as transcribing their notes [2] (Figure 2.1).

This resistance to the adoption of IT innovation within the healthcare sector came as a surprise to many technology vendors. Why would physicians,

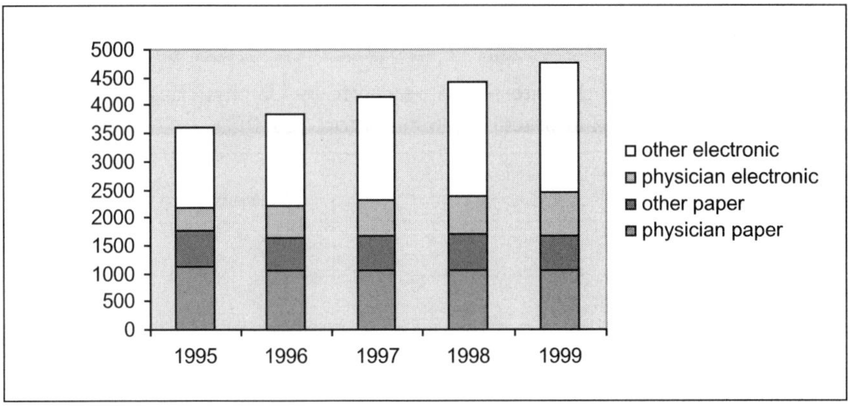

Figure 2.1 Management of US health claims (millions)

Source: [2]

who are the first to use the latest medical devices, from sophisticated scanners to robotic surgery, be so resistant to IT? Similarly, as healthcare is a data-intensive industry (physicians share data with other physicians, hospitals, laboratories, pharmacies, payers/insurers and sometimes even patients), surely everybody would be amenable to more efficient, rapid channels of communication? As George Lundberg, editor in chief of electronic medical record (EMR) provider Medicalogic observed: 'The problem is doctors are very smart, and they're only going to use stuff that will actually help them – they're not going to waste time' [2]. The early e-health vendors arguably made an important mistake – they designed systems without considering how doctors think, work and interact with patients. Given the time and resource pressures that physicians face, this was a critical error. For instance, most US doctors are not reimbursed for talking to patients on the telephone or emailing them, so when a doctor has to communicate with a patient they will use the telephone, as it takes less time. We are undoubtedly seeing a transition in physician attitudes towards Internet-based technologies with information provision and e-prescribing at the vanguard (see Table 2.2). Priority must be given to applications that make the day-to-day jobs of physicians easier. Recently qualified doctors are likely to be far more IT literate and well-thought through applications are likely to appeal to them. It is important to note that when economic incentives and sheer practical ease-of-use supervene, physicians are indeed rapid adopters of digital technologies.

Examples of Internet-based offerings that are increasingly finding favour in the medical community are:

TABLE 2.2

Utility of the Internet as perceived by US physicians and practice administrators (2000)

Respondents who said the Internet is useful for the following (%):	Physicians	Administrators
Providing patient education	25	36
Purchasing products, services	10	23
Obtaining or transferring medical records	10	18
Processing health insurance claims	10	15

Source: [2]

- Carefully screened online medical content and search engines (obviously, to be popular these have to be easier and quicker to use and more comprehensive than standard medical reference works). Ninety per cent of US Internet-using doctors research clinical information online and 78 per cent of doctors read journal articles online [16].
- Handheld devices or personal digital assistants (PDAs) that allow doctors to input patient details, and write and screen prescriptions for possible adverse combinations with other drugs. For example, Allscripts leases wireless PDAs to doctors, giving access to patient records and allowing them to write e-prescriptions.

Standards and the Health Insurance Portability and Accountability Act (HIPAA)

The US government is attempting to overhaul the healthcare industry's outdated administrative practices and introduce open data standards through the Health Insurance Portability and Accountability Act of 1996 (HIPAA), but this is proving to be a difficult task. HIPAA mandates that, over eight years, Internet-based storage and transfer of patient data be standardized, secure and subject to rigorous privacy rules. However, implementation of the act has been slow. Faced with the formidable logistical and administrative task of transforming medical record keeping, many hospitals, physician practices and even some health insurers are adopting a policy of prudent avoidance, in the hope that legislation will be relaxed. The US government estimates it will cost $4 billion to implement the reforms, and unsurprisingly the healthcare industry says the figure will be far higher – in the range of $15 billion. The industry fears a repeat of the Y2K scenario, where it spent about $6.6 billion on consultants. However, it is estimated that HIPAA-related efficiency savings could amount to $3.6 billion annually, and data exchange could be done on a secure website rather than dedicated phone lines [2]. Compliance with the first parts of the Act (standards for electronic transactions) is mandatory from October 2002 (delayed from 2001), although entities that feel they cannot comply may apply for an additional year's extension, providing they submit a concise plan detailing how they will meet the revised deadline. Other parts of the plan (for example standards for identification of providers and employers, electronic signatures, privacy and claims) are due to follow over several years. The HIPAA controversy is in many senses paradigmatic of the debate around digital technology in the health sector, as many of the stakeholders see little immediate use in adopting advances in IT, when transactions remain complex and paper-based. In many senses, we see the repetition of the early history of e-health, where integrators, whose main offering was efficient transactions, failed to develop an attractive business case.

European perspectives

The European Union (EU), characterized by various forms of social health insurance (Table 2.3), does not have the same 'transactional intensity' in its health delivery system, as does the USA. The relatively small number of insurers or final payers has ensured that fairly standardized reimbursement systems with varying levels of IT complexity are in place. However, in the light of recent court decisions and a movement to permit patients to be able to seek care in an EU country of their choice (other than their home country), we are starting to see an increasing interest in standardizing pan-European reimbursement procedures. Similarly, we are seeing initiatives to create a single European medical record standard and growing action on Internet health and privacy issues. For pharmaceutical companies, the introduction of the euro has resulted in a transparency in pricing policy and unrelenting cost-containment pressures can be expected.

Global health systems – implications for IT

While the quality of health systems and their financial stability varies considerably across the globe, the influence of the Internet is becoming pervasive. For example, satellites are being used to transmit health information and provide telemedicine services to remote African hospitals and organizations such as the World Bank are actively supporting electronic patient record

TABLE 2.3

Summary of the healthcare systems in six European countries (2002)

Country	Model	Funding	Reimbursement	Opt out or supplemental private care?	Gatekeeper?	% of GDP spent on healthcare (2001)	% of healthcare paid for by public sector (2001)
France	Social insurance	Compulsory, ring-fenced social insurance premiums topped up by mutual funds	Payment generally made at point of care	Supplemental	No	9.6	76
Germany	Mandatory insurance	90 per cent of population covered by statutory government fund	Largely free at point of care	Both – only those whose salary is above a certain threshold may opt out	No	10.6	75
Italy	National health service (SNN)	Taxation	Largely free at point of care, increasing co-payments, for example, for drugs	Supplemental	Yes	8.4	68

Netherlands	Mandatory insurance	Compulsory public or private insurance funds	Minimal co-payments at point of care	Compulsory opt out for top 40 per cent of earners	Yes	8.6	70
Spain	National health service (INSALUD)	Taxation	Largely free at point of care	Largely supplemental, only government employees may opt out	Yes	7.1	77
UK	National health service (NHS)	Taxation	Largely free at point of care	Supplemental	Yes	6.7	84

Source: OECD data

projects in less-developed countries. Digital technology is seen as a way of 'leapfrogging' ahead in terms of biomedical innovation, especially as fairly simple approaches, such as email and voice-over IP, permit communication between researchers, experts and practitioners. Some pharmaceutical companies have recognized that the Internet provides an excellent channel for communicating with practitioners in countries where sales representative coverage may be limited. Physicians appreciate the contact and often need the information provided. As more households access the Internet, interest in innovative pharmaceutical products is sure to increase, irrespective of whether the drug is marketed or available in a certain country.

Privacy

Health is a delicate and acutely personal issue and hence privacy will remain a vital concern, especially as it pertains to the ultimate customer – the patient or consumer. There is considerable controversy concerning the collection and application of information collected when consumers use health-related websites. A wide range of privacy initiatives, sponsored by industry, consumer organizations, the EU and professional organizations are currently underway. It is not only consumers who are concerned by privacy issues, as physicians may also be reluctant to increase access to information about their online behaviour and prescribing practices. HIPAA rules stipulate that any data that can be used to identify a patient can only be released with the patient's consent, and the patient has the right to correct their data. Nineteen types of data must be removed or concealed before the record is no longer considered a threat to privacy. Providers must also maintain a clear audit trail for the data [2]. The USA, with its complex and transaction-intensive health system, provides a range of exciting opportunities for technological approaches to privacy protection.

Conclusions – 'the take home messages'

A recent report by the US Institute of Medicine recommends that 'private and public purchasers, healthcare organizations, clinicians and patients should work together to redesign healthcare processes in accordance with the following rules':

- *Care based on continuous healing relationships.* Patients should receive care where they need it and in many forms, not just face-to-face visits. This rule implies that the healthcare system should be responsive at all times (24 hours a day, every day).

- *Customization based on patients' needs and values.* The system of care should be designed to meet the most common types of needs, but should have the capability to respond to the needs of individual patients.
- *The patient as the source of control.* Patients should be given the necessary information and the opportunity to exercise the degree of control they choose over healthcare decisions.
- *Shared knowledge and the free flow of information.* Patients should have unfettered access to their own medical records and clinical knowledge. Clinicians and patients should communicate effectively and share information.
- *Evidence-based decision-making.* Patients should receive care based on the best available scientific knowledge. Care should not vary illogically from clinician to clinician or from place to place.
- *Safety as a system property.* Patients should be safe from injury caused by the care system. Reducing risk and increasing safety requires greater attention to systems that help prevent and mitigate errors.
- *The need for transparency.* The healthcare system should make information available to patients and their families that allows them to make informed decisions when selecting a health plan. [17]

While some of these goals may seem in the realm of aspiration, in the short term at least, they do have important implications for the future of digital strategy, and offer promising avenues for enhancing interactions between the pharmaceutical industry and its manifold customers. For example, the seamless, rapid, immediate and automatic transfer of data between all players in the healthcare system will impact across the pharmaceutical value chain, from more efficient clinical trials to better relationships with patients in areas such as disease management and compliance. Better managed medical records will allow easier recruitment of patients with specific conditions into clinical trials and permit easier long-term follow-up. On the other hand, the rapid access and analysis of outcomes data will promote evidence-based medicine (EBM) and a resultant 'shake-out' in terms of non-performing medications and it will be easier to make decisions as to the cost-benefit implications of new therapies.

- The slow but inevitable transformation of health systems in industrialized countries will place an increasing emphasis on IT. The electronic medical record (EMR), e-prescribing and seamless communication between providers, insurers, payers and ultimately consumers is being driven by the need to contain healthcare costs.

- The physician is slowly but surely being drawn into the web of digital innovation, and pharmaceutical companies that can ameliorate daily practice, deal with privacy and safety concerns and provide innovative solutions have the opportunity to use the Internet as a channel for building relationships with prescribers.
- A large number of stakeholders exist at the interface between digital technology and health systems, ranging from consumer groups to large technology companies (medical device and IT). It is difficult to identify the winner in terms of system standardization, but there is increasing pressure to ensure that information can be seamlessly shared between all the players in health and healthcare.

CHAPTER 3

A decade of digital strategy in the pharmaceutical industry

Introduction

The Internet became an issue of interest to pharmaceutical companies in the early 1990s. At the time, excitement was very much focused on what e-commerce and the Internet could do for healthcare delivery (as opposed to the development and sale of pharmaceuticals or medical devices). The concept of the 'health portal', a one-stop site where the user could obtain information, communicate and transact, came to the fore. This was a seductive idea in that the health portal was supposed to facilitate the smooth running of the healthcare system, by providing a system for electronic transactions that would otherwise be performed through paper-based systems, and also offer a single central resource of healthcare-related information (for example health advice for consumers or the latest prescription guidelines for doctors). Companies such as Healtheon/WebMD (co-founded by Netscape pioneer Jim Clark) claimed that the Internet would streamline and standardize communications between physicians, hospitals, insurers, pharmacies, laboratories and patients. The benefits included a reduction in administrative expenses and an increase in customer satisfaction and the quality of care. No longer would a secretary at a local physician's office type up a claim and fax it to an insurance company, where another secretary would re-enter it into their proprietary system; prescriptions would be filled over the Internet and centrally held medical records updated automatically.

The dotcom bubble bursts

The pharmaceutical industry did not fully participate in the phenomenon now described as the technology boom of the late 1990s. We have elucidated some of the reasons for the industry's reticence to embrace the Internet, including an innate conservatism, formidable regulatory constraints and a lack of conviction as to the use of the dotcom model in the relationship-intensive world of pharmaceutical marketing. Notwithstanding these constraints, many senior pharmaceutical executives were indeed extremely interested in the evolution of e-health and this resulted in a mini-boom for consultants and advisers who struggled to formulate the ideal digital strategy for the pharmaceutical giants. At the same time, healthcare was becoming an important component of the dotcom phenomenon.

E-health companies grossly underestimated the complexity and technological inefficiency of the healthcare industry – this is an industry that is heavily regulated, resistant to change and sometimes not driven by either the efficiency or the profit motive. Health portals, connectivity providers and a burgeoning e-health industry have been relentless in trumpeting their message to the global pharmaceutical sector – 'if you do not embrace the Internet, you will be left behind and your interaction with your customers will be mediated by others'. The message of doom has largely fallen on deaf ears. The Internet has certainly not offered any easy solutions when it comes to reaching physicians with a pharmaceutical company's marketing messages. Physicians, already overloaded with information, often see the Internet as yet another competitor for their precious time. Some specialist portals have found that physicians mainly visit their sites to use the leisure offerings that they provide, rather than to seek medical data. As a consequence, physician marketing has been slow to migrate onto the Internet, much to the disappointment of a swarm of start-ups eager for a slice of the huge pharmaceutical marketing pie. Indeed, the large pharmaceutical companies have been employing more, rather than fewer, sales representatives in the knowledge that it is face-to-face contact with physicians that provides the most certain route towards higher drug sales. The Internet also has no easy solution for marketing to patients. Pharmaceutical companies have been quick to register domain names for their drugs and build websites to support marketing in countries where direct-to-consumer (DTC) advertising of prescription drugs is permitted. While these websites may offer slick graphics and leading-edge web design, they are often not more helpful than the stacks of brochures littering every doctor's waiting room. Pharmaceutical executives, always aware of regulatory boundaries, are constrained when exploring e-health's potential to improve patient outcomes.

Large pharmaceutical companies are devoting a very small proportion of their overall marketing budget to the Internet. The less than three per cent of total marketing spend invested in websites and health portals can certainly not be construed as an inexorable commitment by the pharmaceutical industry to becoming e-enabled or virtual. The typical pharmaceutical giant's attitude towards health portals was: 'Which of the hundred horses in the e-health race should we back?' The reason for this hands-off approach is reasonably easy to discern. While WebMD, DrKoop and their thousands of emulators did not offer a compelling and credible solution for patients and their doctors, initially they were the only option for a pharmaceutical company to reach an Internet audience, however small. Consequently, the ten largest global pharmaceutical companies became sponsors, somewhat reluctantly, of hundreds of websites and health portals and even a couple of Internet service providers (ISPs). In order to attract consumers to their sites, health portals undertook expensive advertising campaigns to spread the message that, in a world where physicians have little time or interest in informing their patients, the Internet provides an answer to consumer health concerns. Consumer health sites implicitly justified their offering as a substitute for a physical interaction with a healthcare provider. By promoting business models based on driving a wedge through the doctor–patient relationship, health websites risked alienating physicians. Health websites broadcasting 'anti-physician' messages are not in patients' long-term interests as well as being counterproductive for the pharmaceutical companies that sponsor them.

By the late 1990s, medical information on the Internet had become a plentiful commodity and consumers were faced with a tidal wave of complex, confusing and sometimes contradictory data. Health websites have the challenge of providing customized, relevant information to people with a myriad of health needs and concerns. In order to develop a 'one-size-fits-all' mass-market solution that would be attractive to a pharmaceutical sponsor, many portals veered towards providing shallow, impractical health advice that is largely irrelevant to second-time visitors. The latest medical news gives the impression of fresh content and encourages repeat visits. But how does this help patients when practical therapies lag behind medical breakthroughs by a number of years? The trumpeting of promising, but untested treatments pushed many health sites into an ethical grey area, creating distrust between patients and their physicians. A fleeting, worry-driven interaction with a health website does not provide pharmaceutical companies with the opportunity to pursue sustainable, deep relationships with consumers. Instead of continuing to fuel the myth of an 'informed and empowered' health consumer, the e-health industry should have a priori focused on delivering its promise of creating a seamless interface between consumers, physicians and pharmaceutical companies.

The history of WebMD

Founded in 1996, WebMD's goal was to make the healthcare industry run smoothly by offering a network of services that would turn nearly every piece of paper generated by a healthcare system into an electronic transaction. It soon realized that to do this it would need to offer a wide range of services to all the players in the healthcare system, so it went on an aquisition spree costing billions of dollars, buying capabilities in electronic data interchange (EDI), physician practice management and web content delivery. However, combining these capabilities into an integrated package and persuading conservative healthcare providers to subscribe and adopt these protocols proved more tricky.

WebMD earns the majority of its revenue by charging a commission (typically about 35 cents) on every transaction made over its network. Other revenue streams include subscription by physicians to the WebMD portal and sponsorships.

WebMD promised to make a profit in 2001, but was still making a significant net loss ($30 million loss on revenues of $196 million) in the first quarter of 2002, despite cutting 1500 staff and purchasing physician portal Medscape in an attempt to broaden its appeal to physicians. Jim Clark, the founder of Netscape, quit the WebMD board in October 2000, stating that e-health was not a market he would ever enter again. He argued that the complexity of the healthcare industry made it difficult to offer the simple e-solutions necessary for a viable business model [7].

E-health in Europe

While some European countries, especially in Scandinavia, have attained high levels of Internet connectivity, it has not been an easy market for e-health companies. The different systems for healthcare delivery, reimbursement and cost control and a diversity of language and culture make it difficult to develop a pan-European offering. Also, medical advertising, both to physicians and consumers, is severely restricted, minimizing one potential revenue stream. In fact, with the exception of some chronic diseases, it seems that DTC advertising of prescription drugs will, for the

TABLE 3.1

Hurdles to e-health, pan-European expansion

Content	Cultural differences
	EU restrictions on commercial drug advertising
E-commerce	EU restrictions on commercial drug advertising
	Differences in reimbursement protocols
	Paper-bound national health systems
Connecting payers, providers and consumers	Cultural differences
	Paper-bound national health systems

Source: [2]

foreseeable future at least, not be permitted in Europe. While the opportunities for using the Internet in commercial transactions for healthcare delivery may be limited, we need to be aware that private healthcare is growing, albeit from a small base in Europe. Similarly, opportunities exist in areas such as wholesaling and drug distribution. For example, the Global Healthcare Exchange (GHX), initially a business-to-business (B2B) initiative of the major medical device manufacturers, is actively exploring e-based pharmaceutical distribution and Alliance Unichem, one of Europe's biggest pharmaceutical distributors, has spent £20 million on a B2B exchange for drug manufacturers and pharmacists.

Conclusions – 'the take home messages'

Although none of the first generation of e-health sites was as successful as envisioned, a number of key lessons were learned. Consumers turned out to be a lot more mature in their interaction with health websites than the developers initially envisaged. Health site users wanted specific questions answered, but were not prepared to surrender privacy for service. A study conducted in 2000 found that much of the supposedly private data entered onto some e-health sites could be accessed by third parties such as Internet advertising companies. The flaws in the privacy policies fell into four major categories:

1. Misrepresentation – users who signed up to a newsletter were giving their email address to a third party, contrary to a written policy.

2. Advertisements from third parties that are all but indistinguishable from editorial, allowing the third party to track the user's movement across the site and gain access to any entered information.

3. Unclear policies – few privacy policies stated exactly what data was collected and how it would be used.

4. Accidental leakage of personal data.

DrKoop, a leading US consumer health portal, came under severe criticism for its ethics policy when a supposedly impartial list of 'the 14 most innovative and advanced healthcare institutions in the country' turned out to be a paid advertisement for the featured hospitals, each hospital having paid $40,000 to be on the list [18]. DrKoop filed for bankruptcy protection in December 2001.

A range of global initiatives began some years ago to protect consumers by legislation and self-regulation and we discuss these in Chapter 10. The short history of e-health seems to indicate that while a fringe of dubious and sometimes dangerous promotion of health-related products and services does exist on the Internet, consumers remain reasonably savvy and are more concerned about getting the right information and protecting their privacy.

- The first e-health pioneers were grossly overoptimistic and did not appreciate how difficult it would be to e-enable the healthcare system. Instead of offering an end-to-end service, solution providers are now concentrating on best-of-breed point solutions using open standards. These can then be integrated with other systems as and when adoption becomes a necessity for health providers, allowing the stepwise implementation of solutions.
- The demand for e-health services will grow steadily, but it would be foolhardy to repeat the mistakes of the dotcom years. The focus must be on cost-effective solutions that may only initially cater for small groups as the acceptance of digital technologies in healthcare slowly increases.
- We are only at the beginning of our understanding of how the Internet can be applied to meet the health information and support needs of consumers. Websites that promote collaboration between physicians and their patients, based on clear information and respect of the roles of the various 'players' in healthcare, appear to be an important way forward.
- Pharmaceutical companies continue to explore a wide range of options for using digital technologies to build sustainable relationships with physicians. In the face of inevitable margin pressure and smaller marketing budgets, the lesson from the early history of e-pharma is the importance of seeking value for money when developing e-marketing projects.

CHAPTER

4 Digital strategy is critical across the pharmaceutical value chain

Many regard the pharmaceutical industry as having a fairly simple business model. Therapeutic products are discovered or licensed in from other pharmaceutical or biotechnology companies, developed through a series of clinical trials, manufactured and finally marketed and sold. In reality, the pharmaceutical value chain is indeed fraught with complications. For example, the main customer of a pharmaceutical sales representative is the physician who prescribes the drug. Yet the drug is used by the patient and may be paid for by an insurer or another party. The situation is further complicated by the social, political and health economic environment in each country. While outside the scope of this discussion, we believe that the major trend in the pharmaceutical industry in the forthcoming years will be increasing pressures on margins. National and private healthcare providers around the world are working with tighter budget controls that are transferred into pressure on pharmaceutical prices and thereby pressure on margins throughout the entire supply chain [1]. Pharmaceutical companies will need to offset pressures on margins by lowering transaction costs and increasing revenues. Digital technologies are undoubtedly part of the solution set, as they introduce efficiencies and offer innovative channels for pharmaceutical marketing. Examples include the setting up of an e-supply chain and the disintermediation of wholesalers and pharmacists or a gradual changeover from large, expensive sales forces to new channels for e-sales [19]. More importantly, the industry is faced with a need to both improve service and cut costs due to a growing dissatisfaction with the price and quality of service amongst customers. Information technology and the Internet are seen as the most likely enablers of this, and as a result the industry is belatedly entering the digital age.

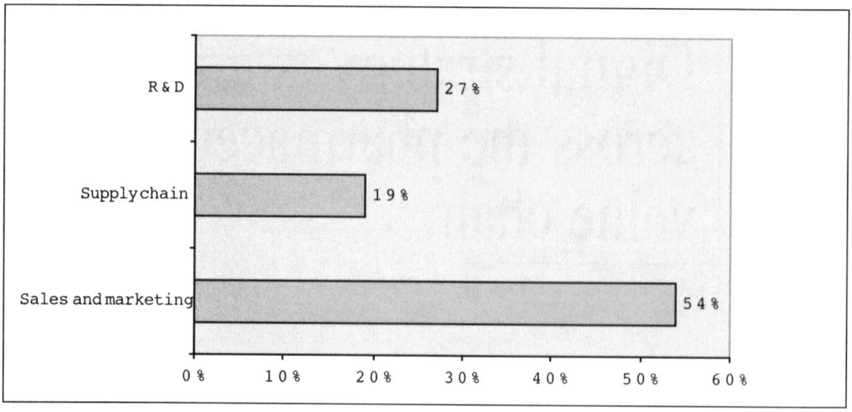

Figure 4.1 E-initiatives across the pharmaceutical value chain (2001)

Source: [7]

In Chapters 5–11 we describe the application of digital strategies across the pharmaceutical value chain. As we see in Figure 4.1, by 2001 pharmaceutical companies had a range of initiatives in e-business with a strong focus on sales and marketing. We are especially interested in distilling lessons as to what, at this relatively early stage in the evolution of pharmaceutical digital strategy, is working well and showing the greatest potential. We should, a priori, make it clear that making a distinction between the silos of R&D, supply chain and sales and marketing is somewhat artificial, especially if one believes that the strength of digital technology lies in the seamless integration of these various functions.

PART II

Digital Strategies: Research and Development

CHAPTER

5 Digital strategies in research and development (R&D)

Introduction: changing paradigms in R&D

> Just three years ago, the computational needs of biology were thought to be minor and irrelevant to the computing industry. Today, biologists are setting the pace of development for the industry. – J. Craig Venter, former president of Celera Genomics [20]

Within a few years, we have seen a dramatic transformation at the interface between digital technologies and biopharmaceutical research. The decoding of the human genome was believed to herald the beginning of an era of bioinformatics, yet many of the companies founded to provide computational services in drug discovery did not do at all well. This serves to illustrate that digital strategy in R&D is certainly not immune to the vagaries of therapeutic innovation. Drug development, always a risky business, is becoming increasingly complicated and expensive. The pharmaceutical industry's spending on R&D has increased from less than 10 per cent of sales in 1970 to approximately 20 per cent in 2000 [21, 23], and overall R&D spending has tripled since 1990 (Figure 5.1). The industry estimates that each approved drug must return between $300 million and $600 million to cover the cost of the failures [22].

Current drug pipelines will not meet growth expectations, especially as double-digit profit growth has been the norm. To meet this ambitious target, Pfizer would have to release three $1 billion blockbusters a year from 2003. From 2007, when key patents expire, it would have to release seven. Historically, the combined Pfizer and Warner-Lambert pipelines have produced fewer than two new drugs a year in the past ten years, few of which have been blockbusters [22]. To make matters worse, drugs are becoming more complex, as we already have a range of reasonably good products in the important

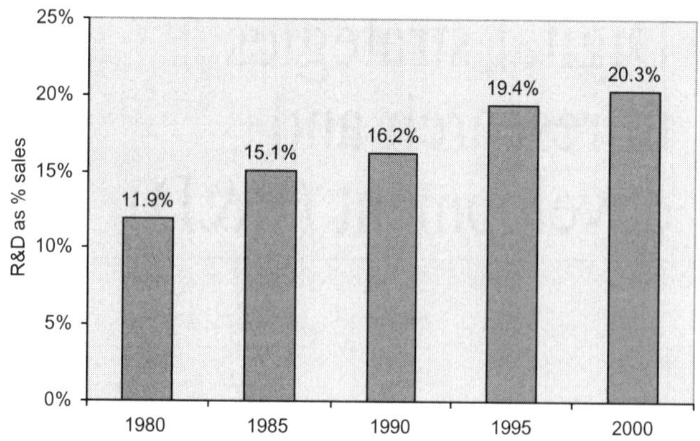

Figure 5.1 R&D expenses as a percentage of sales – US-based pharmaceutical firms

Source: Based on [23]

therapeutic areas, and the industry faces increased pricing scrutiny from payers concerned about a perceived lack of innovation; two-thirds of the prescription drugs approved by the FDA between 1989 and 2000 were identical to or modified versions of existing drugs [24]. New technologies such as genomics will account for some of the shortfall, but the lead time for these to produce new drugs is up to ten years.

The development of diagnostics and treatments based on an individual's genetic make-up has profound implications for the traditional R&D process. Most current treatments are intended for a homogeneous patient population – a one-size-fits-all approach to medicine. However, over the next 15 years we will see a gradual segmentation of patients based on their response to individual drugs and genetic predisposition to disease. Segmented medicine will result in more effective and safer (but more expensive) treatments for high-value patient segments. While personalized medicine (a drug tailor-made to an individual's profile) is in the distant future, segmented medicine will emerge to be a significant new force over the next decade. Segmented medicine will mean more effective, expensive treatments with fewer side effects. The potential for preventing conditions through pharmacological interventions, a concept that was previously mainly applicable to vaccines, will change medical practice. Segmented medicine also has a profound implication for research and development – the challenge is to move from developing a limited number of blockbusters to developing many profitable products for individual segments without greatly increasing R&D costs.

Against this backdrop, we consider the implications of the Internet, and a concomitant 'revolution' in the digital technology arena, for pharmaceutical R&D. A wide range of applications and opportunities exists, from computational power for cracking the genome or proteome to e-based communication of individual risk and personalized therapeutic options.

The human genome – biology as an information science

Genes are the building instructions for life, and genomics is the identification and functional characterization of genes. The human genome contains approximately 30,000 genes, each consisting of a string of DNA letters. By studying our genome, we can identify disease-causing genes, and hence theoretically design targeted therapies for those diseases. We can also predict the susceptibility of individuals to disease, and how effectively they will respond to therapies. The human genome was sequenced in 2001 by the government-funded Human Genome Project and Celera, a US genomics company. It involved sequencing all 3 billion letters of human DNA. However, this was only the first step towards identifying and characterizing every human gene. When it was first mooted in the 1980s, no one imagined that the Human Genome Project would be completed as swiftly or as cheaply as it has been. The unforeseen factor was the vast expansion in computing power available to scientists, who were able to automate much of the laborious sequence assembly and analysis. However, this is only the beginning of the genomics journey as the challenge is to translate the vast amounts of available data into useful knowledge that can be applied to treat disease. The huge enterprise surrounding the decryption of the human genome offers excellent insight into the role of digital technologies in the drug discovery process and particularly the product and service offerings that burgeoned to support genomics research. Some of the major groups involved are:

- Tool-makers (such as PE Biosystems, Amersham, Affymetrix) producing the machines and chemicals needed for DNA sequencing and other related products.
- Information companies building databases of genomic data (such as Celera, Incyte, Myriad), including information on potential drug targets. They can then license this information to pharmaceutical companies, or develop the drugs themselves (early examples being Millennium Pharmaceuticals or Human Genome Sciences, although nearly all database providers are now moving towards drug discovery in an attempt to capture

more of the value created). Other companies do not produce genomic data themselves, but use such data sets to create novel therapies (an example is Cambridge Antibody Technology).

- Bioinformatics companies manage and analyse DNA and protein sequence data in an attempt to identify the best drug targets (such as Genomica, Netgenics).
- Target screening companies (such as Cubist, Igen) have the tools to assess the function of interesting looking genes on a large-scale basis. Until recently, elucidating the function of a gene involved laborious experimental work. Now this can often be fully automated.

The genomics industry represents a convergence of biotechnology and IT. At the root of all genomics developments lies a fundamental shift from drug discovery based on data gleaned from laboratory experiments to drug discovery based on the statistical analysis of sequence and other data derived from genomics. Genomics companies blend information technology and research to make drug discovery faster, cheaper and more efficient. Drug discovery by computer may never replace time-consuming experimental science, but by identifying the most promising targets and leads, it promises to make drug discovery many times more efficient. Not surprisingly, making sense of this data requires considerable investment in IT and it is data-intensive R&D that is driving the explosion in bioscience IT expenditure. This research creates huge data files that must be analysed, stored and moved on secure networks. Biotechnology applications such as the effort to map the human genome have already created some of the world's largest databases, measured in terabytes, or trillions of bytes of information. This is a demanding but high-value market.

The demanding requirements of the biosciences IT market

- *Hardware*. High-end servers and supercomputers, networking gear, workstations and instrumentation.
- *Storage*. In the order of petabytes.
- *Services*. Hosting and application provision services for decoding genomes and analysing their functions.
- *Software*. Knowledge management, database systems, and applications for informatics, sequencing, proteomics, computational chemistry, visualization and much more.

continued from previous page

Celera Genomics, the private company that sequenced the genome in competition with the publicly funded Human Genome Project, utilized the following:

- $1 million of electric power annually.
- 70TB for databases, growing by 15–20GB per day.
- 1.7Teraflops of aggregate processing power.
- 900 Compaq AlphaServer processors.
- Six Paracel GeneMatchers (each with thousands of processors – Paracel is a massively parallel processor manufacturer that Celera purchased last year).
- Additionally, an agreement between Celera and Sandia National Laboratory will develop a supercomputing platform for mining and modelling genetic data. The $25 million project will be powered by multiple Compaq AlphaServers and is expected to provide 100 trillion operations per second (Teraops) of raw computer power, making it the world's largest supercomputer [20].

The completion of the human genome project is only the beginning: the completed genome can be thought of as a crude map, which on its own tells us relatively little. The map needs to be annotated with functional information (for example patterns of gene expression in diseased tissue, protein–protein interactions and genetic differences between individuals). Biocomputational requirements now exceed those of other 'big science' applications, such as weather forecasting, subatomic physics and nuclear weapons research, and making sense of all this additional data will require considerable investment in IT, a fact that has not escaped the major hardware, software and service suppliers (Figure 5.2).

Digital technology – the future R&D market

> With its IT infrastructures and business models still immature, limited supplies of relevant IT expertise, and overwhelming knowledge management requirements, biocomputing's solution space is underpopulated. Current software suppliers (mostly from an academic-based cottage industry) and service providers can't keep up with biocomputing's pace of change and scale of problems . . . in the current economic climate, it is hard to find a more robust IT market than biocomputing. – IDC Executive Insight 2001 [20]

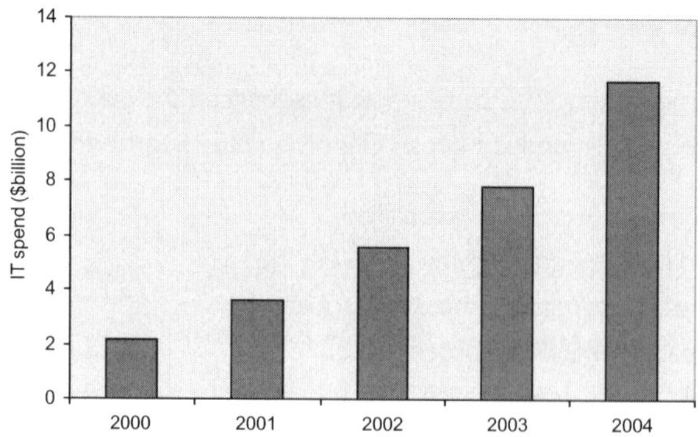

Figure 5.2 Biosciences market IT revenue 2000–04 is expected to grow with a CAGR of 52 per cent

Source: [20]

As genomics has advanced, it has become increasingly dependent on computing systems that can process, store, and analyse massive amounts of data at breakneck speeds. IT companies are beginning to recognize the opportunity that genomics represents, not just as a market for their products, but also as a way of broadening their offerings by obtaining new intellectual property and new skills. Established high-tech companies are entering the e-R&D market, both as biotechnology investors and technology developers. Currently, Compaq and IBM are leaders in the field. Other vendors, such as Hewlett-Packard, NEC, SGI, EMC, Oracle and Sun are aggressively seeking a role in the R&D space. The market is currently dominated by the sale of servers and storage, but services will become increasingly important over time (Figure 5.3). We discuss the evolution of two big players in this field, namely IBM and Compaq.

IBM

IBM has focused on life sciences since the mid-1990s, with development work in computational biology and related areas. IBM has developed a global life sciences consulting business offering computer systems integration, storage management services and other technology outsourcing. IBM also supplies IT outsourcing for AstraZeneca, among others [12], and is involved in proteomics through its stake in MDS Proteomics [25]. IBM is using its expertise in high-performance computing to build a leadership position in the market: NuTec Sciences (a bioinformatics solutions provider) has employed

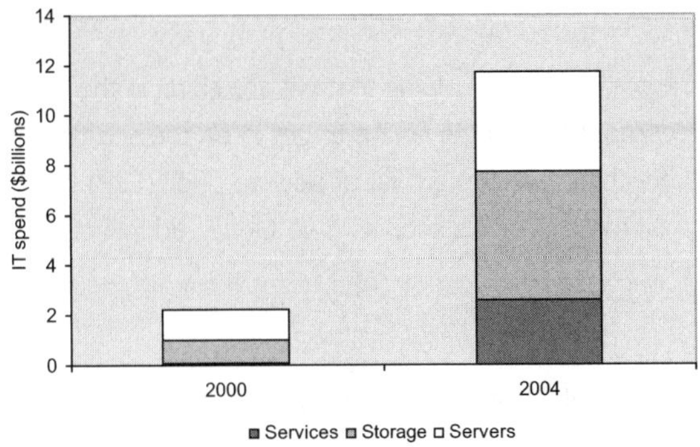

Figure 5.3 Biosciences IT revenue split (2000 and 2004)

Source: [20]

IBM to build a 7.5Teraflops supercomputer, in partnership with the US National Human Genome Research Institute. The cluster will connect 1250 IBM e-Server p640s running IBM's DB2 Universal Database, supported by a NuTec operating system, 2.5TB of memory and 50TB of online storage. NuTec will use it to manage, mine and integrate genetic data and share this information with the life sciences community [26].

Blue Gene

IBM's Blue Gene computer is claimed to be 50 times more powerful than anything available today. Blue Gene has 1000 times the capacity of Deep Blue, which defeated the world chess champion Garry Kasparov in 1997, and is about two million times more powerful than a current desktop PC. It will use that power for a single task – working out how a single human protein is built from the atoms up. Existing computers cannot even accurately model the behaviour of simple water molecules in the human body. IBM is aiming at a machine that will be able to tackle one quadrillion operations per second, making it easily the fastest computer in the world. Proteins are made up of several hundred smaller molecules called amino acids. The unique shape these amino acids form when they are assembled according to a gene's instructions is critical to the protein's job, but scientists still do not understand why what they call 'protein folding' happens as it does. Tim Hubbard, a protein specialist now among the leaders of the British part of the publicly funded Human

continued from previous page

Genome Project, said 'IBM is realising that we are going in the direction of high-performance computing, and they want to get in on the act. It's a good strategy.' However, others think that the arrival of peer-to-peer (P2P) high-performance applications may make projects such as Blue Gene redundant [27].

Compaq (now part of Hewlett-Packard)

> This market isn't just growing, it's exploding. – Bill Blake, Vice President Compaq (2001) [26]

Compaq has achieved high penetration of the expanding life sciences segment. It is focusing on solution development (training, third-party software partnerships and requirements analysis). Like other vendors, it was attracted to the market after 1995 by the raw computer power needed to assemble finished DNA sequence. It has a major strategic alliance with Celera Genomics, the company that sequenced the human genome, to provide integrated bioinformatics hardware, software, networking and service solutions. Celera started with one Compaq high-performance system and expanded to a network of 700 systems in less than 18 months [20].

Encouraged by this, Compaq announced that it was investing $100 million in early-stage life sciences companies in hopes of capitalizing on the genomics industry's burgeoning demand for high-performance computing. Compaq will put some of the $100 million directly in companies and some in venture capital funds that specialize in genomics and bioinformatics. The company said that its goal is to spur the growth of discovery in life sciences and strengthen the company's foothold in the industry. Start-up companies would be expected to purchase Compaq's systems and services when Compaq invests in them [28].

The industrialization of R&D – the role of digital technology

In order to generate the volumes of data required by e-R&D, new high-throughput biological screening tools such as sequencers and biochips were developed. Affymetrix pioneered biochip development in the mid-1990s. A biochip is a piece of silicon that has millions of artificial gene fragments bonded to its surface and permits rapid genetic profiling by computer analysis.

This has important implications for the diagnosis and treatment of any disease with a genetic component (such as breast cancer or schizophrenia). Biochips will also allow us to compare healthy and diseased tissues, quickly pinpointing genetic differences that could constitute new drug targets. The market is estimated to be growing with a CAGR of 65 per cent and will be worth $3.3 billion by 2004 [29]. Whatever the true value of the biochip market, there is the potential for tremendous growth in the long term. If medical diagnostic tests using biochips become widespread, the market for such products could reach the tens of billions of dollars by 2010. Just as the major IT giants currently see pharmaceuticals as a major market, so the industrialization of R&D has aroused the interest of several high-tech manufacturers. Agilent uses ink-jet technology perfected for computer printers to affix genetic material to its chips [26].

Proteomics is the study of all the proteins in the body. Genes store the information for constructing proteins, the more complex molecules such as hormones, enzymes and antibodies that are needed for the structure, function and regulation of cells. The challenge is to go beyond relatively simple genes to understand how more complex proteins work in living organisms. This information has huge commercial potential in terms of new drugs, therapies and even improved food crops. However, this will require massive computing capacity. Hardware maker Hitachi and database giant Oracle joined genomics company Myriad Genetics to launch an ambitious $185 million partnership designed to map all human protein interactions in less than three years. In a competing deal, IBM will be the preferred supplier of a supercomputer infrastructure, software and services to MDS Proteomics. The partnership has been formed specifically to understand the interactions among proteins that trigger chemical reactions in cells and cause diseases such as cancer and depression [25].

The transformation of drug discovery – the role of digital technology

The identification and validation of therapeutic targets is achieved in traditional drug discovery by focusing on the underlying biochemistry of a specific disease, studying the pharmaceutical properties of a novel compound found in nature, or following up a target initially uncovered by an academic laboratory. Today, a company may use a biochip to isolate genes that are only active in diseased tissues, or they may search a genomic database for a likely candidate gene. It is hoped that in future most of this work will be done in silico rather than in vitro (by computer rather than in the test tube). The relevant protein is then isolated and its biochemistry studied. Although genomic technologies have greatly increased the number of drug targets and the ease with which they can be characterized, it is still necessary to do a significant number of time-consuming biochemical studies. However, computer simulation is becoming increasingly important, and may one day largely eliminate time-consuming laboratory work.

In the traditional drug discovery process, thousands of small molecule potential drug candidates are chemically synthesized, and tested in trial-and-error assays against the target biochemical pathway to see if they have the desired effect. Biotechnology allows one to directly create biopharmaceuticals – replacement copies of the defective protein or antibodies that can block the action of the defective protein. However, most new drugs produced (approximately 80 per cent) are still in the small molecule class and computer simulation is increasingly used.

For target validation and lead optimization, the interaction of drug target and drug is studied, and the structure of the potential drug is optimized. As protein structures and protein–protein interactions become better understood, this will be achieved through computer simulation. Currently, most target validation is done using biological screening systems that are either high-throughput or accurate but, crucially, rarely both.

Eli Lilly is focusing on the field of bioinformatics, which uses specialized algorithms and databases to analyse the structure of genes. The analysis helps to identify proteins that cause disease. At Eli Lilly researchers are correlating data in several databases into a single relational database structure.

> Lilly subscribes to a database of gene sequencing information from Incyte Pharmaceuticals Inc., co-owns a database generated by Millennium, and generates its own gene sequencing information internally. In addition, the company downloads information nightly from public databases on the Internet, such as the federal government's Human Genome Project. All the data is stored in Oracle databases that run on Sun Microsystems servers. Eli Lilly's researchers access the databases from their desktop PCs across an intranet, using a mixture of commercial, public domain, and custom-built Web tools to analyse data. Incyte and Millennium provide tools that let researchers compare a particular gene sequence with other genetic information in their databases. In addition, Eli Lilly's developers have built tools that search for gene sequences and proteins that are specific to their needs. [30]

Digital strategy in drug discovery

Before genomics, companies used two basic technologies, chemistry and molecular biology, to develop drugs. Some compared the traditional process of drug development to spending millions to build an aeroplane and then simply sending it off a cliff to see if it flies [31]. In fact, drug developers can take heart from recent developments in aircraft manufacture. Designing aeroplanes was costly and labour intensive. Computer-aided design/computer-aided manufacture (CAD/CAM) systems promised to revolutionize this process into a highly automated and efficient one. However, uptake was slow during the 1970s and 80s, as CAD/CAM was only used in certain R&D niches. Then in the 1990s, Boeing used the system to design the first 'paperless' airplane, the 777. This involved breaking down departmental barriers and encouraging collaboration across all functions [32]. Some predict a similarly dramatic (and perhaps more rapid) change in the way pharmaceutical companies develop medicines. But to implement this will require major organizational changes and overcoming some significant technological challenges.

Using these new technologies creates enormous business challenges for the industry. Over the next five years, the new biology could cause R&D costs to double [33]. Most of this cost will be due to increased failure rates at the later, more expensive stages of drug development (such as phases II/III clinical trials). Many of the new technologies described here are in their infancy, so the biological functions of new drug targets are less well understood than those laboriously studied in the past. Hence the increased failure rate at later stages. A study by Boston Consulting Group also predicts an initial rise in R&D costs, but expects new technologies eventually to reduce both the cost of a drug and the time-to-market. They estimate that it costs $880 million to develop a new drug and 14.7 years to take it to market. Savings of nearly $300 million and two years per drug are predicted, as a result of the combined introduction of biotechnological approaches and digital technologies, largely due to efficiency gains [34].

At the corporate level, the question is: How much to invest in e-R&D? At the R&D departmental level, the question is: Where to invest the money, what technologies are needed (be they genomic or high-throughput technologies, analysis or bioinformatics technologies), whether to buy or partner, and how to organize the processes? These questions are dependent on the size and business model of the company, and the diseases or targets being concentrated on.

In the past five years, most big drug companies have created informatics departments, either by integrating their research and IT departments or creating close ties between the two. But the unofficial origins go back further. 'It started as an outgrowth of the scientific discipline as opposed to IT' says Nathan Siemers, group leader of bioinformatics at Bristol-Myers Squibb.

> Basically it's been a research endeavor, but over its evolution it's become more infrastructure-related. More people need access to this information, and the scale of information we have to disseminate to our clients – the researchers – is growing drastically. So our ties to IT, which originally were almost nonexistent, have become stronger and stronger. [31]

To do informatics correctly you need to blend scientific skills and IT skills. At Merck, the 30-person bioinformatics group is one-third computer scientists, one-third natural scientists and one-third with a dual background in science and IT. That partnership is particularly vital because most pharmaceutical companies are doing a combination of building some tools in-house, licensing software and partnering with or buying companies that already have a piece of the technology. The main reason for these acquisitions is that most companies cannot find enough qualified individuals and the core business of a pharmaceutical company remains drug, not software, development [31].

However, hundreds of vendors in the informatics space combined with varying standards and platforms make integration tricky. Pfizer works with about 15 major vendors in this area. Pfizer uses simulation software from Tripos, chemical databases from MDL Information Systems, and screening and visualization tools from Spotfire, just to name a few. Pfizer tries to sway their partners to build tools according to Pfizer's standards, but integrating the systems is still a major task. For example, Pfizer's scientists often use one database to examine the chemical structures of compounds in order to make assessments about their viability as drug targets. Then they have to transfer that information into a completely different piece of software from another vendor to assess that molecule's biological properties or safety [31].

Some vendors are beginning to offer more modular systems that can plug in to other systems or well-documented APIs (application programming interfaces) in an effort to build market share, but many are still selling closed, stand-alone systems, particularly if they have a monopoly position. The number of mergers and acquisitions in the drug industry further complicates the integration issue. Everyone has different databases, and even making the data accessible can be difficult [31].

Conclusions – 'the take home messages'

Thanks to the slow pace of drug discovery and testing, e-R&D will not lead to a flood of new products overnight. It will probably take a number of years before the drug development process depends on high-throughput, digitally dependent technologies such as genomics, high-throughput screening and computer-aided drug design. Today's challenge lies in the integration of informatics, a process that will require a change in the culture of pharmaceutical industry research. As these new technologies develop, new bottlenecks will form in the drug discovery process (for example until recently, target identification was a major bottleneck). As such, resources will constantly have to be devoted to changing challenges in drug discovery.

Leaders in this emerging field stress that they will never be able to fully develop a drug using only computers, as some analysts have suggested. Scientific experimentation started out in vivo, in real animals and plants. Then it moved to test tubes (in vitro). But in vitro didn't replace in vivo, it simply added value, as e-R&D will. And e-R&D and IT in general will be more useful at some stages of the value chain than others. The early stage of the research process, when big computers are used to discover interesting targets for new drugs, benefits from scale. Size is also an asset at the final stage of the research process, when drugs have to be tested on a large number of patients and then guided through the approval process. The significant time and costs savings will not come until companies have an end-to-end, IT-driven research and development solution. It will be another three or four years before this technology starts to have an effect on drugs already in the clinic and far longer before there is a real effect on the entire drug discovery process. 'So far, informatics spending has been piecemeal, in pockets where the company does understand the impact of the technology' says Vikas Taneja, a project leader at Boston Consulting Group [31].

- The industrialization of pharmaceutical research, heralded by the application of biotechnology in drug discovery, is driving demand for IT solutions, including hardware, infrastructure, analytical tools, software and people. While this transition will lead to cheaper and faster development of therapeutics in the longer term, the short-term challenge is an increase in R&D costs.
- Vendors of bioinformatics services will encounter the inevitable standardization, integration and commoditization of their systems, as

pharmaceutical companies seek robust, sustainable drug discovery technologies.

- While we are still some time away from exclusively in-silico drug discovery, digital technology is already influencing the conduct of pharmaceutical research.

Personalized medicine

Introduction

> We want to be the leader in personalised drug therapies. In fact, our expressed goal is to be the first company to deliver health care tailored to the patient's genetic profile. To achieve that goal, we need to reach all the way to the doctors and the patients. – Mark Levin, CEO Millennium Pharmaceuticals (2001) [35]

> One day you're going to be able to walk into a doctor's office and have a computer analyse a tissue sample, identify the pathogen that ails you and then instantly prescribe a treatment best suited to your specific illness and individual genetic make-up. – Paul Horn, Senior VP of IBM Research (1999) [27]

While many may believe that the time when medical treatment will be customized to individual profiles is in the distant future, we contest that the implications of this advance in biomedical innovation are immediate and have profound relevance for digital strategy in the pharmaceutical industry. Most modern drugs only have the desired effect in a limited proportion of patients, often as low as 33 per cent and most therapies have undesired side effects in some individuals. While our response to therapies is determined by a range of factors, it is our genetic make-up which takes prime importance in determining whether we will be cured or have some dangerous drug reaction. Genetic analysis is slowly but surely giving us the power to identify which personal characteristics lead to the desired drug response, and which lead to an adverse response. The implications of personalized medicine are profound: healthcare providers and patients benefit as drugs are prescribed more effectively and certainly more safely. GlaxoSmithKline is already developing genetic tests that will identify people likely to suffer adverse reactions to their drugs [36], and AstraZeneca is collaborating with the genetic analysis company Orchid Biosciences to create more personalized drugs [37]. However, some major pharmaceutical companies are worried that this approach could reduce sales from existing blockbusters, as certain patient groups are excluded as potential customers [38].

Personalized medicine is currently characterized by two approaches: pharmacogenomic tests and disease-specific genetic tests:

1. *Pharmacogenomic tests* predict the safety and efficacy of a certain drug in any given individual. This will drive the new paradigm in healthcare: 'the right drug for the right person at the right dose', as described by George Poste, SmithKlineBeecham's retired chief science and technology officer. For instance, Orchid Biosciences is studying five enzymes known to interact with 300 of the most commonly used drugs. A genetic test could identify common variants of the enzymes, allowing a physician to predict adverse drug responses or modulate drug dosage [39].
2. Public and private studies of human genetic variability have rapidly increased understanding of the genetic components of disease susceptibility and drug response. This is driving the development of predictive *disease-specific genetic tests*. Over 400 tests are currently available, for diseases such as breast cancer, Huntingdon's disease and cystic fibrosis [40]. Genetic databases are gaining increasing attention, for example with companies such as Salt Lake City's Myriad and Iceland's DeCode using relatively isolated populations with excellent genealogical records to aid in their search for disease genes. Both have had conspicuous successes, for instance DeCode has isolated genes linked to schizophrenia and arthritis. And it is not just private companies that are driving the development of personalized medicine: Britain plans to build the world's largest gene database. Scientists will recruit half a million middle-aged volunteers at a cost of more than $60 million over the next two or three years. Within a decade, this storehouse could lead to a better understanding of how genes affect not only diseases, but also the medicines that treat them [41].

Segmented medicine – just around the corner

Most current treatments are intended for a homogeneous patient population – a one-size-fits-all approach to medicine. However, the next 15 years will see a gradual segmentation of patients based on their response to individual drugs (pharmacogenomics) and genetic predisposition to disease (disease genetics). Segmented medicine will result in more effective and safer (but more expensive) treatments for high-value patient segments. While personalized medicine (a drug tailor-made to an individual's profile) is in the distant future, segmented medicine will emerge as a significant new force over the next decade.

Biomedical advances will lead to an understanding of genetic risk factors, treatment response and predisposition to adverse events at a small group level. Concerns about treatment response and preventable adverse reactions will drive the adoption of segmented medicine in the clinic. Growing healthcare service provision inequality will lead to parallel segmentation of consumers at an economic level. And pharmaceutical companies will target higher value segments of the market with more expensive, but safer, drugs.

Some pharmaceutical companies are less than enthusiastic about segmented medicine, fearing that disqualifying some patients due to their genetic profiles may adversely affect sales of current blockbusters [38]. However, forward-looking companies believe that competitive advantage can be obtained by profiling the responses of different population segments to their drugs. The aim is to exclude those for whom a drug is ineffective and charge a premium to those for whom it is more likely to work. GlaxoSmithKline feels that if it can match patients to the most effective medication, it will be able to enhance the marketing of its biggest drugs by stressing the safety angle: doctors are far more likely to prescribe drugs that they know will have no side effects [36]. And who will be able to afford those drugs? High-value consumer segments with adequate healthcare coverage. Predictive tests for GSK's AIDS drugs are expected to be available in three to five years time. According to Allen Roses of GlaxoSmithKline, these type of tests 'have the potential to change pharmaco-economics' [36]. Innovative companies will move to carve themselves segmented medicine niches and develop intellectual property. For example, Genaissance Pharmaceuticals is linking patients' specific genetic markers with their clinical response to four popular cholesterol-lowering drugs [42], while DeCode Genetics and Affymetrix have formed an alliance to determine the genes responsible for the effectiveness of depression, asthma and hypertension drugs [43]. Thanks to these and similar efforts, many drugs will soon be bundled with diagnostic tests.

Personalized medicine has immediate applications, as it will permit a better selection of suitable patients for clinical trials, with a consequent cost saving for pharmaceutical companies. This is particularly true when the drug itself only targets a specific genetic subsection of patients – the classic example being Herceptin, a breast cancer drug that only benefits (and was subsequently only tested on) the 25–33 per cent of patients who expressed the HER2 oncogene. Without this selection, the drug would not have passed the clinical trial process. Conversely, the rarity of certain adverse drug reactions will make it difficult to link a gene to the reaction with any statistical certainty [44]. One analysis suggested that, in time, a 25 per cent reduction in drug development costs might be achieved using genomic data [45].

Clearly the benefits of finding the best responders, patients more likely to have a certain common adverse drug reaction, and the identification of opportunities to modify the drug or dosage for small patient groups could be substantial. On the other hand, companies need to carefully weigh the economic implications of personalized medicine (Figure 5.4). Today, large companies are reluctant to develop drugs that are projected to have less than $500 million in annual sales and a margin of less than 70 per cent but, in the age of segmented medicine, smaller market niches and lower margins will become the norm. Thus, segmented medicine will necessitate major organizational changes within major pharmaceutical companies. The greater use of diagnostics and preventive treatments will eventually open up a whole new class of consumers – the 'symptomless ill' – and this is a potential market for pharmaceutical companies. Indeed, William Haseltine, CEO of Human Genome Sciences, believes that we will see a huge shift in the ratio of doctors' bills to pharmaceutical costs from around nine to one now to around one to one in 25 years [46].

Implications for digital strategy

The growth of personalized medicine will promote the widespread application of the Internet and advance IT systems in healthcare. Besides the sheer

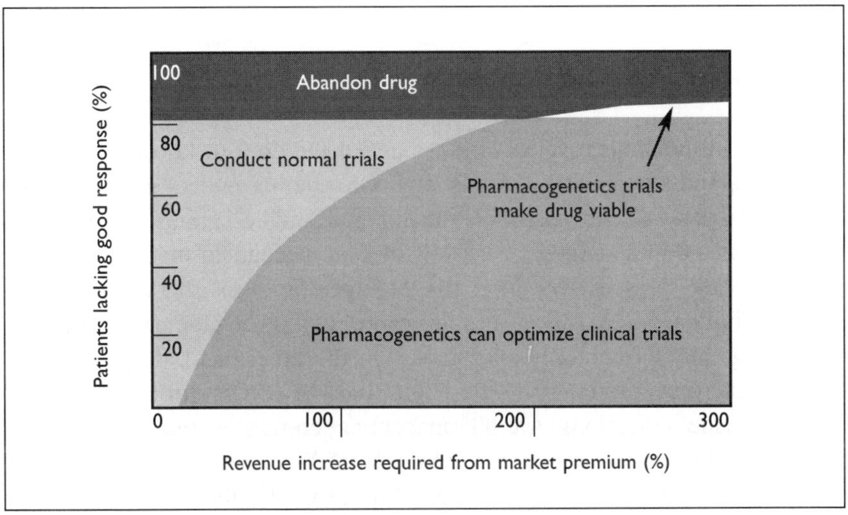

Figure 5.4 The economics of personalized medicine require careful consideration

Source: [32]

computing power required to undertake pharmacogenomic research, both at a population and laboratory level, the administration of complex clinical trials and patient tracking is dependent on e-tools. In order to identify patients with the appropriate genetic profile to participate in clinical trials, pharmaceutical companies and their contract research organizations (CROs) are going to have to cast the net wide, using the Internet and health websites for patient recruitment. As personalized medicine does indeed become part of a standardized therapeutic approach, the data will be managed using a range of analytic and warehousing tools.

We are already seeing a range of web-based offering for consumers aimed at measuring predisposition to disease. As personalized medicine becomes a real option, the Internet will be the main tool for obtaining information and conducting the transactions related to individual testing and therapeutic choice. Companies, such as Roche Diagnostics, that currently have dominant platform technologies have been quick to seize the opportunity, already piloting online patient consultations in the USA, where the regulatory climate is more amenable to such innovation. The e-market for personalized medicine is certainly in a state of early flux, as we see players offering biochip-based pharmacogenomic testing explore the consumer market via the Internet. It is difficult to predict the size of the opportunity, but we are certain that economic segmentation exists in personalized medicine, ensuring that a group, probably not insubstantial, will be willing to pay well for innovative testing managed via the Internet.

Conclusions – 'the take home messages'

Advances in biomedical science have opened the door to far more specific diagnostic and therapeutic options and the pharmaceutical industry will have to respond to the needs of smaller and smaller groups. Segmented medicine is a double-edged sword for the pharmaceutical industry. From a customer value perspective, drugs that are specific to the therapeutic needs of an individual are highly desirable, especially if development times for these drugs are substantially shortened. On the other hand, drugs are sold today on the basis of being slightly better than the competitor's product and for fairly wide indications. Are pharmaceutical companies ready to compete with each other in very specific niche markets? We are seeing an inexorable move towards personalized medicine. For example, the FDA sometimes asks for pharmacogenomic profiling as part of the clinical trial design and in the case of highly specialized therapeutic new drug applications, FDA advisers are already requesting genomics data on small target groups.

- The implications of personalized medicine for pharmaceutical marketing are immediate. Drugs will have to be sold to individual patient segments rather than to the entire patient population, greatly reducing potential market size. To manage this new market, companies will have to penetrate segments deeply, by adjusting pricing strategies and developing new promotional approaches. In order to mitigate the disappearance of the blockbuster drug, companies are going to have to extract maximum value from smaller segments, either selected on economic or genomic criteria. The Internet offers a cost-effective channel for reaching smaller customer segments, be they physicians or consumers. Online segmentation permits a pharmaceutical marketer to customize messages to particular groups and measure response.
- Smaller customer segments will result in tighter marketing budgets and pharmaceutical companies will have to focus on better market analytics and more experimentation and innovation in their interaction with customer groups.
- Personalized medicine will drive closer interaction between the various silos that constitute a global research-based pharmaceutical company, especially collaboration between R&D and sales and marketing.

E-clinical trials

Introduction

Clinical trials aim to establish the safety and efficacy of a new drug in humans. They are highly regulated and, as a result, extremely paper intensive. It is not unusual for a single subject in a trial to generate 60 binders of documentation, and some trials involve over a thousand patients. The amount of data required for the registration of new drugs will rise as regulatory bodies are now not only concerned with the safety and efficacy of new treatments, they also take into account cost-effectiveness, placing a greater emphasis than ever on credible pharmaco-economic data. Personalized medicine and pharmacogenomics will add to the data burden in clinical trials, as genetic testing of participants becomes routine and increasing safety concerns will mean a greater emphasis on post-approval monitoring. As large comparative trials are now the norm (especially in chronic diseases), we are seeing the number of patients in individual trials increase substantially. The Internet, if properly harnessed, has the potential to greatly streamline the clinical trials' process. Companies can use the Internet to improve communication between investigators, share pertinent regulatory information, recruit participants, speed analysis (and 'time to data lock') and manage trial data.

The clinical trials' time-line and process

Promising drugs that have shown no significant toxicity in pre-clinical testing then enter clinical trials in humans. This is when regulatory bodies, such as the FDA, become heavily involved in the drug development process, and this is where most R&D costs are incurred. The US approval process is outlined below, and a similar process is used in the EU [45, 47].

Phase I

Duration: 1–3 years
Average cost: $7 million *Chance of success*: A drug entering phase I trials has approximately a 20 per cent chance of reaching the market

Phase I trials concentrate on developing the drug's safety profile. The human subjects in the study are normally healthy volunteers, although sometimes patients who have terminal illnesses and no other therapeutic alternative will take part in phase I studies. Usually no more than 100 patients are involved.

Phase II

Duration: 2 years on average
Average cost: $19 million *Chance of success*: A drug entering phase II trials has approximately a 29 per cent chance of reaching the market

The statistical efficacy of a drug is preliminarily established by phase II trials. These trials are also used to establish the safety of the drug in a larger pool of patients. The drugs are given to volunteers (usually between 100 and 300 patients) who suffer from the disease or condition targeted by the drug.

Phase III

Duration: 3–4 years on average
Average cost: $43 million *Chance of success*: A drug entering phase III trials has approximately a 61 per cent chance of reaching the market

Phase III testing is intended to verify the effectiveness of the drug against the condition that it targets. The study also continues to build the safety profile of the drug and record possible side effects resulting from long-term use. Phase III studies involve anything from several hundred to several thousand patients. If the drug proves to be effective in this stage, the trial is deemed to be successful (pivotal). Normally, two pivotal trials are required for regulatory approval.

Marketing approval and phase IV

If a drug successfully makes its way through all the clinical trials, the sponsor must then submit a final request for marketing approval (known as a new drug application, or NDA, in the US). Over two-thirds of all NDAs are approved. Once marketing approval and other costs have been taken into account, the total cost of the clinical trials' process is, on average, over $250 million. Further trials may then be carried out in an attempt to broaden the conditions for which the drug can be prescribed.

All phases of a clinical trial involve a similar process, although obviously the complexity of managing the trial increases with the number of patients enrolled (Figure 5.5).

The application of e-clinical trials

Faced with formidable challenges in terms of communicating between clinical trial sites, often scattered across the world, and the need to manage, analyse and submit large amounts of data in a cost-effective and timely manner, pharmaceutical companies have for a number of years been exploring and implementing digital technologies in drug development. E-clinical trials was one of the areas that attracted interest at the beginning of the dotcom boom and

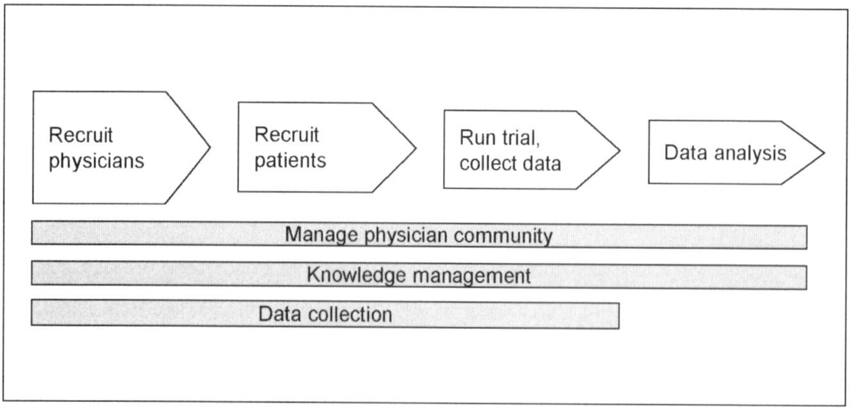

Figure 5.5 The clinical trials' process

companies such as Phase Forward have grown to provide comprehensive e-clinical trials' services. The benefits of e-trials at each stage of the process are outlined below.

Recruitment

A quarter of all delays in drug development are due to difficulties in recruiting patients [7]. Pharmaceutical and biotechnology companies have begun to use the web to recruit patients and physicians, as well as efficiently and effectively manage patient information, identify risk factors and communicate with patients. In the US, the potential of e-recruiting is substantial, as demonstrated by the approximately 150,000 patients who visit the online CenterWatch Trials Listing Service every month [48]. And disease-specific websites, often visited by newly diagnosed patients who want to learn more about their conditions, are increasingly being used as portals for clinical trial recruitment.

Electronic data capture

The collection of clinical trial data, especially from remote sites, is a prime candidate for Internet applications. Analysts predict double-digit growth in the use of EDC (electronic data capture) technologies over the next five years. The upward trend is due, in part, to the increasing number of trials conducted outside the United States and Western Europe, leading to growing acceptance and use of EDC technology for clinical trials across the globe. Participants in a 2001 survey cited cost savings and shorter time-to-market as the major benefits of EDC technology. Nearly half (44 per cent) of survey participants indicated that they were currently using EDC technology in their clinical trials. Another 6 per cent reported that they are not presently using EDC, but have in past trials. The remaining half of respondents indicated they have not yet implemented an EDC system for clinical trials. However, of those not currently using EDC, 28 per cent indicated they had plans to begin using EDC over the next 18 months. When asked to rate their experience with EDC, the majority of respondents (52 per cent) indicated that their companies have had either a positive (29 per cent) or neutral (23 per cent) experience with the technology. Only 7 per cent reported having a negative experience. The majority of respondents (70 per cent) believe EDC generates revenue by getting drugs to market faster (26 per cent), saves on the costs associated with clinical trials (16 per cent) or does both (28 per cent) [49]. Interestingly, 57 per cent of trial coordinators were positive about the technology and only 9 per cent negative, despite the fact that the responsibility of data entry shifts from the sponsor to them [50] (Figure 5.6).

A recent report concluded that the use of simple mobile devices for data submission by patients during phase III and IV trials was the most cost-effective use of wireless EDC to date. Because mobile phones are such an integral part of consumers' lives, engaging in two-way communication with the patient is relatively easy. They also present the opportunity to collect new kinds of data such as emotional response to the drug packaging and symptom histories that may be useful for later CRM and pharmaco-economic efforts. As participating physicians need access to a considerable amount of complex data, their needs are well served by a laptop (perhaps, in the near future, with a wireless modem) [51].

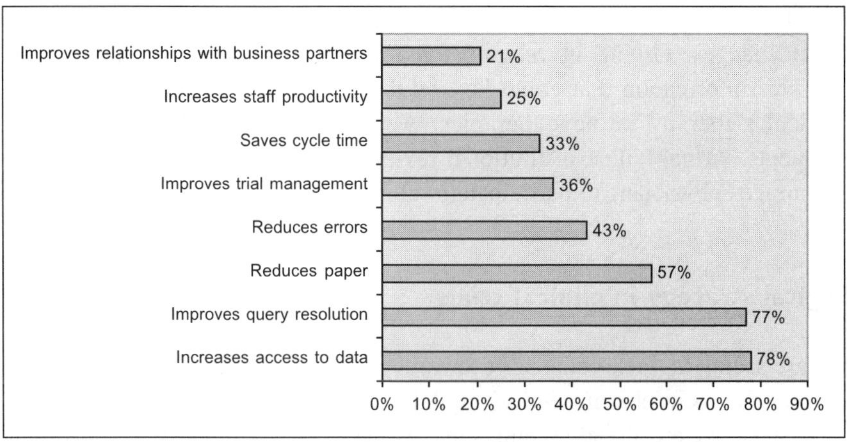

Figure 5.6 Significant advantages of web-enabled or patient diary data capture systems (base: 400 trial professionals in 2001)

Source: [50]

When it comes to integrating EDC with other technologies, respondents wanted to be able to link to sensors (41 per cent) and interactive voice response systems (40 per cent). Thirty-five per cent felt that integration with PDAs (personal digital assistants) is important and 32 per cent want to see integration with other wireless systems [49].

EDC is becoming an increasingly important technology as the life sciences industry looks for ways to cut costs and speed time-to-market in an effort to meet the growing pressures of both its customers and investors. But in order for the technology adequately to meet the dynamic needs of the industry, EDC systems require levels of functionality and flexibility that are only slowly being attained.

Data analysis, drug approval and stakeholder management

Electronic records can cut weeks or months off the time needed to establish if a drug is safe and effective and new software can help investigators write up their results simultaneously for multiple regulatory agencies (such as the FDA and EMEA – European Agency for the Evaluation of Medicinal Products). Early approval can mean more than an extra million dollars per day in revenue for a blockbuster drug. Some companies are reporting a 40 per cent reduction in the time it takes to move from finishing clinical trials to submitting dossiers for regulatory approval, as a result of implementing an e-clinical trial system [7].

By including physicians earlier and longer in the drug development process or clinical trials, pharmaceutical company researchers will have access to important information that otherwise might not have been raised until the investigators' meeting, by which time it may have been too late to make changes. Giving investigators a forum for ongoing communication provides information that could be useful in the further development of the particular therapy or new therapies. Adding features such as automated payments, virtual online institutional review boards and other functionalities encourages physicians to participate in clinical trials [52].

Digital strategy in clinical trials

We are seeing an inexorable shift towards e-clinical trials, perhaps one of the success stories in pharmaceutical digital strategy. While the field is still at an early stage, we are already seeing some evidence of best practice in areas such as data infrastructure, patient recruitment and trial standardization. Perhaps the most important recent advance has been the progress towards the development of a global uniform design for e-clinical software supported by some

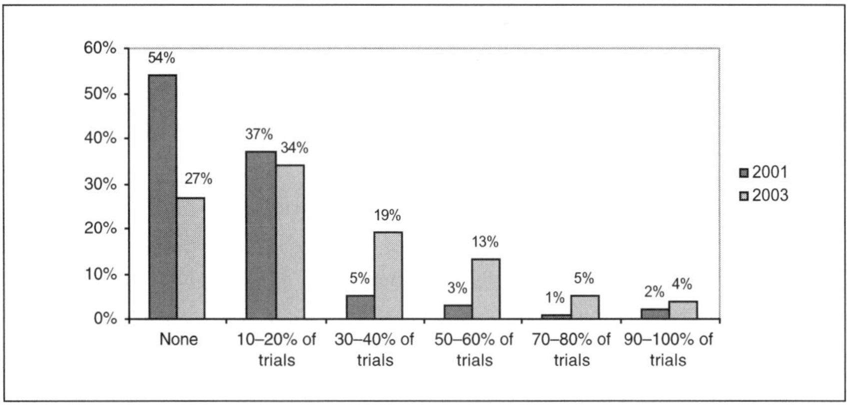

Figure 5.7 Proportion of trials using the web for data collection in 2001 and 2003 (base: 400 trial professionals)

Source: [50]

of the major players in this area. The Clinical Data Interchange Standards Consortium (CDISC) is an open, multidisciplinary, non-profit organization aiming to develop standards to support the electronic acquisition, exchange, submission and archiving of clinical trials' data for pharmaceutical product development. CDISC data models are intended ultimately to support end-to-end data flow in clinical trials, from the source into an operational database, through analysis to regulatory submission. The data that is relevant to CDISC includes patient records (clinical report forms), laboratory data, data from contract research organizations, shared data between companies and development partners, and numerous other sources. CDISC has unveiled metadata models for electronic FDA submissions and a new XML-based data acquisition and archiving model. Leading pharmaceutical, biotechnology and information technology companies are providing funding to accelerate the progress of CDISC activities [53] (Figure 5.7).

- The US NIH (National Institutes of Health) has partnered with VitalLink.net to produce a series of six interactive presentations on hepatitis C. These will be delivered to the 400 participants of an NIH hepatitis C clinical trial either by touch screen or PDA. The presentations are aimed at educating patients, gaining consent and collecting data. It is hoped that they will also prove a speedy way of allaying participant anxiety and improving the doctor–patient relationship [54].

continued from previous page

- American Home Products is attempting to speed time-to-market by standardizing its worldwide operations on one global IT infrastructure. The network will help the company roll out a global system for running simultaneous clinical trials in multiple countries. The system will use Oracle Clinical for clinical data management, Fraser Williams' Impact for clinical trials' management and a custom-built application for adverse events tracking [30].
- CenterWatch has a wireless PDA suite of searchable databases, called CenterWatch-Mobile, designed for clinical research and healthcare professionals seeking clinical trials' information in a portable format. The databases are intended to allow research and healthcare professionals to gain access to information about investigational new drugs and active clinical trials at the point of patient care. This information is designed to assist professionals in determining treatment programmes and identifying potential clinical trials for their patients. CenterWatch-Mobile is made up of three databases that include detailed listings of more than 8000 ongoing industry-sponsored clinical trials; summary descriptions of hundreds of drugs recently approved by the FDA; and more than 1500 profiles of drugs in phases I–III clinical trials. Instead of spending time investigating a printed index or surfing through a website, clinical professionals can search any one of these resources whenever and wherever they need to and know that the information is up to date [55].
- PDAs can also be used by trial participants to collect, record and transmit relevant data. For instance, 250 participants in a type I diabetes trial used software provided by electronic diary firm Invivodata to record and upload data, allowing sponsors Amylin Pharmaceuticals to monitor the trial in real time [56]. And some companies are experimenting with a truly innovative form of EDC – clothing that can monitor various physiological functions such as heart rate and blood pressure, and relay this information to investigators via the Internet [57].
- Eli Lilly has deployed Phase Forward's InForm software as its standard global platform for managing web-based clinical trials. Lilly is using Phase Forward's technology to speed the collection and management of phases I–IV trial data. By streamlining these processes, Phase Forward's solutions are expected to help Lilly reduce product development time. Lilly would like to see the industry begin to adopt common standards for the capture, collection and analysis of clinical trial data [58].

continued from previous page

- DataLabs is collaborating with Microsoft to bring its DataLabs CTMS (clinical trial management system) to pharmaceutical companies. DataLabs gains the respectability associated with the Microsoft name, whilst Microsoft gains an opportunity to push its NET technology to pharmaceutical companies. DataLabs CTMS is designed to lower drug development costs, accelerate the time-to-market, increase efficiencies and improve the quality of research [59].

Another strategic imperative is for companies to appropriately use pharmaco-economic data as a marketing tool. It has been argued that drug company-sponsored pharmaco-economic studies can be inherently biased. Indeed, it has been found that studies funded by drug companies are eight times less likely to reach unfavourable conclusions as compared with non-profit organization-funded studies [60]. If products and services are to be reimbursed, it is vital to show a convincing, positive cost-benefit analysis to the payer. Pharmaceutical companies must build credible pharmaco-economic analysis into the trials of drug/diagnostic/service bundles in order to convince payers of their usefulness. Companies should also seek to demonstrate the overall benefits of their treatments, including societal and quality of life impacts. The Internet is certainly the most rapid and focused channel for communicating a strong case concerning the value of innovative therapeutics.

Getting physicians online for the purpose of conducting research and collecting and sharing information on medical therapies is an important challenge to increasing the use of the Internet for R&D. 'E-hubs' used in clinical trials encourage sustained involvement of physicians in the development and use of the product, increasing their trust in the product [52]. Physicians considering the use of a new therapy will often look to the physicians who participated in the clinical trials. E-hubs can provide physicians with immediate access to the investigators from specific clinical trials [52].

Conclusions – 'the take home messages'

Although 90 per cent of pharmaceutical executives believe that the clinical trials' process will be changed radically by the Internet, only 13 per cent expect a significant bottom-line impact [7]. However, some argue that the bottom-line impact will be significant. Cost savings made as sponsor coordinators visit trial sites less often are significant in larger (that is, phase III) trials, but the major benefits (up to $66 million in increased revenue) will come from quicker time-to-market [50]. We believe the latter analysis to be closer to the truth, if somewhat overoptimistic. The reason? Trials can be streamlined and made more efficient, but they will not get significantly shorter, as this is largely a function of a therapeutic end point. But significant time savings will be made at the front and back ends of the trial, therefore there will be some time-to-market benefit, but less than predicted, due to the paucity of blockbuster products.

The current drug approval process places a high hurdle cost on new drug development, effectively restricting the ability of companies to deliver products suitable for only a narrow segment of the population. Therefore, new regulations may be required, for example, to make the clinical trials more appropriate for products that target only a small segment of the population. And as EDC takes off, it is possible to submit data to regulators in real time, allowing them to request modifications while the trial is still taking place. It is inevitable that consumers will get more involved with trials as they become more incentivized to manage the quality of their healthcare. Evidence suggests that their involvement can have major positive benefits. Twenty-three out of 62 government-sponsored clinical trial centres in the UK involved consumers in the design of trials. Most researchers thought that the input from consumers was useful, particularly in areas such as refining research questions, improving the quality of patient information and making the trial more relevant to patient needs [61].

- Clinical trials, already data intensive and highly regulated, are set to become more so. However, new digital technologies afford the opportunity to shorten upstream and downstream elements (recruitment, analysis and submission) and streamline the entire process through the use of EDC and management.

- The conduct of large phase III clinical trials remains an important financial barrier to entry for a smaller biotechnology company wishing to commercialize a drug. The extent to which e-clinical trials would permit biotechnology companies to develop drugs without pharmaceutical industry partners is debatable, especially as drug registration remains extremely expensive. However, we should remember that if we do indeed see an increase in niche or personalized medicine products, it is reasonable to expect that new and cheaper avenues for getting a drug to market will appear.

- As pharmaceutical companies seek to extract more value from marketing budgets, clinical trials are increasingly being seen as a way of establishing sustainable relationships with key opinion-leaders and potential high prescribers. We are already seeing the application of e-hubs or clinical trial portals as a tool for establishing communities of investigators and serving the scientific information and administrative needs of trial participants.
- As consumers are increasingly segmented into smaller groups for economic and genomic reasons, clinical trials offer options for building relationships, in areas ranging from cancer treatment to more lifestyle-oriented drugs. Following the example of e-panels used extensively in the consumer goods industry, small experiments will be conducted to explore the market for a specific therapeutic product. This will result in a very different and certainly more cost-effective market research paradigm, where focused interactions with target customers will replace expensive generalized surveys.

Managing knowledge and collaboration

Introduction

> Companies believe, as an article of faith, that they should link scientists and researchers across the enterprise. How they go about doing this is another matter. We're seeing a lot of testing of federated and virtual warehouses and other middleware solutions but no clear answers so far. – Emmett Power, CEO of Silico Research (2001) [62]

Biopharmaceutical research is a knowledge- and collaboration-intensive pursuit. By the early 1990s, it was not unusual for academic and industry scientists to collaborate on projects entirely by email, without having ever met. Although cheap, this is not ideal, as the authors of this book can testify. Writing emails is time consuming, and the time-lag between receiving an email and answering it makes truly creative collaboration problematic. Problems increase exponentially if more than two scientists are involved. Today, specialized web-based applications allow large groups of scientists to collaborate remotely, publishing results to each other and automatically updating key data on every linked computer. Faced with unspectacular drug pipelines and a growing belief, in the financial markets at least, that innovative discovery is now in the domain of small, nimble biotechnology companies, the pharmaceutical industry is devoting considerable expense and reflection into how to leverage knowledge and promote collaboration across its huge research establishment. First we explore some of the modalities available and then discuss the strategic implications.

Knowledge and collaboration tools

Intuitively, it would appear that the Internet and the web in particular are ideal platforms for sharing knowledge and managing collaboration. The reality has been a burgeoning industry offering a wide range of tools and approaches. This is not unexpected in the light of the range of environments and specialized contexts in which research and development knowledge is shared across the pharmaceutical industry.

Laboratory information management systems (LIMS)

LIMS is software that facilitates experiments by collecting and processing data in the laboratory, as well as streamlining day-to-day operations by automating such tasks as alerting staff when, where and how to take samples. Before the advent of LIMS, all lab information was kept on paper. Not only was this labour intensive, it could also cause problems if a regulator requested a certain piece of data. LIMS systems normally run on PCs connected to a central database. If LIMS data is needed throughout the company, the database needs to be linked to the company's ERP system or some other central database. There are at least 40 vendors selling LIMS solutions, mostly for the pharmaceutical and chemical industries [63].

Corporate portals and intranets

Intranets are being deployed across all pharmaceutical departments with the aim of sharing knowledge faster and encouraging collaboration. A wide range of knowledge is generated including business intelligence (what an organization knows about its internal workings and status of projects, such as the latest R&D findings of a particular group) or competitive intelligence (knowledge generated by studying the strategies and actions of competitors, including the latest status of their clinical trials).

Business and competitive intelligence is of limited value unless it can be distributed to relevant individuals in the organization at the right time and place. Valuable information is easily obscured in the torrents of dispersed data generated by a modern business. Most organizations deploy business and competitive intelligence in an ad hoc manner. Ideally, corporate portals should allow users to select the types of information they wish to see (a personalized view), or generate custom reports, in a way that suits their particular role. Solutions can gather data from relevant databases and warehouses (see the section in Chapter 12 on data warehouses) and publish it as individuals require. As such, these systems are similar to content management systems.

Document and content management

Document management allows automatic indexing, storing, securing, revising and searching of documents. It has long been used by heavily regulated industries such as pharmaceuticals to manage regulatory paperwork, and in the 1970s this was known as 'paperwork simplification'. Document management is a combination of processes and technologies. The ease with which new technologies such as the Internet and XML allow documents to be stored, retrieved and published has led to great advances in document management systems. The most advanced of these are known as 'content management systems'.

Content management applications allow authors to rapidly publish large amounts of content, in any format. Ideally, content is created by the author and approved by the editor(s) in a structured work-flow process. For instance, a physician in London can write a web article on clinical trials' procedures and submit it to the staff editor in Chicago for approval. When the editor logs into the content management system, she sees the article submitted for editing in her task list. Once she edits and approves the article, the system notifies the publisher that the article is ready for publication. The publisher then publishes the content to the appropriate section of the corporate portal. Approved content is then automatically metafile-tagged (using a system such as Autonomy) and stored in a format that allows rapid indexing (XML-tagged data in an Oracle database). Articles on clinical trials' procedures stored in a central database could then be located and published as a printed page on a portal or sent to a PDA at the push of a button. This streamlined process improves the efficiency of web publication, letting organizations increase the amount of content published on their websites and ensuring that this content has been through a formal review process. Key benefits of a content management system are:

- High-quality content is published more quickly, allowing the creation of richer, more dynamic publications (including websites, reports, advertising material).

- Content is tagged with metafiles and archived, allowing rapid search and retrieval.
- Content is stored in an open format that can be displayed correctly in a number of publishing media, such as web or PDA pages.

Content management has obvious applications in research (storing and retrieving internal and external scientific results), development (storing and managing clinical trial data) and marketing (personalizing marketing material to be sent to customers over the web or by mail). Pfizer provides a good example of the savings achievable by content management. By managing the FDA submission for Viagra over the web, the approval time-line was cut nearly in half, as researchers no longer had to sift through mountains of paperwork [64].

Intellectual property management

Intellectual property (IP) is proprietary knowledge owned or controlled by a company. IP can be protected by law with patents, copyrights and trademarks, or be a trade secret (where the IP is not made public). In a world where value is created by innovation and ideas, the management of intellectual property is a required core competence, as IP is one of a company's most valuable and flexible assets. Strategic management and use of patents can significantly enhance a company's success. Global revenues from the licensing of patent rights have rocketed from $15 billion in 1990 to $110 billion in 2000 [65]. IP is particularly valuable to the pharmaceutical industry. Approximately 65 per cent of pharmaceutical products would not have been developed or launched if patent protection were not available. Because of the extra development time needed for regulatory approval, pharmaceutical products have a shorter patent-protected commercial lifetime than those in other industries (the average for a new drug in the 1990s was 11–12 years) [66].

But much intellectual property is wasted. A 1998 survey reported that 67 per cent of US companies owned technology assets that they failed to exploit. These companies fail to exploit more than 35 per cent of their patents because they can see no immediate use for them. The value of these wasted assets was conservatively estimated to be $115 billion [65]. The reason? Few companies systematically mine their IP portfolios looking for revenue-generating opportunities; those that do tend to do so only under times of severe financial pressure. And licensing revenues are not the only benefit – refound patents can be used to make new products or block competitors' patents, while an analysis of the patent universe can allow a company to make informed decisions on R&D projects, and identify possible alliance partners who have IP that may be valuable to a particular project. Indeed, many argue that a company that puts protection of intellectual property in the same hands as those who select and manage R&D projects produces higher returns. One of the best-known patent portfolio mining efforts was undertaken by Dow Chemical in 1994, as part of a cost-cutting effort. The year-long audit of its IP assets allowed each of the company's 29,000 patents to be valued and assigned to one of 15 business units [65]. IBM reviewed its patents in the 1990s, and now makes nearly $1 billion per annum from licensing its IP [65].

Automated software can be deployed by a company to analyse its own or a competitor's patent portfolio, allowing rapid analysis of unused IP or a competitor's relative strength. Some systems permit users to search multiple patent libraries by keyword or Boolean logic. Users can then build, save and store customized groups of patents, examine how and where their patents are cited and annotate patents for competitive intelligence or litigation purposes. Pharmaceutical IP management is a highly specialized domain often housed within legal departments. New e-tools allow more communication and a more rigorous decision process concerning the management and defence of IP.

E-learning

Manufacturers of drugs and medical devices are starting to use the Internet not only to deliver training, but also to assure regulators that training projects comply with strict standards. Failing to prove that people are qualified to do their jobs can mean warning letters and fines from the FDA. Good manufacturing practices (GMPs) are now vitally important, as the FDA, to ensure patient safety, has indeed closed a number of pharmaceutical plants. Procter & Gamble's (P&G) pharmaceuticals unit has begun testing software that keeps track of training compliance. The goal is to automate the reporting of employee training, a required task because training certifications expire periodically. Training for skills such as running an assembly line or testing products is documented largely through paper forms or PC spreadsheets. Systems now automatically alert employees when their skills need to be refreshed or when new skills are needed. This requires integration into email servers and databases that store employee records and contact information. P&G is, for example, integrating the training system with the financial and human resource modules built into their ERP software, using XML interfaces [67].

Digital strategy in knowledge and collaboration management

The opportunity to communicate using video-conferencing and web-based tools has changed the dynamics of scientific collaboration across pharmaceutical companies. It is difficult to measure the impact of innovation in communication, a challenge that has long existed when we look at the telephone, fax and email. Similarly, it is not easy to quantify ROI (return on investment) for a range of clearly useful technologies such as secure data warehouses, document management systems and corporate intranets. Many of these tools have been difficult to implement and have not been very user-friendly. We describe some current best practice in this area:

- Bristol-Myers Squibb uses the web and its enterprise portal to let its researchers communicate in virtual conferences. Researchers in the company around the world make use of the company's web system to hold virtual conferences on work of mutual interest [11].
- All biotechnology and pharmaceutical companies need to store information for decades while research and regulation processes are completed. Traditionally, this information has been kept in volumes of scientific notebooks and spreadsheets, but the FDA has stipulated that it must be moved online. Eli Lilly's Molecule Library is a knowledge management application linked to the portal that lets regulatory, scientific and other workers find information about molecules in seconds. The Molecule Library cost $2 million and Lilly estimates that, primarily through time saved searching for information, savings will total $27 million during the next ten years [5].
- GlaxoSmithKline has invested in peer-to-peer (P2P) technology – the file-swapping method made famous by the Napster music service. The company uses P2P to link its scientists with researchers at biotechnology companies and universities across the world (it has purchased 10,000 licences), allowing them to share the same virtual workspace and edit the same documents without using a company server [68].
- The Lilly corporate portal, known as myELVIS (for Eli Lilly Virtual Information Service), integrates technology to automate the categorization of content from thousands of Lotus Notes and Documentum databases, speeding searches for information and helping to spread expertise across the global Lilly enterprise. In addition, Lilly has integrated taxonomy technology to facilitate the automated categorization of documents, web pages and messages in the portal's document directory,

speeding the creation of a global knowledge base. Lilly's sales, marketing, manufacturing and scientific communities will gain access from the desktop to patent information, market news, biomedical research and competitive intelligence. The myELVIS portal is the framework for an enterprise-wide web experience extending from the laboratory and the boardroom to the field. It will provide Lilly employees with a single destination for healthcare news, patent services, reference works and the results of clinical trials [69].

- ActiveCyte is a start-up developing Internet-based tools and services to support the technology licensing process. ActiveCyte hopes to optimize and automate screening and preliminary due diligence processes using a database that aggregates available patents from sources around the world and classifies them with a purpose-built taxonomy [7].

- In 1998, Bristol-Myers Squibb built its own laboratory information management system (LIMS), a database that allows the company to track DNA samples as they are sequenced, stored and analysed by scores of different scientists. The choice to build rather than buy at that time was out of necessity. None of the vendors offered a system that could be accessed easily by a scientist who was working at the bench with only three samples as well as by researchers examining 30,000 samples with a high-throughput screening device [31].

- Real-time software applications will make remote collaboration far more efficient. Juice Software has developed a program that allows spreadsheets linked to a corporate database to be updated automatically. Collaborators can also link all their spreadsheets so if one updates a cell, all can see the change. OurProject.com gives teams all the tools they need to run a project on the web. A graphical interface can be used to assign tasks, track budgets and view time sheets. Needless to say, Microsoft is getting in on the act, updating its Excel and Project applications so they can be shared by multiple users and updated in real time [70].

Conclusions – 'the take home messages'

Effective collaboration is the key to creative, innovative scientific research. Modern communications technologies allow collaboration to take place at great physical distances and we now have robust technologies to store necessary data in a warehouse, and search and disseminate it as needed. Knowledge management will become increasingly crucial as e-R&D, changes in the regulatory environment, the demands of payers and segmented medicine increase the data intensity of drug development by several orders of magnitude.

- The tools exist for optimized information flow across the pharmaceutical value chain. Standards (such as XML) ensure that data is formatted, stored and distributed consistently. The main barriers to better management of knowledge and collaboration are institutional, rather than technological.
- A centralized knowledge management system has a numbers of virtues, as it captures and stores research and development data, combines it with external data and makes it available throughout the company. The missing link is often the analytic tools required to mine and make sense of the data and the people to implement this analytic focus.
- Knowledge and collaboration technologies are getting a lot cheaper. Currently, it is difficult to justify the building of highly customized tools, as often very basic approaches are appropriate. The bad reputation of knowledge management is attributable to the fact that companies spent large amounts of money on systems that were never fully used. The first step in specifying these systems is in defining and meeting the real needs of the users.

Managing alliances and partnerships

Introduction

> I am not certain yet that we [the research operations] are any better than a biotech company, a small pharmaceuticals company or a university department. – Tachi Yamada, head of R&D at GlaxoSmithKline [71]

The economic and technological pressures we describe, as well as the pressures of globalization and regulation, are forcing pharmaceutical companies to operate in an R&D environment that is increasingly specialized and complex. New technologies could double R&D costs over the next five years and companies are concerned about the productivity of their research units. Pfizer has split its research department into eight separate discovery sites (although clinical development, which benefits from scale, has been consolidated into a single site) [72]. GlaxoSmithKline has also divided parts of its research group into autonomous units and has also promised stock options to successful scientists in a bid to recreate the entrepreneurial climate of biotechnology companies. Indeed, it will consider selling a large part of its research operations if the rate at which they discover new drugs does not improve over the next few years. Few companies now have the capabilities or resources to cover the entire value chain, from research to development to manufacturing to marketing. The traditional response to these pressures has been to merge to form ever-larger groups but, beyond short-term cost savings, the results of these mergers have tended to be disappointing. For example, the market share of GlaxoWellcome in 1998 was 15 per cent lower than the separate market shares of Glaxo and Wellcome in 1994 [73].

The pharmaceutical industry is becoming a network of joint ventures, alliances, partnerships and outsourcing. Global giants, faced with the expiry of patents on key products, are in-licensing new therapeutic leads and compounds from specialist R&D players, and outsourcing clinical trials to service organizations. In addition, the race to patent and commercialize new discoveries in the life sciences (in 2000 alone, more than 20,000 gene patent applications were submitted to the US Patent and Trademarks Office [32]) will force even the largest companies to act quickly to develop or in-license the intellectual property they need to create new products and services.

Types of alliance

Companies can enter into alliances to gain competencies at any stage of the value chain and with a wide range of partners, each of which will now be discussed.

Partnering with academic institutions, research agencies and government laboratories

The healthcare industry, and pharmaceuticals, is regarded as a vital part of the economy of the industrialized world. The promotion of research innovation, and its commercialization, fuels important collaborations between pharmaceutical companies and a range of institutions. The US NIH, with a budget exceeding $20 billion, is a global force in biomedical research. Drug development requires the collaboration of a global network of academic physicians and universities.

In-licensing drugs or technology to boost research capabilities

Currently, about 40 per cent of pharmaceutical industry revenues are derived from in-licensed products. The balance of power between big pharma and

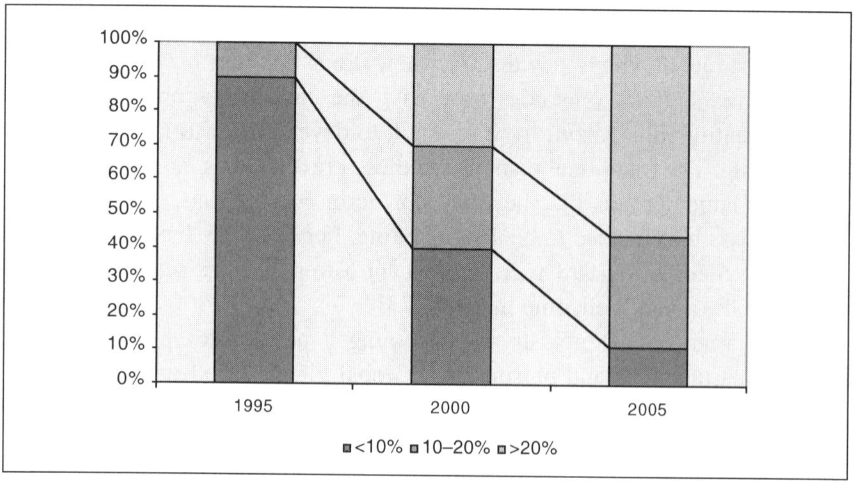

Figure 5.8 Licensing as a percentage of R&D spending (survey of large pharmaceutical companies)

Source: [74]

biotechnology companies is in a state of constant flux, as on the one hand pharmaceutical companies need innovative products urgently, whereas most biotechnology companies do not have the resources to commercialize the drugs that they discover (Figure 5.8).

Partnering with contract research organizations (CROs) to boost development capabilities

Faced with the need to speed up drug development, pharmaceutical companies are using CROs. But as e-clinical trial systems become the standard, we may see new business models with hospitals and even individual physicians managing contract research. The large CROs are looking for higher return arrangements (revenue sharing) rather than the traditional model (fee for service), especially in their relationship with biotechnology companies. The risk-sharing model is gaining in popularity, especially as smaller biotechnology companies, in the current financial market, cannot afford to build drug development capacity.

Partnering with contract manufacturers to gain capability and flexibility

Outsourcing of manufacturing is becoming increasingly common (Table 5.1), and we discuss this in detail in Chapter 6 on manufacturing and the supply chain.

TABLE 5.1

Number of contract manufacturers in North America and Europe (1980–2000)

	1980	2000
North America	36	75
Europe	156	306

Source: [75]

Partnering with contract sales organizations (CSOs)

As the sheer number of representatives visiting physicians remains a major determinant of pharmaceutical sales, it is likely that the sales representative 'arms race' will continue into the near future. As sales budgets come under pressure, and for small companies without sales forces, the market for contract sales organizations that pay their representatives 25–30 per cent less than an in-house pharma representative [21] will increase.

Structuring alliances

While alliances can certainly range in terms of scope and scale, four structures predominate:

1. *Cooperative alliances.* Cooperative partnerships are the most popular, and do not entail the creation of a separate enterprise. Instead they take the form of virtual organizations. Sixty per cent of alliances undertaken within the biopharmaceutical and medical device and diagnostic sectors fall into this category.
2. *Minority equity alliances.* In this form of alliance, one partner takes a minority equity position in another, and the companies cooperate in management and operations. Such arrangements can stimulate the sharing of technology and joint development of products.
3. *Joint ventures.* A joint venture entails the formation of a stand-alone operating company with a distinct identity. This type of alliance requires an explicit statement of business strategy and organization.
4. *Consortia.* Consortia involve the alliance of several companies through a combination of different types of partnerships [76].

However, whatever legal form an alliance takes, it is worth remembering this maxim: an alliance is any business arrangement in which the success of one partner is tied to the success of both. Anything else is nothing more than an arms-length contractual arrangement [76].

Digital strategy in alliance management

Industry experts estimate that up to two-thirds of alliances fail to meet their goals [77]. However, if pharmaceutical companies are expecting to obtain a significant proportion of their revenues from alliances, then it is vital to manage them well. The key features of a good alliance have been well documented and include involvement by senior management, finding the right people, devoting adequate financial resources, setting realistic goals and milestones, clarifying responsibilities, frequent communication, promoting collaborative decision-making, constant performance monitoring and ensuring that critical systems are compatible. Alliances require constant attention lest they languish and cause enmity. For example, when Eli Lilly realized that it was losing out on potential business transactions by not paying enough attention to its partners, of which it had about 140, it set up a special alliance oversight group which it trained and staffed not with scientists but with managers fitted to the task of managing and smoothing relationships [78].

Pharmaceutical companies, used to being in a position of strength in relationships, have traditionally done little to actively enhance alliances and ensure that partners were satisfied. One manifestation of this is the fact that pharmaceutical companies are about half as likely to have implemented an IT strategy to support collaboration as health insurers or payers [79] (Figure 5.9).

Conclusions – 'the take home messages'

Digital technology makes monitoring of relationships, alliances and contracts much cheaper, and it can be argued that good monitoring makes for good relationships. A classic example is video rentals, where before 1998 outlets generally paid distributors $70 for each tape and thus could not afford enough copies of the most popular movies to satisfy demand. Now they pay $3–8 upfront and a royalty of 40–60 per cent on each rental, as smart cash registers and network connections are cheap enough to allow distributors to monitor rentals on a daily basis. Pharmaceutical in-licensing based on royalties and

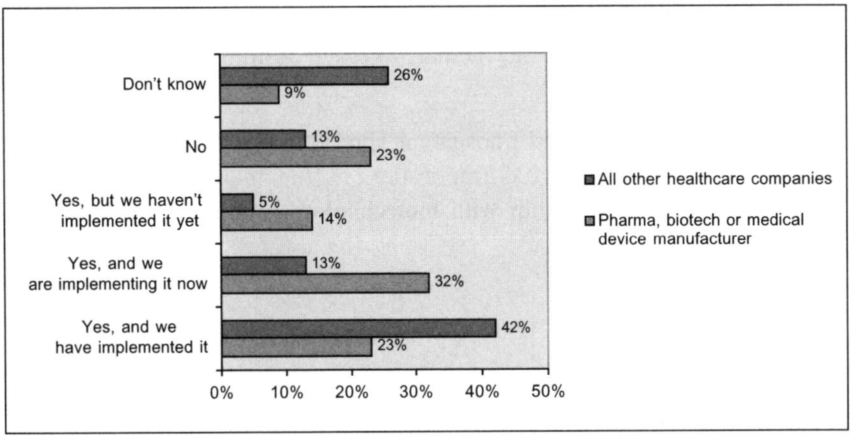

Figure 5.9 Percentage of healthcare companies with an IT strategy in place to support collaboration with partners (base: 60 healthcare professionals, 2000)

Source: [76]

shared risk will benefit from similar arrangements, making alliances more secure for both parties.

The pharmaceutical industry is becoming less vertically integrated and more dependent on networks (despite the attempts of many biotechnology companies to boost their valuations by moving into drug development and marketing). However, evidence suggests that many industry players have not yet developed best-practice IT collaboration strategies. Currently, some companies attempt to build franchises around a single disease or customer group. However, if a disease is segmented into many sub-conditions needing different treatment regimes, it will become increasingly difficult for one company to provide all the necessary treatments without forming a network of alliances. Pharmaceutical companies will also have to partner and share data with disease management firms (to get the data needed to develop and market products) and healthcare providers (to understand the new dynamics of personalized medicine).

- As in the case of knowledge management, pharmaceutical companies are being forced to extract maximum value from alliances across the value chain. Digital technologies are an avenue for managing alliances better and more cheaply.

- The loyalty of alliance partners is becoming crucial to pharmaceutical companies that not only need access to products and services, but also want to appear to be attractive potential partners to companies offering innovative therapeutics or channels to reach customers (both physicians and patients).

- IT offers a traceable and transparent approach to documenting alliances. This has become of vital importance as the industry faces scrutiny concerning its relationship with biotechnology partners and its financial management of alliances.

PART III

Digital Strategies: Manufacturing, Supply Chain and Distribution

CHAPTER

6 Digital strategies in manufacturing and supply chain

Introduction

As biomedical products must have an excellent safety profile, the pharmaceutical manufacturing and supply chain is highly regulated, but is otherwise similar to those of many other industries. Companies purchase raw materials for bulk synthesis of active and inactive ingredients, thereafter drugs are formulated and packaged into various delivery mechanisms (solutions for injection, inhalers and pills of various types). Despite this similarity with other industries, there is substantial potential to improve the pharmaceutical supply chain and increase asset utilization (Table 6.1).

TABLE 6.1

Gross margins and inventory turnover of indicative companies (2000)

	Pfizer	Schering-Plough	Merck	Coca-Cola	Intel	Cisco	IBM	Dell
Gross margins	82%	80%	47%	69%	59%	65%	37%	21%
Inventory turnover	1.5	2.0	6.5	6.6	7.2	8.5	10.6	59.8

Note:
Inventory turnover is defined as the cost of goods sold for the trailing six months divided by average inventory. Generally the higher the number the lower the inventory costs.

Source: [80].

There are several reasons for the relative inefficiency of pharmaceutical manufacturing:

- High product margins and public health concerns make lost sales due to stock-outs undesirable and hence inventory turnover tends to be low.
- Individual plant managers have traditionally been given a considerable degree of autonomy, their prime directive being to avoid stock-outs.
- Plants were often built in particular countries as a political trade-off.

However, increased R&D and marketing costs and drug pricing pressure are forcing pharmaceutical companies to focus more on saving money (as opposed to increasing revenues through increased expenditures on R&D or sales or marketing). Automation and the use of IT have led to demand projections that are more accurate, a supply chain that is better managed, and asset utilization targets of up to 90 per cent are now common. Pharmaceutical manufacturing facilities are becoming increasingly centralized. In the past, pharmaceutical companies would often site a manufacturing facility in a certain country as a concession to the government (it could even be a precondition of product approval and regulation), and local manufacturing divisions were highly autonomous. The drive to cut costs and the globalization of regulations, especially those concerning good manufacturing practice (GMP), are reversing this situation.

The transforming supply chain

Many pharmaceutical companies rely on very few products for the vast majority of their sales. However, industry consolidation and more complex therapeutics are resulting in a changing manufacturing environment. Mergers mean larger companies with larger product portfolios, and some of the more innovative drugs (such as antibodies or complex small molecules) require a new range of competencies and technologies. As we enter the age of personalized medicine (where individual patient segments are treated with different drugs according to their genetic susceptibility to disease and response to those drugs), companies will have to produce smaller batches of highly customized products. One consequence of this will be the need to make manufacturing facilities more flexible, as most would currently have difficulty in moving between different manufacturing processes. Regulatory hurdles make repurposing even more difficult, as approval is required both for process and material changes.

Globalization is putting new demands on pharmaceutical companies. They are faced with increasing numbers of partners in manufacturing and distribution. At the same time, these partners are located at greater distances from company headquarters and each other. While such changes provide significant opportunities for pharmaceutical companies to generate new revenues and cut costs through increased outsourcing of manufacturing processes, the increased complexities require significant changes in communication and supply chain management.

In 2001, Forrester Research identified the following obstacles to developing the type of flexible manufacturing system needed to deal with a flood of new drugs [81]:

- Rigid and constrained global manufacturing – custom-built plants with non-standard production equipment, long lead times for raw materials and varying regulatory regimes lead to manufacturing capacity that is inflexible.
- Limited demand visibility due to poor demand forecasts.
- Poor trading partner integration – the Internet is hardly used to communicate with supply chain partners such as suppliers, contract manufacturers and distributors.

Supply chains are becoming transparent through the deployment of tools such as supply chain management software and digital marketplaces. Advanced planning software optimizes production activities by letting companies more easily communicate their production needs to suppliers, keep buyers abreast of production cycles, and respond quickly to changes in supply and demand. The software works by comparing order data from several ERP systems, from within or outside the company. Many of these applications are web-based, allowing all partners in a supply chain easily to access relevant information.

Online marketplaces for both procurement and sales should introduce transparency, information availability and streamlined systems into the supply chain. Employees are able to self-purchase supplies, thus reducing the role of a purchasing department. Exchanges can automate processes such as ordering, catalogue maintenance, inventory and shipment tracking, volume forecasting and invoicing.

E-procurement from B2B marketplaces will offer immediate savings in terms of purchasing compliance, and further savings are possible from inventory control and competitive tendering. However, given the limited number of suppliers for some raw ingredients (such as biologic ingredients for protein drugs), B2B competitive tendering is only likely to be implemented for true commodity products (such as non-specialist plant equipment or basic supplies) [7]. Even so, it is predicted that nine per cent of the European health-care industry trade, totalling 53 billion, will be online by 2005, compared with 0.5 billion in 2001 [82]. Some healthcare companies are already participating in exchanges, but data standards, competitive, regulatory and privacy concerns are preventing others from joining. And joining is costly, as companies looking to buy or sell on exchanges are likely to have to spend an average of $6 million to $23 million on systems integration [83].

Traceability in the value chain

As pharmaceutical product transaction volumes are far less than those in fast-moving consumer goods, and the number of outlets (such as hospitals and retail pharmacies) is limited, we have not seen a major impetus to adopt universal product coding. However, drug packaging already has a high level of traceability, as it is important to know when, where and how medications are manufactured, in case of undesirable effects or product tampering. The need for traceability and tightened EPA (Environmental Protection Agency) and FDA requirements is fuelling the growth of batch control systems. Total global shipments of batch control systems, including hardware, software, supplier and third-party services, which were US$2.4 billion in 2000, will exceed US$3.2 billion by the end of 2005, a compound annual growth rate (CAGR) of nearly six per cent. With the approval of electronic batch records and electronic signatures by the FDA, there is now a greater incentive for regulated industries, such as pharmaceutical and biotechnology, to move to paper-free systems. Large, sophisticated users are now demanding comprehensive and integrated batch control solutions with seamless interfaces to production management and business planning systems. Manufacturers of pharmaceuticals and fine chemicals are building flexible plants where many different products can be manufactured, and product changes can be made more quickly and easily. This is creating demand for more automated batch control systems [84] (Figure 6.1).

Supply chain networks and control

Supply chain pioneers are leveraging Internet technologies and adding functionality to enterprise-wide resource planning systems to capture key customer information. Forging alliances with domestic and overseas partners and outsourcing are also key to improving supply chain efficiency [85].

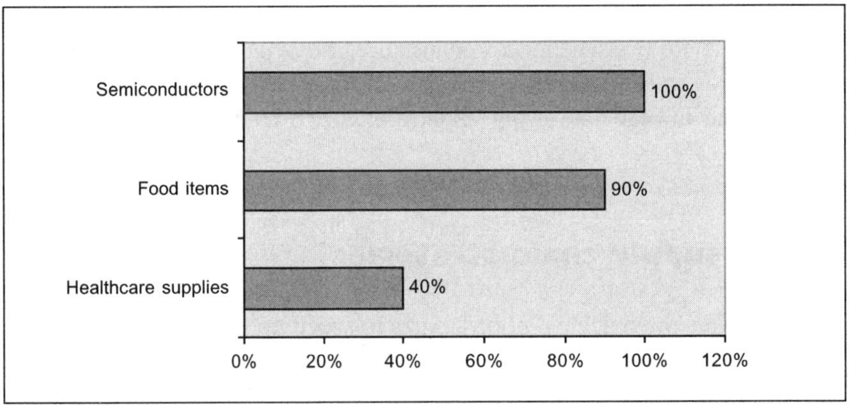

Figure 6.1 Percentage of products with universal product codes (2001)

Source: [83]

As companies seek greater flexibility and efficiency, there is a trend towards outsourcing. Pharmaceutical companies tend to retain control of formulation and labelling, and some refuse to outsource the manufacturing of their most critical products because of secrecy concerns. But outsourcing remains a valued option in an industry where it takes three to five years to build new manufacturing capabilities. For instance, Sanofi-Synthelabo outsources all of its US manufacturing. Digital technologies provide strategic partners with new possibilities for communication and feedback and multiple strategic partnerships in manufacturing can certainly be managed effectively. This will help pharmaceutical companies to deal more efficiently with their increasingly complex and diverse product lines.

At the same time as manufacturing capabilities are spread among a network of partners, control of manufacturing is becoming increasingly centralized. For example, many companies have consolidated bulk chemical synthesis – Pfizer now only has four bulk synthesis plants [80]. Good control systems permit flexible networks to operate optimally.

Companies can attain speedier time-to-market as collaborative processes improve interaction with R&D and marketing using collaborative tools, data management and seamless collaboration with sales and marketing [81]. Similarly, agile production becomes a reality when better visibility of internal and external capacity is improved. This involves the application of a manufacturing execution system (MES) to maintain constant manufacturing conditions throughout the complex manufacturing process, for example Genentech uses Aspen Technology's MES to ensure all its complex protein drugs are manufactured in a uniform manner. Linking plant-reporting systems to ERP systems allows global managers to know where there is spare capacity, and where plants are overwhelmed. For instance, Novartis uses Viewlocity to tie plant systems to central ERP and supply chain systems. Production planning can be done in real time using applications such as Manugistics, currently deployed by Pfizer.

Digital supply chain strategies

A range of technological solutions exists to speed up transactions across the manufacturing component of the pharmaceutical value chain. These include improved sourcing by linking with suppliers in B2B exchanges and using strategic sourcing tools and the prediction and management of demand using real-time product tracking. For example, ArcLight Systems, founded in 2001, is a data collection service managed by ten major pharmacy operators, including CVS, Wal-Mart and Albertson's. It harnesses the real-time monitoring potential of the web to deliver sales trends more quickly to pharmaceutical companies. Its pharmacy data service, R(x)ealTime, is updated online every ten minutes, and annual aggregated data from almost one billion filled prescriptions is used to provide custom reports revealing prescription drug use trends. Several major pharmaceutical companies signed onto the R(x)ealTime service for contracts typically ranging from one to three years. The firm is now also measuring patient compliance, switching and persistence [86].

GlaxoSmithKline's (GSK) procurement process

GSK has implemented e-enabled worldwide procurement. It has 1200 procurement professionals and purchased £8.2 billion in goods, services and supplies in 2001. GSK's procurement is based on a strategic sourcing process that works collaboratively across the business, sharing successes, rewards and recognition. *The Purchasing Machine*, a book by Dave Nelson, ranks GSK among the top ten purchasing organizations across all industries. Goals include delivering savings greater than ten per cent of total spend for purchased goods and services over the next three years, while ensuring all business requirements (that is, assurance of supply, quality/regulatory, service and so on) are met or exceeded in the process.

continued from previous page

The various modules of the system allow for detailed tracking of spending and savings, as well as contract management and creation. In addition, GSK has entered into an association with FreeMarkets, a reverse auction marketplace, to facilitate much of its procurement activity. GSK is also utilizing a buyer website of 'preferred suppliers' and is taking a 'plug and play' approach designed to take advantage of technology advancements as they occur in the marketplace. Any new implementations are rolled out first in the United States and United Kingdom and then in the company's facilities in the rest of the world. Specific point solution applications will be added to the system and horizontal exchanges and vertical marketplaces will be added when applicable. GSK predicts e-trade exchanges will be introduced in the industry, albeit at a slower pace than most had originally predicted, and will transform relationships in the industry and beyond [87].

One of the challenges that companies face in adopting e-commerce strategies is standardization across systems. Different departments throughout the companies use varying software programs and machines for information management and transfer. These programs or machines are often not compatible, thereby limiting the potential for information transfer and management across functional areas. In addition, the new software still does not provide complete solutions for such standardization; a problem exacerbated by the multiple systems in place in newly merged entities. Supply chain software selection is a challenge for many companies as it is unclear which programs will become the pharmaceutical industry standard. Choosing the software that does not become the industry standard could reduce opportunities for future strategic partnerships. Pharmaceutical manufacturing has to comply with strict regulations, such as the FDA's GMP. Compliance is often paper-based and voluminous, so transferring to an e-based system is no trivial task.

To gain manufacturing flexibility, pharmaceutical manufacturers need to invest in applications that create asset transparency, automate links between manufacturing and R&D and facilitate online collaboration with supply chain partners [81]. Pharmaceutical manufacturers will, according to Forrester Research, move to a more innovative and flexible networked approach in three phases, as shown in Table 6.2.

TABLE 6.2

Changing manufacturing environment – a blue-skies prediction

	Phase I – 2002–05	Phase II – 2005–10	Phase III – 2010+
Production environment	Make to forecast, pack to order	Make to forecast, pack to order	Make to order
Dominant customers	Wholesalers	Retailers, pharmacies and provider networks	Retailers, pharmacies and provider networks (and genetically affiliated customer groups)
VP of operations' mandate	Optimize asset use	Manage partnerships	Address customer needs
Production output per year	3 blockbusters	5 blockbusters, each with 5 configurations (for major genetic segments)	20 drugs, each with 10 configurations (for major genetic segments)
Demand change frequency	Monthly	Weekly	Daily
Capacity planning	Weekly	Daily	Continuous
Outsourced manufacturing	20 per cent	50 per cent	80 per cent
Order to delivery lag	Weeks	Days	1 day if possible
Finished goods inventory	< 15 per cent sales	< 8 per cent sales	< 2 per cent sales

Source: [81], modified by the authors

Conclusions – 'the take home messages'

Most pharmaceutical companies tend to see improving the supply chain as an operational necessity, whereas 85 per cent of medical device manufacturers see the supply chain as an area of strategic importance. This finding is not surprising, given the more commoditized nature of the medical device industry, where order fulfilment and margin control are of vital importance [7].

Some reports predict a future where goods are manufactured in 'batches of one' for individual consumers [81]. This will probably never be cost effective using existing manufacturing synthesis processes (be they chemical or biological). However, a degree of personalized medicine is still achievable in the next 20 years, with different people with different genetic needs receiving different mixtures of products bundled with services that will be unique to their needs and profiles. This is an impossible dream without innovative digital technology.

While we are some way off from a seamless interaction between R&D and manufacturing, the exigencies of producing increasingly complex drugs and growing capacity constraints in areas such as specialized fermentation are forcing communication and integration.

Manufacturing commodity exchanges for pharmaceuticals are already operational. The challenge is to develop product identification standards, centralized transaction and product information databases and integrate with existing supply chain management systems [83].

- Faced with margin pressures, pharmaceutical companies are certainly beginning to focus on better control of manufacturing costs. Similarly, following a number of high-profile warnings and plant closures by the FDA, GMP is becoming a strategic imperative. Innovative drugs are now fairly difficult to manufacture on an industrial scale. These factors are driving the diffusion of sophisticated digital technology into the manufacturing component of the pharmaceutical value chain.
- The barriers to creating a seamless link between R&D, manufacturing, distribution, sales and marketing, in order to be nimble enough to exploit market opportunities and react to the range of regulatory, health economic and innovation-based challenges that global pharmaceutical companies face, are institutional rather than technological.

CHAPTER

7 Digital strategies in pharmaceutical distribution

Introduction

Effective management control of distribution is particularly important in the highly regulated context of the pharmaceutical industry. The distribution process has, until recently, been regarded as relatively simple. Products are transported from company warehouses to pharmaceutical wholesale distributors. From there (based on demand) they are distributed to retail pharmacies and medical institutions, and thereon to patients or consumers. Globally, the majority of pharmaceutical distribution is controlled by a small number of wholesalers. Manufacturers do, in some cases, supply physicians, hospitals and even patients directly but have largely relied on distributors or wholesalers to manage the physical movement of products. While the final price of a drug may be high, it generally costs very little to produce (this is certainly changing in terms of innovative biotechnology products) and it was not generally in a manufacturer's interest to become too deeply enmeshed in the distribution chain (Figure 7.1).

Customer service departments have to work closely with the distribution network so they can resolve any problems concerning orders. Wholesalers and distributors also need to know policies concerning outdated, unsold or returned goods. Companies also have to be able to offer discounts to large buyers. Information systems are also needed to track all lot numbers and expiry dates for regulatory bodies, in case there is ever a product recall. The optimal distribution network manages factors such as the storage and handling characteristics of each product and the control of free samples.

One area that has been of interest to pharmaceutical companies is 'stocking the pipeline', or ensuring that all outlets have stock of a new product within

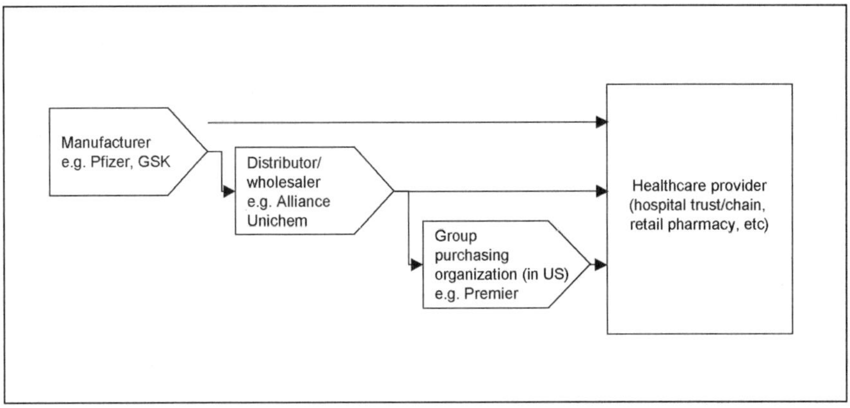

Figure 7.1 Pharmaceutical distribution – a simplified schematic

two to three days of regulatory approval. This is an expensive and planning-intensive process, particularly important for new products competing against established brands. The distribution strategy is often guided by a launch plan to incentivize physicians to prescribe, pharmacists to stock and, increasingly, patients to demand the new drug.

A changing pharmaceutical procurement environment

The purchase and distribution of medical products is in an increasing state of flux. Cost-containment pressures, whether a result of government or insurer scrutiny of pharmaceutical expenses, are forcing a degree of transparency across the distribution chain. Similarly, forces such as parallel imports in the EU or cross-border drug purchasing involving the USA and Canada are forcing consideration of the modalities for moving medicines from manufacturers to patients. Pharmaceutical manufacturers seeking to extract every penny from the value chain are looking at distributing directly to pharmacies and hospitals. The result will be a profound change in areas such as inventory control, delivery processes and customer service.

Johnson & Johnson, GE Medical Systems, Baxter International, Abbott Labs, Siemens, Medtronic and a range of partners formed the Global Healthcare Exchange (GHX) in 2000 to enable hospitals and other healthcare providers to buy directly from a single website [19]. The venture is an independent company and the founding companies do not have access to competitors' contract pricing. The participating companies supplied the funds to establish the new site, and suppliers pay to be listed. The site includes online product catalogues, ordering, order status enquiries and confirmation, and contract price information [88]. In the case of medical devices and disposables, the economic advantages of facilitating and integrating transactions are considerable.

The fact that pharmaceutical companies are already investigating lowering transaction costs by joining together with competitors to create online exchanges or marketplaces (such as GHXRx), through which pharmacies and other healthcare providers can purchase their products directly, would have been regarded just a few years ago as completely implausible. The economic imperative is to bypass distributors and increase the value that pharmaceutical companies derive from the supply chain, even at the expense of losing some competitive advantage.

Wholesalers and other large distributors are also using the Internet to eliminate inefficiencies in the supply chain. So, while some pharmaceutical companies are attempting to bypass wholesalers by using the Internet, the wholesalers are trying to make themselves more attractive to health providers and manufacturers. In the US, more than 100 distributors supply more than 220,000 providers via dozens of group purchasing organizations (GPOs) [83]. In Europe, there are two main types of distributors or wholesalers; those providing a full range of products and services (such as GEHE and Alliance Unichem which offer a one-stop shop for retail pharmacists and hospitals) and so-called 'short-liners' or wholesalers offering a deeply discounted but limited range of products. As most hospitals and pharmacists in Europe are reimbursed at a fixed rate for drugs, this offers the potential for the pharmacist to make a considerable profit. Alliance Unichem, one of Europe's biggest pharmaceutical distributors, spent £20 million on a B2B exchange for drug manufacturers and pharmacists. The inertia that characterizes health systems will ensure that wholesalers do not disappear overnight and, in fact, some of their offerings may become even more important as the dynamics of health service delivery change.

At the same time, healthcare providers are grouping together to form more powerful bargaining entities [89]. Therefore, there are attempts from both ends to compress the supply chain and squeeze out more value. IT permits the creation of ad hoc coalitions of buyers and forces unprecedented levels of price transparency. Also, most industrialized world hospitals already have a sophisticated communications backbone for the operation and maintenance of expensive technologies such as scanners and this 'pipe' can be used for communication with suppliers (Figure 7.2).

At the interface with the consumer or patient, we have hospital and retail pharmacies. Here global variation is great, with a spectrum ranging from the

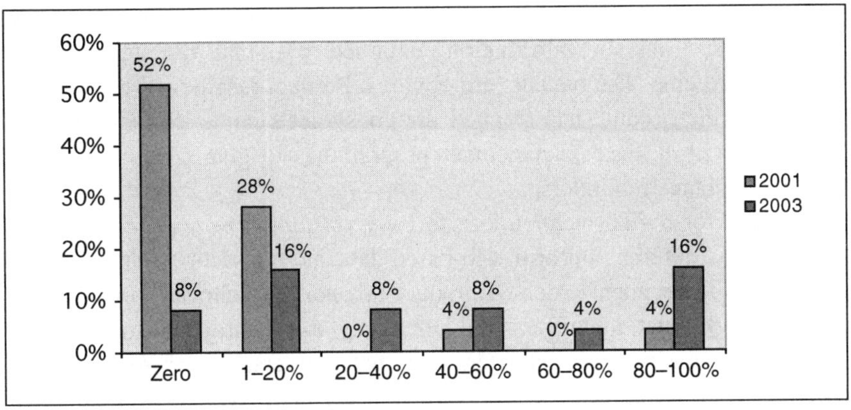

Figure 7.2 Percentage of European hospitals procuring on the Internet (2001 and 2003)

Source: [82]

huge US pharmacy benefit management organizations (PBMs), to retail chains such as Boots in the UK to small, privately owned pharmacies throughout Europe. The technological needs of these organizations differ substantially, but all use various forms of pharmacy management software for managing inventory, ordering, labelling and reimbursement and checking for interactions between dispensed drugs.

The scope for innovation in the distribution chain is virtually limitless. One technology that will have a major impact on manufacturing and distribution is remote sensors and automatic identification (auto-ID). The cost of remote wireless transponders will soon fall to a level that will allow them to be placed on just about any object in a supply chain – raw chemicals, fork-lift trucks, packets of finished products or even individual capsules of medicine. They will be able to carry large amounts of information and will be a key driver of real-time technologies that give almost unlimited visibility of manufacturing and distribution processes. Sensors are nothing new in expensive machinery that is subject to breakdown, or when any malfunction is undesirable (for instance in aircraft engines). But cheaper and smarter wireless chips are allowing the formation of real-time networks. Soon, smart wireless tags could replace bar-code readers. Shoppers will be able to walk through the checkout and their bill will be automatically calculated. And, if they bought packets of pharmaceutical X, the shop will automatically order more, an order that will move instantly up the supply chain through the manufacturer's own real-time network. It is not inconceivable to imagine an intelligent medicine cabinet in a bathroom with a small screen that will convey instructions and information contained in a small tag attached to a bottle of medicine. The benefits are obvious. Product recalls will be possible even when the product has reached the consumer's home. Sensors will be integrated with disease management programmes to give consumers automatic compliance reminders.

In order for digital technologies to truly revolutionize healthcare supply chain and distribution, uniform web-based data and transaction standards will be required for elements such as product taxonomy, healthcare organization identifiers, product identifiers and pharmacy e-standards. Historically, as discussed in the previous chapter, very few universal standards (such as product codes) have been used by the healthcare industry. However, attempts are being made to set such standards, most importantly by the Coalition for Healthcare Standards (CHeS) [90].

Conclusions – 'the take home messages'

Until recently, there has been very little economic incentive to build a lean, coordinated pharmaceutical product supply chain. This is manifested in the lack of universal product coding that creates integration problems which are difficult and expensive to resolve [91]. We have outlined a range of health economic, scientific and social forces that are making better management of pharmaceutical distribution a priority.

It is unclear what the ultimate impact of digital technologies will have on distributors and wholesalers. Some pharmaceutical executives think that the time is ripe to bypass wholesalers and deal directly with pharmacists and ultimately consumers. Similarly, there is considerable debate on the future of retail pharmacy, both in terms of structure (for example will pharmacy chains eventually proliferate all over Europe or will most pharmacies in the USA ultimately be situated in stores such as Wal-Mart?) and function (in an information society, what is the role of the pharmacist, when consumers will ultimately be able to get reliable information using the Internet or mobile devices?).

We will discuss e-pharmacies in Chapter 11, but it is important to note that even the final leg of the distribution chain, between pharmacist and patient, is in transition. Patients, especially those with chronic diseases, are actively seeking out Internet-based suppliers that can offer deep discounts, especially if these orders can be fulfilled using the mail or courier services.

- Faced with an inexorable increase in the importance of distribution, pharmaceutical companies will need to be in position to act quickly to take advantage of changes in the relationships between the current stakeholders.
- The role of wholesalers is changing and we have already seen defensive action such as vertical integration in this sector. Wholesalers are seeking to consolidate their position with customers by offering a range of services, many of which are IT-based.
- Payers and insurers, especially in the USA, are staking a claim in the distribution chain in order to monitor and control drug prescription costs. With a few notable exceptions, Merck-Medco being the best example, pharmaceutical companies are no longer involved in the management of patient prescriptions. New alliances are being built to contain prescription drug spending and IT is being extensively used for tracking and analysing drug costs.

PART IV

Digital Strategies: Marketing and Sales

CHAPTER 8 Digital strategies in marketing and sales

The pharmaceutical industry has, until fairly recently, operated in a 'walled garden' of patent protection, growing demand for high-value prescription drugs and an easily manageable global market. Creating the demand for a new drug remains a relatively straightforward, although increasingly difficult, process of marketing to physicians (and more and more to consumers) through a range of channels, but has mainly been driven by a sales force that maintains close physical contact with key prescribers. Over the past 20 years, the role of regulatory agencies, government and payers (especially managed care) has become pivotal in drug sales. Today, account management teams ensure that the drug is on the healthcare provider's formulary (a list of drugs approved for use in that particular institution) and providers and payers may reach a contractual agreement with the manufacturer to allow a drug (sold at a discount) to be prescribed and reimbursed.

The overarching pharmaceutical marketing model is one of 'push' – where the company uses salespeople to influence physicians, pharmacists and payers to prescribe, stock or reimburse the product (Figure 8.1). The current reality is that the pharmaceutical sales force size remains the key driver of sales [92]. This finding is intuitively supported by the fact that prescription drug selling is relationship-driven.

The historical success of Pfizer and Merck has largely been attributed to their world-class sales and marketing organizations. It was felt that while Pfizer has benefited from some excellent research, its success has been due to its ability to use its sales force to turn in-licensed drugs into billion dollar blockbusters.

Direct-to-consumer (DTC) advertising is becoming an important alternative promotion method, particularly in the US. In other markets such as the EU, DTC is currently constrained by strict advertising regulations, but

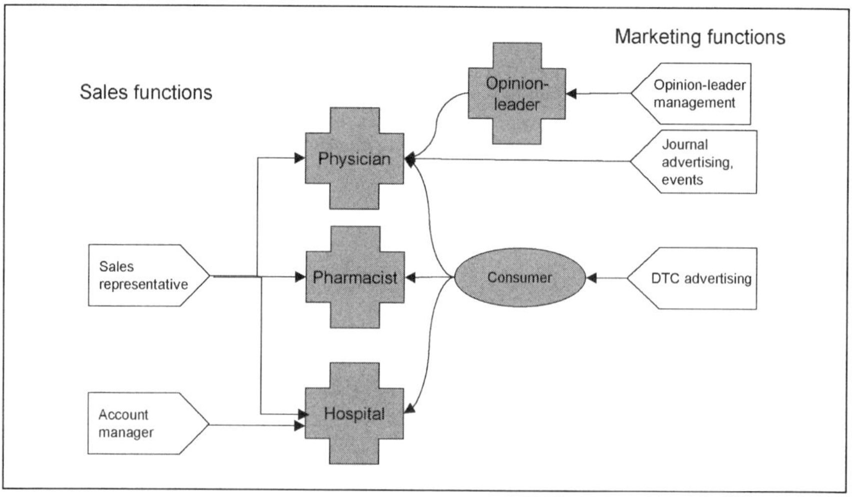

Figure 8.1 Traditional 'push' promotional channels

pharmaceutical companies still use a range of innovative informational strategies to inform consumers of new therapeutic options. Pharmaceutical companies segment their customers by tracking and analysing prescribing data supplied by vendors such as IMS Health, or retail consumption data supplied by parties such as AC Nielsen. Focus groups and attitudinal surveys may also be used to segment targets.

Pharmaceutical companies aim to build sustainable partnerships with target physicians, but this must be achieved at the lowest possible cost. As margin pressure increases, marketers are faced with difficult resource allocation choices such as between putting more resources into gaining market share in the highly competitive segment of high-prescribing physicians or developing new market opportunities.

From random push to focused pull – Dr Foster

Pharmaceutical marketers are acutely aware of the limitations of available data on target physicians. The availability of accurate practice and prescribing data, even when combined with sales representative qualitative input and market research surveys provides only a limited understanding of the true prescribing decision drivers and support needs of physicians. Ideally, customers (be they physicians, patients or payers) would provide pharma-

continued from previous page

ceutical companies with fine-grained information to permit the establishing of value-laden, sustained relationships.

In the United Kingdom, Dr Foster is a private company that is the leading independent provider of comprehensive and authoritative comparative data on health services. Dr Foster obtains and analyses data from the Department of Health, NHS, regional and local health trusts and physicians to create high-value sources of aggregated information that are published in the form of newspaper supplements (such as the Good Hospital Guide), websites (sponsored by Boots) and books. Having built up considerable expertise in the management of public databases, Dr Foster also relies on top health research institutions for analytic support. The public health benefits of providing impartial rankings of hospitals and health service providers are clear, especially as the NHS faces constant controversy concerning quality, resource allocation and safety. For the pharmaceutical industry, Dr Foster's approach offers manifold benefits, including the first accurate data set of hospital admissions giving weight to arguments concerning specific therapeutic approaches. For example, the correlation of regional differences in the prescription of lipid-lowering drugs with admissions for cardiac disease could make a strong case for aggressive early pharmacological intervention.

Perhaps the most exciting of Dr Foster's current activities relates to the establishment, in collaboration with the Wellcome Trust, of a database of specialist physicians (consultants). This tool will facilitate more efficient referrals by primary care doctors. The database contains information on the specific research interests of the specialists, merit awards, important publications and the types of procedure that they regularly perform. Of particular interest is the fact that many specialists actively provide supplementary information to this database, motivated to some extent by the positive implications for their reputations and private practices. The specialist database is recognized by a number of professional societies as an important tool to inform and empower family doctors and patients in the referral process. The Dr Foster experience opens our eyes to the possibilities for customer-driven relationships. Physicians who trust impartial parties and are driven by clear economic incentives are indeed prepared to share information and explore innovative, health-promoting partnerships.

The potential for digital technologies in pharmaceutical marketing and sales

We have already discussed the growing margin pressures that are being faced by the industry and our belief that digital technologies will come to the fore, especially in marketing and sales, due to their cost-saving and efficiency attributes. Automating elements of the sales and marketing process using e-business technologies should result in major cost savings. A recent report states that aggressively pursuing e-enabled solutions throughout the supply chain could lead to revenue increases of up to 14 per cent for early adopters. The majority of this saving is realized by minimizing duplication of effort and inefficient use of time. For example, IT solutions reduce the amount of time spent on tedious administrative tasks (between 25 and 49 per cent of a sales representative's time) [93]. It has also been suggested that using wireless technologies to actively schedule sales representative visits, reducing the time spent in physician waiting rooms, could be the 'killer application' needed to drive widespread adoption of wireless technologies by the pharmaceutical industry [94]. The reality remains that many digital tools, such as sales force automation (SFA), are badly designed and poorly implemented, resulting in a growing resistance in the field to technological innovation. It is certainly reasonable to expect that pharmaceutical companies, forced to reduce sales and marketing budgets and unable to deploy more salespeople, will increasingly rely on a range of e-solutions.

The attractiveness of digital technologies in pharmaceutical sales and marketing does not only relate to the cost-saving virtues, but more importantly to a range of opportunities that the Internet especially presents. In Chapter 9, we will present evidence of the generally increasing use of the Internet by physicians and consumers. In the case of physicians, there are a number of inexorable forces that drive them to engage in e-business transactions on a daily basis. Besides changes in the economics of medicine and healthcare that are bringing digital technologies to the fore, we are beginning to see the impact of advances in biomedical science that will make it imperative that pharmaceutical marketing be focused on smaller patient segments. Certainly, we can expect a stratification of markets based on a willingness to pay and insurance coverage, especially as consumers are presented with a cornucopia of diagnostic and therapeutic choices. To manage this new market dynamic, companies will have to understand and penetrate segments deeply, adjusting pricing strategies and developing new promotional approaches. We will explore the role of customer relationship management (CRM) technologies, a future operational necessity in a more complicated pharmaceutical marketing environment.

CHAPTER

9 Digital strategies in marketing to the physician

Introduction

The personal contact between a pharmaceutical company and physicians, epitomized in the sales representative visit to a doctor's office, is the gold standard against which all marketing interventions in this sector are judged. However, pharmaceutical companies are now caught in a vicious cycle, as they employ an ever-increasing number of sales representatives for the same pool of target physicians. A few years ago, 2000 sales representatives in the US affiliate was considered a reasonable target. Now, the major pharmaceutical companies employ 5000 or more, and are spending more than twice the amount on sales, marketing and administration as they spend on R&D [22]. US sales forces nearly doubled in size between 1996 and 2001, but the number of detailing visits to physicians rose by only 15 per cent, as doctors succumbed to 'salesperson fatigue' [95]. The competitive environment demands that pharmaceutical companies continue the sales force arms race in the absence of viable alternatives.

In the early years of managed care, it was thought that sales force size would have to be reduced, as physicians would be forced to prescribe according to strict guidelines, formularies would be introduced and companies would only have to focus on a limited number of managed care decision-makers. Many companies reduced the sizes of their sales forces in the USA, only to increase them again when it was realized that physicians were still the key decision-makers, and maintained high levels of autonomy. However, the failure of formularies and prescribing guidelines may be temporary, as this is more a reflection on the relative failure of managed care to control physician behaviour, and the relatively low penetration of evidence-based prescribing, than it is on the overall effectiveness of the sales representative process. Ironically, there is some evidence that the managed care organizations (MCOs) themselves have contributed to the increase in the prescribing of expensive drugs, as they used generous drug benefit offerings to differentiate themselves in the battle to recruit enrolees.

Although other methods are also used to promote drugs, notably events, symposia and medical journal advertising, sales force detailing remains the dominant approach, consuming over 70 per cent of marketing budgets (not including the cost of drug samples) [95]. The evolution of sales force size (Figure 9.1) is a source of interest to pharmaceutical companies, who would certainly like to be in a position to replace more of the sales force with equally or more effective, but cheaper channels.

The relationship between the sales representative and the physician is critical to the industry, and represents a major barrier to entry. However, this model of pharmaceutical marketing is regarded as increasingly inefficient. There are approximately 225,000 pharmaceutical sales representatives worldwide [21], but access to physicians has diminished, with an estimated 43 per cent of sales visits failing to get past the receptionist's desk [97]. The major reason that physicians limit sales representative access to their offices is that they are seeing less value in sales representative calls. In a recent survey, 78 per cent of physicians said they felt that detailers give biased information [95]. Whereas sales representatives were previously often the easiest source of thera-

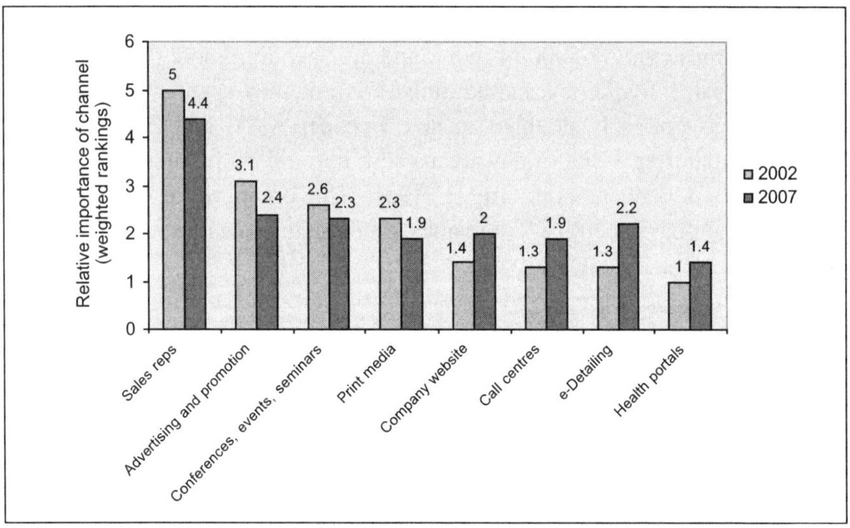

Figure 9.1 Relative importance of channels in 2002 and 2007 (survey of 60 senior pharmaceutical industry executives)

Source: [96]

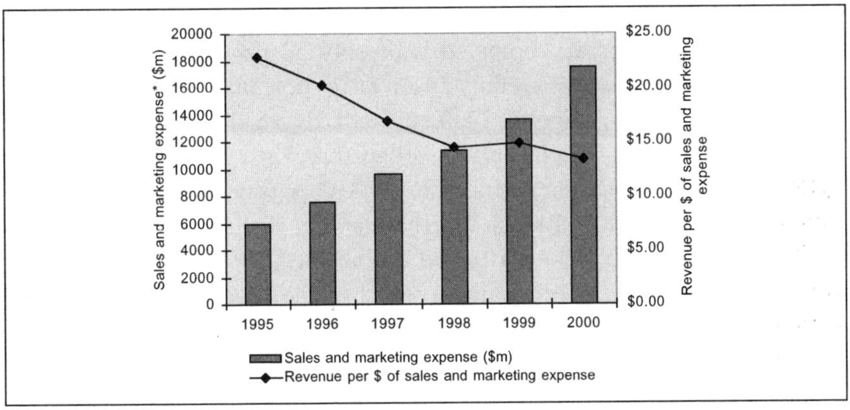

Figure 9.2 Sales and marketing expenses have increased while the revenue generated by that spending has decreased

Note: *Sales and marketing expense includes detailing expenses, journal advertising, convention spending, promotions and DTC
Source: Rosetta Marketing Strategies

peutic information (and this information was invariably delivered with a small gift or food), physicians, like all consumers, are bombarded continuously by print, media and Internet channels and are forced to choose when, how, and how often to interact with pharmaceutical companies (Figure 9.2).

If the current model of the sales representative–physician interaction were to change (and current levels of physician dissatisfaction suggest it must), then pharmaceutical companies will face a major internal upheaval. In recent years, contract sales organizations (CSOs) have emerged to provide services such as sales force recruitment, training, deployment and management. Outsourcing of detailing has a stronger tradition in Europe than in the US, with an estimated 25–30 per cent of sales representatives in the UK working for a CSO, compared with about 14 per cent in the US [21].

Digital technologies may not, as yet, have radically changed the pharmaceutical business model, but as a revolutionary new way of communicating with customers they will have a particular impact on sales and marketing.

Physicians and digital technology

Within the next five years, most healthcare organizations will largely communicate with payers, regulators, physicians and consumers over the Internet. Large pharmaceutical companies now have groups responsible for e-business, and most of these groups have a primary focus on sales and marketing. A 2000 poll showed that 75 per cent of medical professionals in the US used the Internet, compared with only 52 per cent of the general public [95]. Physicians are certainly aware of the potential of the Internet, yet they are resistant to change. A 2000 study of 20 small physician practices (ranging from one to 19 physicians) found that 5 per cent used email for patient contact, 25 per cent had a website (10 per cent developed in-house and 15 per cent developed by an external partner, such as a pharmaceutical company), and 30 per cent performed online medical searches [98]. Most estimates put the overall promotional spend of the pharmaceutical industry on the Internet at less that one per cent of total sales, which is not an insubstantial amount, for a $300 billion plus industry [99].

An ongoing and fascinating insight into the diffusion of digital technology into the medical profession is in the area of handheld portable computing devices or personal digital assistants (PDAs). According to a 2001 survey based on interviews with 834 US practising physicians, the proportion of all physicians using handheld devices increased from 15 per cent in 1999 to 26 per cent that year, and more recent data indicates that close to half of US physicians working in some specialty areas and many more in fully computerized hospitals are using PDAs. Unsurprisingly, the use of handheld devices is highest among doctors under 45 years of age (33 per cent versus 21 per cent among older doctors in a 2000 survey) [100]. Practical issues seem to be driving physicians to use PDAs. For example, if the easiest way to enter patient details, access test results or participate in a clinical trial is via a wireless device, then subject to the constraints of usability and portability, the device will enter mainstream clinical practice. Similarly, for the busy primary care physician in a managed care environment, e-prescribing on a wireless PDA can save time, ensure compliance with a formulary and avoid dangerous drug interactions or incorrect dosing.

For a pharmaceutical company, the entry of digital technologies into daily practice is an exciting opportunity to explore new channels for interacting with target physicians and building relationships. One of the lessons of the dotcom crash is that first-mover advantage is invariably superseded by those companies that can offer something simpler, more robust and sustainable, over the longer term. In a nascent area, such as digital strategy, the rules are still unclear. For example, high levels of personal Internet use among physicians, an expected finding for an affluent, educated group, has certainly not translated into a great enthusiasm for e-health. The reasons for this lie in a web of economic, social and scientific complexity that is physician behaviour.

Physician portals

Introduction

The first 'e-health revolution' revolved very much around the interface between users, be they consumers or physicians, and the Internet. A prevailing idea was that whoever controlled the portal or entrance through which a user interacted with the web was in a position to extract value by offering information, selling advertising and sponsorship and providing a range of value-added services. The reality, clearly manifested at the end of the technology boom of the 1990s, was that customers are fickle, their needs complex and constantly changing, and that Internet uptake and use did not become pervasive enough to ensure the survival of the portal as a business model. Notwithstanding these constraints, the portal does indeed offer physicians access to a range of increasingly important services including:

- Scientific information and medical news
- Communities and chat rooms
- Participation in e-clinical trials
- Formulary guidelines and updates
- E-prescribing tools
- Evidence-based medicine (EBM) guidelines
- Communication with pharmaceutical companies for questions, representative visits and sample requests
- Access to e-detailing and continuing medical education
- Regulatory reporting
- Practice management guidance and software
- Medical politics and leisure activities.

The American Medical Association (AMA) released findings that showed that many of the physicians surveyed in 2001 were using the Internet for medical research and other tasks [16] (Figure 9.3).

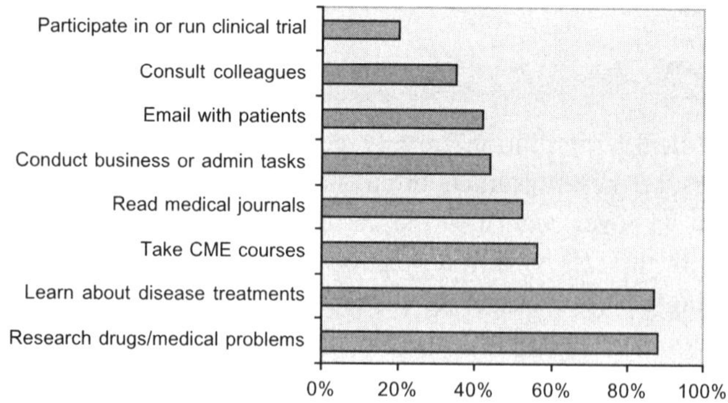

Figure 9.3 US physician Internet use (2001 survey of 201 physicians)

Source: [95]

Best practice in physician portals

Pharmaceutical companies, uneasy with the quality, intensity and results of their interaction with customers, are attempting to increase their understanding of customer needs. Physician portals represent an ideal opportunity to gather physicians' views and study their behaviour. Market research currently covers two main areas. Prescribing data, competitive ranking and descriptions of the market environment are provided by IMS Health and similar organizations, whereas segmentation and targeting data are mainly gathered prior to drug launches by specialist pharmaceutical market research organizations. Although the US market for medical market research exceeds $1 billion annually [101], it is by no means a perfect way for pharmaceutical companies to understand the customer. Market research is targeted almost entirely towards physicians, and largely deals with post hoc prescription patterns. The emergence of new Internet-based market research services has made it easier, cheaper and quicker to obtain specific information on the attitudes and needs of physicians. One medical device company employed an Internet market research organization to obtain data on the treatment preferences of cardiologists, a notoriously hard to reach group. A traditional market research study would have taken one to two months. Using the market researcher's physician database and an emailed survey, the company had responses from 175 cardiologists within a week [101].

Physicians are only likely to embrace the Internet when it offers a true killer application: value-added tools that synchronize well with what doctors are already doing, offer time or cost savings and do not create extra work. Some innovative websites are aiming to supply just this:

- Aventis launched MyDocOnline.com, a suite of online services designed to help physicians enhance practice management and patient care [102]. The service includes scheduling, billing, referrals, prescription refills, laboratory results, physician–patient communication and healthcare information provision.
- Most physicians cannot practice the most up-to-date evidence-based medicine, as they simply do not have time to wade through the mountains of medical literature. WebEBM.com hopes to provide physicians and patients with evidence-based treatment guidelines online, offering guidelines for 45 conditions, including congestive heart failure, diabetes, pregnancy and high cholesterol. Tools for monitoring patient compliance include satisfaction questionnaires, risk calculators, calendars, weight trackers, blood pressure trackers, glucose trackers and exercise calendars [103].
- Elan sponsors neurohub.com, a neurology site owned by California web company Salu. About 45 per cent of US neurologists are members of neurohub.com and use its services to run more efficient and profitable practices. Services include advice on practice operations, billing and coding, regulatory requirements, legal issues and technology. Through the site, Elan deploys marketing, education and research initiatives, providing educational content and e-detailing, obtaining market research and recruiting patients for clinical trials. Elan's sales representatives reportedly now spend longer with neurologists, offering some proof that neurohub.com is offering them increased value [104].
- Baxter Healthcare Corporation initiated three Internet-based continuing education programmes on nutritional therapies for nurses and pharmacists. Baxter posted online continuing education home study programmes that provide immediate test results and are free to all clinicians with access to the Internet (www.baxter.com/ce-program). Successful completion of each of the three programmes gives nurses and pharmacists certified hours of continuing education. Baxter offers ten other accredited online educational programmes. The courses are nationally accredited by the American College of Pharmaceutical Education and the American Nurses Credentialing Center [105].
- During 2001, Merck launched a website offering physicians a variety of information and practice management services. Merckmedicus.com, a free reference portal for physicians, includes medical news, CME accreditation and medical dictionaries. Merck chose a 'soft launch', promoting its site to doctors solely through members of its sales force [16].

Conclusions – 'the take home messages'

Physicians are fairly conservative and unwilling to adopt new technology if it does not have an immediate impact on either the quality of care that they offer to their patients or the ease with which they carry out their jobs. A 2001 poll of 101 physicians from a variety of specialties assessed the most important attributes of medical Internet sites and whether existing sites meet doctors' expectations. The majority of respondents rated physician-focused websites as average or below average in terms of ease of use and overall comprehensiveness. Seventy-eight per cent of respondents indicated that the provision of accurate, credible information was extremely important. When it came to how to gain credibility, a full 60 per cent of physicians surveyed felt that the absence of advertising on a medical website enhances the credibility of the site. Ease of navigation was rated a top priority by 58 per cent of survey participants, yet only 38 per cent gave typical existing physician websites a positive rating on this dimension. In fact, more than half of those surveyed (52 per cent) said poor navigation performance keeps them from using the Internet as often as they would like to in their practices [100].

The brief, yet turbulent history of physician portals teaches us that practical issues such as simple usability and a 'feeling' for the real needs of physicians promote sustainable relationships. It has been difficult for many to accept that customer loyalty on the web is a relative concept, when the next site is just a click away.

- Portals are an excellent channel for communicating with physicians and providing a range of innovative and useful services. It is foolish to attempt to correlate levels of use with the sophistication (or expense) of a web offering and companies should avoid spending too much on fancy sites when users simply want speedy access to information. More effort should be devoted to designing sites that meet specific needs, a process which requires resource allocation to understand the market.
- We should not underestimate the importance of a pharmaceutical company website, especially as a source of current product information for physicians. The next step is using company sites to support the interaction (in areas such as disease management) between physicians and patients. They can also be used to gain a better understanding of physician behaviour and those offerings that physicians particularly value.
- Segmented medicine will greatly increase the complexity of the physicians' tasks, as they eventually have to deal with ten different treatments

for a disease when before there was only one. Physicians will become ever-more dependent on prescription guidelines and formularies, and products will be bundled with full usage guidelines and support services delivered via web portals.

Customer service centres (CSCs)

Introduction

The customer service centre (CSC) is becoming an important part of the physician-facing pharmaceutical marketing mix. The terms 'CSC' and 'call centre' are used interchangeably, but we prefer CSC in order to stress that communication is now 'multichannel' (using the Internet, automated response and web tools), as compared to previously being almost exclusively telephone-based. The CSC is usually classified as a pull or customer-driven vehicle (although outgoing CSCs are gaining in importance) where high levels of personal interaction are attained. CSCs are fairly expensive to maintain, especially in pharmaceuticals where highly trained personnel (often nurses or physicians) and strict regulatory compliance are requirements. While traditional sales representative visits (push, high personal interaction) will continue to be the mainstay of pharmaceutical marketing, we foresee that personal contact will be complemented by new channels, such as CSCs and e-detailing.

The drivers of increased CSC use are similar to those for digital technologies across the industry. As competition increases, especially in areas such as specialty products for acute hospital care, pharmaceutical companies are moving from a product to a services approach. For example, an interventional cardiologist is now offered 24x7 access to a CSC where he can get super-specialist advice concerning the product, report successes and adverse events and interact with peers. Important opinion-leaders, specialists or high prescribers who do not want to be bothered by representatives when they are busy may be interested in a CSC that can deal with specific queries and provide on-demand information using tools such as e-detailing. Complex products will have to come with a service and support offering provided via a CSC and the US FDA is increasingly demanding that such services be made available.

Integrating CSCs into digital strategies

A CSC permits a company to provide a high quality 'baseline' service including query management, product information provision, adverse event reporting and transaction management. Where customers are ordering products, the CSC can be directly integrated into the company ERP system. The CSC can also be deployed to better manage the sales force, treating sales representatives in the field as 'internal customers'. For example, an outgoing CSC strategy can be used to train representatives through the web and telephone for a forthcoming product launch, or the CSC can be used as an IT help desk for SFA tools or processing free sample requests.

The real-time nature of CSC interactions permits companies to use analytical CRM approaches that are common in the banking sector. The aim is to predict the needs of the customer in order to meet specific needs, offer a certain service or automate the transaction. A more predictive CSC design requires innovative approaches to customer segmentation.

There is considerable debate concerning the return on CSC investment in the pharmaceutical industry. Physician CSCs usually have a fairly low volume of customer interactions that makes it difficult to justify installing sophisticated and expensive call centre systems. As qualified nurses and physicians have to be employed to respond to the queries of medical personnel, a CSC remains a costly undertaking. CSCs should be evaluated in the light of their role in a coordinated programme to improve customer satisfaction, promote loyalty and increase prescribing. Unlike call centres in the technology and financial services sectors, it is difficult, for regulatory and technical reasons (such as language and operator expertise), to either outsource (except to specialized service providers) or relocate CSCs to countries or regions with cheaper labour costs.

Pharmacia's Genotropin, a growth hormone used for paediatric growth disorders, is mainly marketed to specialist endocrinologists, who have strong global networks and similar needs. Pharmacia has put together a service offering for 2000 participating clinics, aggregating patient data in a data warehouse, and supplying interesting or useful data to participating physicians. The key competitive edge for Pharmacia is the quality of the data. Pharmacia supports the publication of scientific papers based on the stored data and distributes the information mined from the global outcomes research system to participating physicians through their PDAs. A physician can thereby use the data to guide the course of treatment of individual patients at the 'bedside'. Pharmacia is sharing the patient outcomes' data and the resulting evidence-based best-practice information with participating physicians through a CSC [106].

Conclusions – 'the take home messages'

The CSC model will evolve, especially with the segmentation of customers based on their service needs. This will permit better triage of incoming calls and the handling of more basic requests through automated response systems. This type of market segmentation is still at an early stage of development, but is certainly becoming more important as companies face budget pressure. It is difficult to predict how the role of pharmaceutical companies in patient care will change. For example, CSCs are being used as a point of interaction between physicians, nurses and patients, especially in the case of diseases requiring long-term management, such as diabetes. CSCs can be deployed for contacting patients that have opted into a reminder or 'treatment diary' service with a resultant improvement in compliance.

For smaller companies, including biotechnology companies that may be bringing a few products to market, CSCs will be vital, especially if the company has a small sales force (or no sales force at all). In the case of highly specialized products, for example some oncology and ophthalmology drugs, marketing, ordering and information provision is already being almost exclusively being conducted using CSCs.

- The linkage of web, telephone and other customer contact channels in a CSC is becoming standard practice.
- Physicians value timely, efficient service and this will inevitably be a source of competitive differentiation at a time when the industry will have to extract more value from each customer. CSC deployment is a mandatory component of an improved CRM package.
- CSCs are a real-time tool for measuring the impact of promotional experiments. While adhering to strict legal, data privacy and ethical rules, pharmaceutical companies must mine customer data, especially data concerning outcomes and service needs. CSCs will be an important source of aggregated customer data.

E-detailing

Introduction

The term 'detailing' is generally used to describe the sales representative drug promotion process. This involves the representative visiting the physician with information packs, free samples and small gifts to 'detail' how the drug works and why it is superior to its competitors. Detailing and free samples constitute most of the spending on direct-to-physician promotion (DTP).

The definition of 'e-detailing' is somewhat controversial as it can entail a range of activities varying in complexity, expense and the types of participant. We believe that e-detailing is best defined as the 'digital-enablement' of information delivery to physicians (and other stakeholders), creating new digital channels for interaction between the pharmaceutical company and the physicians. The Internet is an ideal medium for providing physicians and consumers with real-time, personalized information on drugs, side effects, disease management and pharmacogenomics. E-detailing programs enable physicians to learn about pharmaceuticals and medical devices at convenient times (often after office hours) and locations (often from home) and to have the opportunity to focus on the issues that they think are important (and to have the opportunity to revisit the information as many times as they want). E-detailing is thought to be particularly useful as a tool to interact with so-called hard-to-reach physicians, such as those in super-specialty practices or those who refuse to see sales representatives or participate in pharmaceutical company promotional activities. Of course, e-detailing is only suitable for physicians who are comfortable with modern communications technology, but this number is bound to rise over time.

E-detailing encompasses a spectrum of interaction levels ranging from simple web-based provision of promotional material; to virtual e-detailing where sales representatives are available for discussion via the Internet or telephone; to video detailing, where physicians interact with sales representatives in real time over high-speed digital lines. Examples of e-detailing include:

- Handheld/PDA e-detailing is suitable for those products that are simple to prescribe (as the amount of information that can be displayed on a PDA is limited), but where there is a big advantage in being able to detail at the point of care or the time of prescription. This is particularly useful when competition in a certain product class is intense. PDA e-detailing is also of great use to sales representatives who can access requested information during the course of a detailing session.

- Interactive website detailing is most appropriate as a baseline information service for all products and the active promotion of the 'tail' (products that have been on the market for some time, may be coming off patent and where the sales force is not active). In order to attract physicians to an interactive website, focused email campaigns can be used. Sales representatives should be encouraged to mention the website in their detailing discussions and the website should be highlighted on all written promotional materials.

- Websites that provide training courses, detailed animation and tools for patients such as diaries, quizzes and reminders can be deployed as part of a product launch or where a complex product requires a range of value-added services.
- E-detailing with direct communication between the physician and a sales representative in a CSC is expensive, especially if this is done using video. This form of detailing should only be employed after careful consideration of the ROI. As the high-speed Internet becomes more widely used, it may be possible to use video-conferencing as a pharmaceutical marketing tool. For example, a sales representative may schedule the occasional video-conference, at a physician's convenience, to cover a new product or some important issue.

E-detailing strategies

The drivers of the e-promotion channel include the growing use of PCs and PDAs in medical practice. Physicians are adopting PDAs and mobile Internet devices, and it is only a matter of time before their use at the point of care, and when writing prescriptions, becomes standardized. The consequences of this include cost savings and improved safety as illegible prescriptions are eliminated, and dangerous drug interactions and incorrect dosages automatically identified. The battle for the physician's desktop or PDA will intensify as pharmaceutical companies see the benefits of being near to the physician when crucial treatment and prescribing decisions are made. The nature of the opportunity is unclear, as the prescribing decision is extremely complex and physicians do not like the direct or unsubtle promotion of products. As we have previously discussed, loyalty in a digital world is relative, as a competitor is generally just a mouse click away.

Online versions of detailing and continuing medical education are believed to be 25–90 per cent cheaper than the face-to-face variety. E-detailing is certainly cheaper than traditional detailing, which costs $150–200 per representative visit [95]. The variation in savings depends on the technology used; detailing by instant messaging and online training courses is obviously cheaper than detailing by video-conference. But whatever the e-detailing technology used, opinion as to its likely effectiveness is mixed. Many feel that e-detailing is just another way of flooding physicians with the same information by a different channel. However, several companies are piloting e-detailing and have been pleased with initial results [107], and although only four per cent of online physician marketing budgets were spent on e-detailing in 2000, this is projected to rise to 25 per cent in the future [99].

A 2001 study showed that a growing number of physicians are using PDAs and participating in e-marketing activities, including e-detailing. Based on specialist focus groups and 600 responses to an online questionnaire, the work showed that 19 per cent of physicians participated in e-marketing, and 44 per cent used a PDA. Family practitioners reported the highest participation in e-marketing activities (27 per cent), followed by neurologists (23 per cent) [108]. Research commissioned by Novartis showed an e-detailing ROI that was 20 per cent higher than for the deployment of field representatives, when measured against prescribing results [16]. Substantial imprecision exists in the evaluation of e-detailing. The pharmaceutical industry does not have a robust tradition of measuring ROI on many of its marketing activities and it is difficult, for example, to quantify the impact of inviting an opinion-leader to a medical conference. While the unit cost of a single e-detail (such as an email invitation to visit an interactive website) may be low (relative to a sales representative visit), we cannot accurately quantify the value of personal customer contact.

E-detailing has the potential to address some of the complaints that physicians have about traditional sales representative detailing, with the exception of the concern about biased information (Figure 9.4). Our experience is that while surveys show that physicians favour e-detailing over representative visits, this finding has to be viewed with a modicum of scepticism. What physicians may indeed be saying is that it is much easier to avoid or turn off an e-detail than it is to turn away a sales representative who has been patiently sitting for hours in the waiting room.

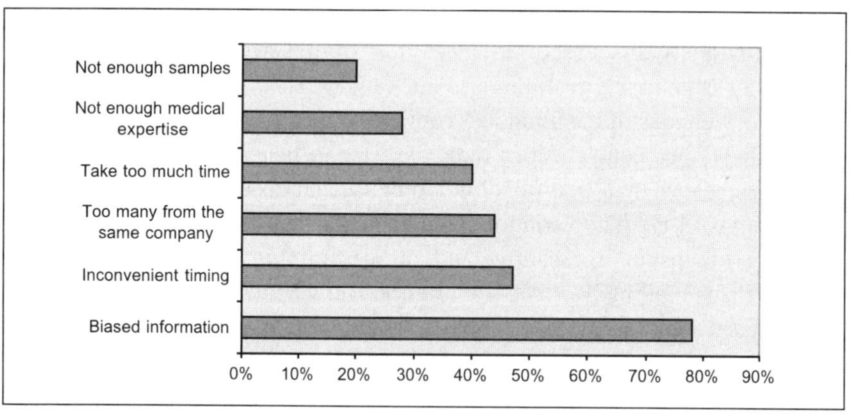

Figure 9.4 What are your top complaints about sales representative detailing? (2001 online poll of 201 US physicians)

Source: [95]

Currently, representatives are exhorted to concentrate on the top-prescribing physicians. The logic is seductive; a detailing visit has a fixed cost, but top-prescribing physicians will prescribe more of your product if convinced, leading to a greater ROI. This means that while pharmaceutical companies tend to spend a lot of time understanding these top-prescribers, they often neglect and poorly understand some of the other market segments. The top 20–30 per cent of physicians are saturated with sales representative visits and approaches such as e-detailing do allow marketers to profile and reach lower prescribing physicians in a cost-effective and personalized manner.

The e-detailing provider market is in a state of constant flux, as some of the smaller providers fight for survival. While it is outside the scope of this book to describe all the service companies providing the various e-detailing options we describe, it is important to look at what sort of in-house capacity a pharmaceutical company needs to develop to take advantage of the e-channel. Within the constraints of regulatory compliance, it is reasonable to outsource e-detailing, whether this be to a division of an advertising agency or a specialized e-detailing company. Issues such as global reach and sustainability should be carefully considered when choosing a provider. However, in the light of the inevitable margin pressures that the pharmaceutical industry will face, companies should certainly be looking at building small e-detailing solutions in-house that are scalable and easily deployable by affiliates throughout the world.

Conclusions – 'the take home messages'

> E-detailing will become the mainstream way of doing business. I believe in five years from now 70 per cent of all detailing will be done electronically. – pharmaceutical executive interviewed in 2001 [7]

The digital channel will increase in importance. This transition will be driven by the diffusion of computers, PDAs and the Internet into daily medical practice and the need to find new ways of communicating a pharmaceutical promotion message to physicians and healthcare stakeholders. E-detailing is a promising, if somewhat limited, approach to using digital technologies to push a product message. Some of the promise of e-detailing lies in the possibilities of building partnerships between physicians, patients and pharmaceutical companies through the provision of interactive tools (such as diaries, reminders and ultimately, biomonitoring) and in the possibilities for creating highly customized services for physicians.

Pharmaceutical companies are seeking value-for-money e-detailing solutions, as initial uptake among physicians is usually low to moderate. The unit cost of a single e-detailing 'intervention' may be small, but when multiplied by the number of campaigns required and the number of physicians per campaign, the investment can be substantial.

E-detailing success stories are not common and companies tend to be very secretive about ROI. The anecdotal evidence seems to indicate that:

- E-detailing campaign success is a function of personalization of the offering rather than sophistication.
- Sales representative buy-in is vital; for example sales representatives should be rewarded for steering physicians to a product training website.
- 'Mixed' campaigns work well; for example combining e-detailing with an outgoing CSC where the representative discusses the e-detail with the participating physician over the telephone.
- E-detailing works well for selling the 'tail' products; drugs that are not actively promoted or are off-patent and where e-commerce may be an option.
- E-detailing works well in less-developed markets where sales representative coverage is extremely limited and physicians appreciate product information. Even when Internet access levels are low, innovative approaches (such as inviting groups of physicians to an Internet café) are possible.
- The 'devil is in the detail' in e-detailing; campaigns often fail because the targets have not been properly identified or the lists of physicians provided are not accurate.
- Price is everything; physicians will lose interest in video-conferencing-based e-detailing and companies could be better served by ensuring that robust on-demand information and training tools are available on the web.

The industry is still at an early stage on the e-detailing learning curve. For e-detailing to be successful, systems will have to give customers the information they need in the right place at the right time, rather than just flooding them with the same information by a different channel. This requires a focus on better understanding the needs and motivations of the customer. The integration of e-detailing with CRM databases and data-mining tools in order to infer customer preferences and needs is critical.

- E-detailing is not a marketing panacea, but should make detailing cheaper, at least in the medium term. It is a tool that allows coverage of all prescribing physicians and participants in the prescription process, permitting companies to move away from an exclusive focus on high-prescribers.

- The two-way interaction between an e-detailing system and a customer database permits the deployment of a range of real-time analytic options.
- E-detailing is an ideal laboratory for customer segmentation, as it is possible to track the interactions and behaviour of participants. Thus it should be used as a market research tool, rather than simply as another component of the marketing mix.

Customer relationship management (CRM)

Introduction

Many pharmaceutical companies are exploring ways to enhance their relationships with physicians. The concept of better responding to the needs of physicians at every point of contact (or touch point) (Figure 9.5) through a range of channels, and using the information gathered to improve sales and marketing effectiveness is described as customer relationship management (CRM). The goal of the physician facing marketing initiatives that we have described is

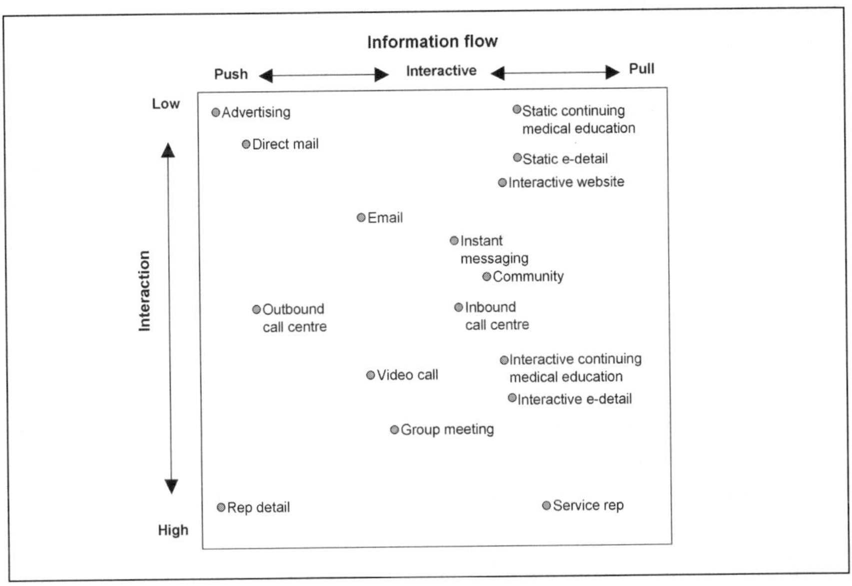

Figure 9.5 Customer touch points

Source: Adapted from ZS Associates

effective CRM. The growing interest in health sector CRM mirrors a trend in other sectors, where spending on CRM technology in the US is predicted to reach $16.5 billion by 2006 [109]. The ultimate goal is to incorporate sales force automation, customer intelligence and a range of channels, including the Internet and CSCs, into a seamless interface with the customer, thereby increasing the effectiveness of customer acquisition, loyalty and retention.

Many pharmaceutical companies are exploring CRM as a way to unify their marketing initiatives and increase the return on sales force investment. CRM theoretically allows companies to give their customers a consistent, two-way, personalized service via any channel – sales representatives, the Internet or CSCs. Customer details are stored in a centralized database and accessed by all customer-facing functions. These databases allow more effective mining of customer information, further increasing the effectiveness of marketing efforts. However, trying to achieve all these goals in a single project is seen as close to impossible. Companies tend to concentrate on only one or two goals in their initial CRM implementation [110]:

- *Enabling the sales force*. The first CRM-related systems (such as sales force automation (SFA) and electronic territory management systems (ETMS)) equip the sales representative with tools to aid in call planning and customer data recording. However, initial systems were largely designed to aid management surveillance and control rather than making the sales representative's job easier. Newer systems offer additional functionality to aid in the selling process (such as access to medical information and customer history).
- *Understanding the customer*. Pharmaceutical companies want to become better at turning information about customers into useful insights for improved marketing. Some pharmaceutical companies are adopting CRM so they can better segment their customers (be they physicians, pharmacists, payers or consumers) and develop more appropriate services for each segment.
- *Building a single customer database*. Some companies approach CRM as a data management project, the aim being to combine customer information held in separate silos for the benefits of all departments. In a 2000 survey from the research house Jupiter, over 80 per cent of pharmaceutical executives interviewed said they intended to increase investment in developing databases to support CRM efforts [99].
- *Connecting with the supply chain*. The aim is to connect sales and marketing with manufacturing and distribution, with the rationale that a

better understanding of customer requirements permits redesign of the supply chain to ensure improved customer service.

A CRM-enabled pharmaceutical company can expect to achieve benefits in terms of accelerated time to peak sales for new products, improved sales force productivity and enhanced returns from promotional expenditure.

Implementing CRM

Any company intending to implement a CRM system must set clear strategic goals before the technology is chosen [111]:

- What are the company's business goals?
- Who are the company's customers?
- What value can the company offer to each customer segment (and, by definition, what value do these customers have for the company)?
- What channels are necessary to offer the most value to the customers (for example key account management, CSCs, telemedicine, portals, education or disease management)?
- What service package should each segment receive?

Once these questions have been answered, a CRM solution can be designed to meet the defined needs (Figure 9.6). A CRM system should be specified against five key capabilities or abilities [112]:

- To collect and clean customer data
- To store securely or warehouse customer data
- To access and analyse customer data
- To report and act on data analytics
- To achieve meaningful ROI on CRM efforts.

There is considerable discussion concerning the architecture of a CRM system. This stems from the early technology-intensive approach to CRM, where considerable systems integration was required. In a sense, the prevailing paradigm equates CRM with enterprise resource planning (ERP) and notably SAP, where it is necessary to connect disparate accounting, supply chain and

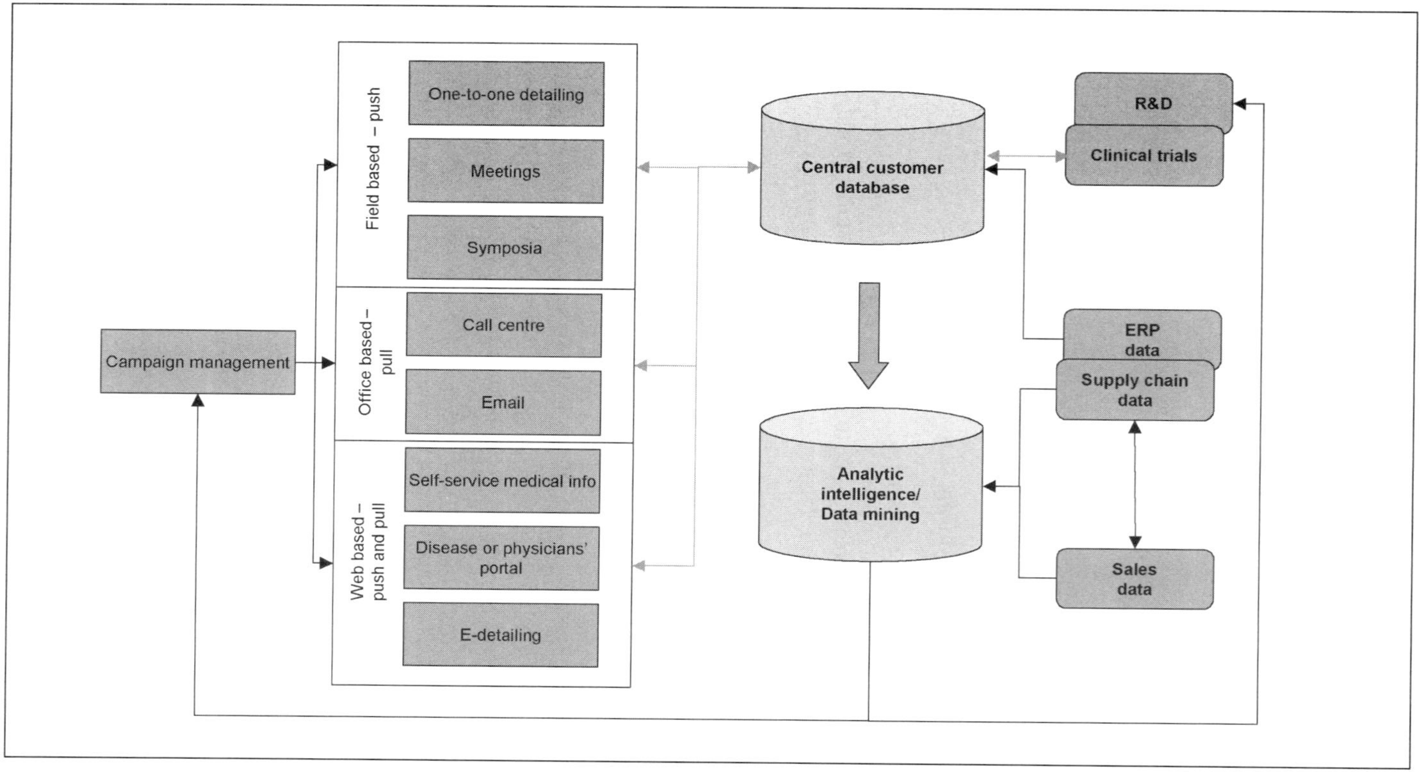

Figure 9.6 An idealized CRM schematic

TABLE 9.1

Contrasting ERP and CRM

	ERP	CRM
Investment	Massive	Moderate
Foundation	Changing existing processes, systems	*De novo* culture
Implications of failure	Moderate	Potentially catastrophic due to breakdown in relationships with customers
'Hype factor'	Started off high, then increasing scepticism	Hype and ignorance in pharmaceutical industry

human resource systems to produce a coordinated management reporting and control system. Contrary to a widely held belief, CRM is not essentially about technology. CRM is a way of managing and exploiting customer-related data within the organization. As such, technology makes up a key part of any CRM solution. Early, generic CRM packages were not suited to the complex customer relationships and regulatory requirements prevalent in the pharmaceutical industry. Now, all-in-one CRM vendors such as Siebel and the Oracle/Dendrite joint venture claim to provide CRM solutions tailored for the industry. Large-scale CRM implementations are still fairly rare across the pharmaceutical industry, as companies are justifiably wary of committing large sums into improving sales and marketing when the traditional sales representative approach is working well. Similarly, companies are concerned that country affiliates may react negatively to the centralized monitoring and control of marketing that well-implemented CRM systems permit. As compared to other industries, such as banking and financial services, where CRM is standard technology, the pharmaceutical industry does not generate the volume of transactions that fully justify the ROI from large-scale CRM implementations.

Sales force automation (SFA) and electronic territory management systems (ETMS)

Historically, CRM has revolved around targeted sales productivity through SFA and ETMS to lower costs and better leverage the sales organization across the globally extended supply chain. Only a small amount of sales force time (usually 10–20 per cent) is spent in front of customers, the rest is spent preparing, travelling, sitting in waiting rooms and doing administrative tasks. SFA and ETMS applications allow salespeople to call on more customers, spend more time with each customer and see each customer more often. In theory, combining SFA/ETMS with CRM allows representatives to better target physicians, understand the customer's needs and offer better customer service. However, salespeople have often resisted SFA/ETMS implementations. The reasons for this resistance included the poor usability of the technologies, the burden of having to carry around heavy laptop computers, the problems with connecting to central databases to upload and download information and the perception that the tools provided were designed more for management information, command and control, than to aid the salesperson in the field. Resistance to more sophisticated CRM systems often comes from senior sales representatives and sales managers who are reluctant to share their knowledge, gained over years of customer contact, with senior management.

Wireless and other functionalities

Pharmaceutical CRM is a prime candidate for the flexibility and mobility that wireless systems provide. It is beyond the scope of this book to discuss the advantages and pitfalls of the multiple standards that exist globally, but we reiterate our confidence that mobile applications are indeed the future of pharmaceutical CRM. Instead of salespeople updating the SFA system on their laptop several days after a meeting, they can do it whenever they next have free time – for example by using a wireless PDA when they are in a physician's waiting room. They can also access vital information at the physician's request to improve the quality of the detail, increasing the likelihood of cost-effective repeat visits. Wireless technologies should make SFA systems user-friendlier for the sales force, thereby overcoming some of the reluctance to use these systems and improving ROI.

A mobile solution should integrate not only with a company's SFA system, but should also be connected to other back-end systems such as pricing, product catalogues, inventories, order status and customer care information. An effective mobile system will:

- Support multiple types of mobile devices – there are many such devices available on the market (from makers such as Palm, Microsoft, Handspring, Compaq, RIM Blackberry and Nokia) and it is unclear who will dominate it in the long term.

- Use open standards such as XML and Java, and be compatible with multiple network standards such as GSM, 3G, GPRS and Bluetooth; in order to provide flexibility across geographies and with different technology partners.

The FDA's Regulation 21 CFR Part 11, which regulates the management of electronic records throughout the value chain, has introduced new challenges for all software providers including CRM vendors. Wireless technologies and Internet-based applications are being introduced to support sample management, data capture, patient feedback, and digital signature authorizations to increase the effectiveness of data capture and information reach in the clinical trials and customer-facing process. With security issues adequately addressed, wireless and Internet technologies will become a cornerstone of CRM.

The CRM market now includes a diverse set of technology providers. For example, Blue Martini and Broadvision support communities built around particular ailments and product experiences so that manufacturers can tap into consumer information and share content with patients. Others, such as iMany and SAP with its acquisition of Infinite Data Structures, are addressing the complex contract management issues in the healthcare supply chain. Advanced marketing vendors, such as E.piphany, support analytic-based marketing campaigns, and vendors Siebel and Dendrite are attempting to provide suites of functionality across many of these areas.

Managing CRM data

We believe that the management and analysis of data lies at the heart of good CRM. A basic classification of the data collected and generated from external and internal sources in today's pharmaceutical marketing environment includes:

- *Descriptive data* – databases of target customers including demographics, prescription behaviour, attitudinal information, professional status and so on.
- *Activity data* – sales calls, visits, samples and promotional items, meetings and corporate event invitations, requests for information and so on. This can be divided into the activities of various parties such as the sales representative, physician and even the consumer.
- *Sales data* – this can be divided into company-generated (direct sales, value of product) or secondary (IMS, Cegedim) data.

- *Profiling data* – segmentation of target physicians, consumers or other customers. Various approaches exist for the calculation of potential of each group and the design of marketing interventions.

The performance of current CRM systems is often hampered by the application of segmentation and target weighting models that have not been rigorously validated. Similarly, the rules for the prediction of physician response to a marketing intervention are often not experimentally tested. In a nascent area such as pharmaceutical CRM, companies have difficulty creating dynamic data models. For example, when a physician calls a CSC for some product information, this may require that the particular physician be automatically moved from one segment to another.

The link between the vast amount of data collected and bought and the final output is often opaque and tenuous. For example, 20 profiling indicators are collected to generate a basic ranking that is often not validated. End-users such as sales representatives are faced with a complex array of data and questions and have difficulty in seeing the value of many of these questions when the feedback from headquarters is a 'simplistic' ranking of targets. No standardized approach exists for identifying the most important indicators (leading indicators) for simplifying the sales force tasks and testing the segmentation, weighting and intervention model in the CRM. The data collected and the questions asked in CRM systems are often badly chosen, open to subjective interpretation and even manipulation in the field. The CRM needs to be coordinated with and support the sales cycle – sales managers think on a three-to-six-month horizon and activities tend to be sporadic rather than continuous (sales campaigns and so on), whereas the CRM system is often predicated on a continuous, stable supply of data.

A good CRM system is based on a 'data context' that, to some extent, is unique to the pharmaceutical industry. For example, customer transactions are limited in pharmaceutical marketing (perhaps 20–30 contacts per year with a high-prescribing physician, as compared to hundreds of individual credit card transactions in consumer banking per year). Yet, while discrete quantitative data points may be limited, sales representatives and many pharmaceutical managers have rich long-term relationships with physicians, a source of invaluable qualitative insights. Pharmaceutical CRM has to be designed for a 'quantitative-poor, qualitative-rich' environment.

Dako – the database is the foundation

For Dako, a Danish company and global leader in specialized diagnostics based on immunology and protein chemistry, the foundation of its CRM strategy is a robust, accurate and powerful global customer database. With 97 per cent of its sales outside Denmark and a record of growth and success since its founding in 1966, Dako looks forward to expanding into new areas such as pharmacodiagnostics (linking diagnostic tests to specific treatments) and flow cytometry (sophisticated cell diagnostics). Dako prides itself on a close, collaborative and innovation-driven relationship with its customers – specialists, laboratories, medical technologists and hospital purchasing agents.

Dako is exploring a concept of 'scientific CRM', or being the science-based partner of choice for its customers. Aiming to stick to its core business of laboratory diagnostics, Dako wants to use CRM as a vehicle for improving its human contacts, managing customer information and providing customers with the expertise and knowledge sharing that they expect from a trusted partner. How does Dako achieve this close relationship, while at the same time expanding in terms of personnel and product offerings? Dako sales representatives have multiple roles, sharing cutting-edge knowledge, being the first line for most technical 'troubleshooting' and encouraging scientific collaboration. Operating in a highly specialized market, Dako cannot rely on external data providers such as IMS, and its decentralized structure makes it vital to identify the customer interactions and needs that are important globally. Speed is important in the rapidly evolving molecular pathology and diagnostics space and Dako is seeking a tool that can allow it to signal clearly to existing and potential customers, that it is the partner of choice.

With these exigencies and opportunities in mind, Dako began exploring the development of a fully integrated customer database, adapted particularly to the highly collaborative, scientific, but decentralized Dako operational approach. Dako is seeking to set up the structures and customer segmentation that will ensure that everyone across the Dako family sees the value of, and participates enthusiastically in, the customer database initiative. Early in the project, in parallel with the database design, a series of workshops at headquarters and subsidiary level were organized to obtain detailed input on customer segmentation and user expectations. Similarly, a global customer survey was undertaken to identify evolving needs and important relationship drivers.

continued from previous page

Why a database? Dako sees benefits both in cost reduction and improved customer service and has opted to make the system as 'usable' as possible. With this in mind, a number of core principles have been adopted:

- Providing a working model early in the project to ensure a high level of 'buy-in'. Subsidiaries are being encouraged to 'play' with the prototype system.
- Ensuring that the data is 'respected' – accurate, relevant and timely.
- Defining the data collection, management, analytic and output processes upfront and ensuring that these rules are respected.
- Using the database to 'standardize' activities, such as product launches, globally.

The longer term vision for the customer database is clear. Using this foundation, it will be possible to further integrate customer support, manufacturing and R&D for improved customer service. Relevant integration with existing databases is being explored, especially as Dako enters into markets that require extensive interactions with regulatory authorities. Dako also see the virtues of using this database for cross-company knowledge sharing and e-learning and becoming more 'visionary' in the scope and depth of customer interactions. Building on the database, Dako envisions a range of mobile tools to ensure that its field force can provide an even better first-line technical and scientific service. In the specialized diagnostic environment, where customers purchase expensive solutions and 'know what they are talking about', Dako views good science, good service and good relationships as inseparable and seeks to reflect a unique competency as scientific partner of choice, in its CRM.

CRM strategy

A 2002 study conducted by INSEAD and CGEY developed a model of CRM based on the customer communication channels used, analytical approach and IT and organization architecture. Some of the findings from this work are illustrated in Table 9.2. As a whole, the pharmaceutical industry is committed to the CRM 'idea', although most companies are not very far ahead in implementation. Clearly, sales force size and effectiveness are a source of major concern especially as margin pressure becomes relentless. CRM is seen as a way of

TABLE 9.2

Key pharmaceutical CRM findings and implications

Topic	Findings	Implications
Channels	With sales rep productivity decreasing in saturated markets, the sales force arms race is at a turning point	New channels will not replace the sales representatives, but selectively complement them
	New channels will grow in importance, increasing reach to customers and speed of interaction as well as feeding back customer data	Companies need to coordinate their messages across multiple channels
		Companies need to build the organizational flexibility to sustain better and faster customer dialogue
Analytics	Companies are rediscovering analytics – seeking ways to integrate customer and market profiles into daily operations	Moving from passive data to information to actionable knowledge
	Challenges are in collecting, prioritizing or integrating data and using the insights from analysis and segmentation models	Companies need to move beyond traditional static segmentation and seek useful answers to the 'why' of the prescribing decision
IT architecture	CRM IT investment in the industry will focus first on extracting the benefits from existing systems and second on building analytical capability	Companies need to review their IT priorities in the light of future cost considerations
Organizational architecture	CRM will increase data transparency, alignment along segmentation models and more rigorous processes based on codified best practices	A super sales force will emerge
		CRM will find an organizational home
		Companies will develop more formal processes for customer interaction
		Team-based work across organizational boundaries will break down internal barriers

Source: [96]

extracting more value from the sales force, which will probably decrease in size at least within the medium term. The e-channel (including e-detailing, websites, interactive tools) will become more important and CRM systems will be required to manage multichannel, real-time interactions with customers. Similarly, companies are beginning to realize that in order to act more effectively, a better understanding of the customer (and customer data) is vital. Hence, the growing interest in managing, storing and analysing customer data. There is much confusion concerning both the ideal IT and organizational architecture for implementing CRM. Companies are interested in more robust, simpler CRM solutions and in better connecting existing systems, rather than in undertaking expensive 'greenfield' implementations [96].

CRM is a way of breaking down artificial barriers between sales and marketing organizations, especially at a time when the industry has to do 'more with less'. Cooperation between sales groups and marketing teams is often minimal with, at best, one-way communication from marketing to sales about promotional events. Sales and marketing divisions using different metrics to measure success can exacerbate problems. In 2001, Forrester asked a panel of 22 pharmaceutical executives to identify the most challenging strategic problems that they faced. More than one-third identified cross-functional coordination as their biggest hurdle. Companies that believe that CRM can be accomplished with a simple SFA implementation are wrong. Internal sales and marketing processes must be examined as part of the same customer experience to drive accurate assessment of ROI on all components of the marketing mix, consistent data collection and meaningful understanding of the value of each customer [113]. Ideally, CRM will allow companies to use data mining to move from simplistic models that are focused exclusively on high-value customers to approaches that estimate the appropriate investment, service offering and channel for all customer segments.

No discussion of CRM strategy would be complete without a note of extreme caution. CRM can become a costly failure. It is rumoured that one major pharmaceutical company spent $200 million on a CRM system that was never launched because it failed to meet expectations [7]. Current advice is to implement CRM in defined stages around one or more central databases, defining clear goals and ROI targets for each stage. Many pharmaceutical executives are of the opinion that no single technology 'solution' provider exists for pharmaceutical companies launching CRM initiatives, as no single CRM provider can meet a global pharmaceutical company's diverse needs. As with ERP, the main barriers to successful CRM implementation are political and organizational rather than technical.

The measurement of ROI is a mandatory and early component of CRM implementation. Simple quantitative metrics such as improvements in number of visits and sample requests to qualitative measures of customer (and CRM-user) satisfaction should be included.

Conclusions – 'the take home messages'

The value of CRM lies in the potential to increase sales through more efficient processes: better targeting (target identification); better communication (getting the appropriate marketing message to the identified target); and improved service (responding better to customer needs). CRM facilitates more accurate market segmentation (dynamic testing of a customer model) and predictive marketing (being proactive in customer relationships).

Currently, few comprehensive CRM implementations have been completed; however, it is likely that we will see advanced CRM systems in the pharmaceutical industry within the next five years. CRM implementation in pharmaceutical companies requires a complex aggregation and integration of different approaches and technologies. Integrating around business processes is a necessity because no one vendor has a complete system to address all these requirements.

It is best to regard CRM as a 'journey' rather than a specific technology implementation. The road to action starts with improvements in data management (descriptive CRM), then turning the data into useful information (dynamic CRM) and finally developing useful knowledge for action (predictive CRM). While this model may sound somewhat in the realm of aspiration, it does highlight the series of practical steps required to extract value from a CRM implementation (Figure 9.7).

CRM has been criticised as the latest technology 'fad', and implementing a successful CRM system is extremely difficult. However, there is little doubt that the potential of CRM to improve the relationship between pharmaceutical companies and their customers is enormous.

- CRM implementation requires a rigorous focus on the quality of incoming data – the art of the possible – ensuring that each indicator is valuable, accurate and can be cleanly and consistently collected.
- Making CRM accessible, easy and part of the everyday life of the key users will change the dynamics of sales and marketing by introducing transparency and making it easier to realign the sales force in a changing market.
- Pharmaceutical companies need to invest more in analytical capacity to simplify the task of people who interface with customers. How many phar-

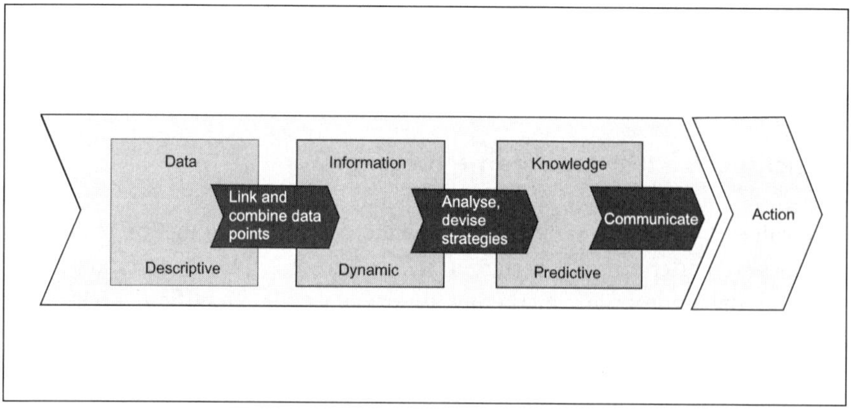

Figure 9.7 Analytics – turning passive customer data into targeted action

Source: [96]

maceutical companies can identify ten priority indicators in their CRM databases that are important for predictive marketing?

- CRM permits a clear focus on the important and valuable customers interactions. How many pharmaceutical companies can identify vital cross-channel interactions that require an action on their part?

CHAPTER

10 Digital strategies in marketing to the consumer

Over the past decade, the consumer has emerged as a significant partner in the complex universe of health and healthcare. Governments, insurers, physicians and pharmaceutical companies increasingly use the terms 'patient' and 'healthcare consumer' interchangeably, conceding that the end-users in the health value chain are indeed concerned with quality, cost and access to care and information. Healthcare consumers, as compared to passive patients, play a role, both real and perceived, in the healthcare decision-making process. Health consumers are demanding, more interested in self-determination and more likely to develop loyalty to products or healthcare and pharmaceutical companies that partner with them and consider them as a partner [114]. While there is still considerable debate as to the extent of consumer empowerment in healthcare, we believe that increasing involvement in the healthcare financial transaction, either directly or through insurance schemes, is indeed forcing citizens of industrialized countries to take a far greater interest in the quality and price of health services and products. Similarly, we face a daily barrage of scientific and lifestyle information in a world where health is extremely newsworthy, but the best methods of building relationships with and marketing to health consumers are still to be found.

As consumers take their rightful place in the health purchasing process, providers of products and services are prioritizing consumers in their advertising and promotion campaigns. However the interaction between the consumer, the physician and the payer remains complex:

- Internet users from all income brackets search for health or provider information online, according to a 2001 US Commerce Department study,

'A Nation Online: How Americans Are Expanding Their Use of the Internet', which surveyed more than 137,000 individuals nationwide. Almost 35 per cent of all Internet users surveyed used the web to search for health information. Specifically, 30 per cent of respondents with web access and incomes below $15,000 had used the Internet for health searches within the last year, compared to 39 per cent of those with incomes greater than $75,000 [115].

- A 2001 Canadian study of oncologists and their patients found that 86 per cent of patients wanted as much information about their illness as possible, but 53 per cent reported receiving insufficient information; 71 per cent actively searched for information and 50 per cent used the Internet. However, both patients and oncologists agreed that information seeking did not directly impact on the patient–physician relationship [116].

Freely available information to the consumer does not necessarily result in accurate knowledge: 'as physicians are discovering, the increasingly empowered and demanding health consumer is still, by professional standards, poorly informed' [117]. However, there is no doubt that informed consumers are influencing physician prescribing. In a 2001 survey, 71 per cent of patients who requested a specific drug from their physicians were indeed prescribed that product [118]. As consumers have access to more information, products and service quality and, in particular, medical errors are becoming a real public concern. Patients are now being forced to deal with reports that the health industry is facing a crisis in quality. In the US, a widely publicized 2001 report claiming that errors in medical settings resulted in between 44,000 and 98,000 patient deaths annually has not increased patient confidence [114].

The public is being exposed to a biomedical world that, on the one hand, is incredibly complex yet, on the other, offers almost daily news of breakthrough discoveries with the potential to cure (in the longer term at least) many serious diseases. Pharmacogenomics, as it slowly enters mainstream medical practice, offers a myriad of diagnostic, preventive and ultimately therapeutic choices. Informing people of the choices, let alone marketing tests and drugs, poses huge educational and ethical problems. For example, a drug for a certain group of patients with high cholesterol will require genetic testing, but genetic records will certainly remain the private property of individuals, thus making individualized information campaigns (through email, for example) difficult to implement.

A small but growing proportion of pharmaceutical marketing budgets is spent on consumer marketing, and this seems destined to be an important channel, despite wariness and opposition on the part of some physicians and consumer groups. However, companies remain unsure about how best to spend this money, or how effective their spend is.

Consumer activism

Consumers are not only increasingly important to pharmaceutical companies as purchasers of their products. In a world where health is indeed a major concern and health issues a media priority, consumer power in health and healthcare is amply demonstrated by the rise of activism, ranging from concerns about prices, animal welfare, global equity and social justice to the demand for the rapid approval of experimental drugs for rare or rapidly fatal diseases. Many pharmaceutical executives may see this as a distant concern, but it is one that all will have to address soon, as several leading companies have found:

- Huntingdon Life Sciences (HLS), a UK animal testing company, and service provider to most global pharmaceutical companies, was all but destroyed by a small group of activists who not only targeted HLS facilities and executives, but also their bankers, brokers, shareholders and customers. The HLS situation highlights the need for companies in sensitive areas (such as healthcare) to actively manage consumer opinion. Consumer activism is certainly a global phenomenon as health issues, from the impact of globalization to drug prices in less-developed countries to animal rights, are on the agenda of non-governmental and activist organizations [119].
- Europe's public backlash against genetically modified (GM) food forced Gerber, the Novartis baby food division, to stop using GM ingredients, despite the fact that Novartis was a major producer of GM seeds [46].
- GlaxoSmithKline and several other firms have felt the force of AIDS activists' fury, who argued that the pharmaceutical giants should allow less-developed countries cheap access to branded AIDS drugs, or permission to make generic versions prior to patent expiration. The corporate argument that the problem was not the price of the drugs, but widespread corruption and healthcare systems unable to deliver the drugs properly, failed to persuade popular opinion, forcing the pharmaceutical multinationals to concede defeat on some key issues. In April 2001, 39 pharmaceutical companies that sued the South African government over legislation that allegedly contravened constitutional patent law dropped

their case unconditionally. Jean-Pierre Garnier, Chief Executive of GlaxoSmithKline, one of the pharmaceutical companies that led the industry's retreat from what had become a public relations catastrophe, said he had been influenced by the concerns of investors, shareholders and the public about equitable access to medicines [120].

- The accelerated regulatory approval of Glivec, an innovative anti-cancer treatment developed by Novartis, can to a great extent be attributed to the activism of leukaemia patients and their families, who demanded that the drug, after showing near-spectacular efficacy in early clinical trials, be made available without delay. The Internet played an important role in the campaign to make Glivec available, connecting patient support groups and allowing them to communicate their concerns rapidly to the company and governments.

Managing consumer expectations and negotiating with a range of interest groups, some extremely radical in their beliefs and actions, has become a major challenge for pharmaceutical companies. On the one hand, the Internet permits companies rapidly to disseminate important news and provides a window into the corporate philanthropic activities and values, yet it also allows opponents to mobilize quickly and spread counter-arguments.

In the face of intense and rapid communications, companies are finding that just doing good works is not enough. Many companies have made the mistake of confusing social responsibility with philanthropy. Nike long prided itself on supporting charities in the US. But for a global brand, that wasn't enough when activists attacked the company because of working conditions and the use of child labour in its Asian factories. The pharmaceutical industry has an exemplary record of corporate philanthropy, but this has not stopped the media from increasingly equating pharmaceutical companies with the tobacco industry (ironically, another industry known for its generosity to charitable causes, the arts and culture), primarily due to its use of legions of lawyers to fight against generic competition and drug price controls. It is often difficult to identify the important partners with whom to open a dialogue. While radical animal rights protesters will not be interested in talking with a pharmaceutical company, many other organizations would indeed wish to debate and seek just solutions. The Internet makes it possible to organize a global community around a certain issue in a 'split second'. Many of tomorrow's issues, particularly in the fields of environmentalism and international human rights, get an airing in Europe before they do in the US. Monsanto, a world leader in biotechnology, is a classic example of a company that thought it could adopt American tactics and 'resist and fight' those Europeans who opposed genetically modified crops. It lost [121].

The Internet has changed the rules of interaction with consumers for the pharmaceutical industry, in that it has introduced elements of speed, transparency and intensity that make every contact (be it with a customer, potential customer or concerned citizen) important and urgent.

Direct-to-consumer (DTC) advertising

Introduction

In the US, pharmaceutical companies have been aggressively targeting consumers since 1997, when pharmaceutical advertising regulations were relaxed. Since then, expenditure on direct-to-consumer (DTC) advertising of prescription drugs has rocketed. Pharmaceutical companies spent an estimated $2.3 billion on DTC advertising in 2000, and are boosting their spends by 25–35 per cent annually [122]. Contrary to reports in the summer of 2001, the EU is not considering relaxing a ban on DTC advertising for AIDS, diabetes and asthma drugs in member nations. Instead, commissioners debated a provision allowing pharmaceutical companies to provide the public with non-promotional data about prescription drugs for those conditions. The confusion arose as the English-language translation of the proposal used the wording 'public advertising' instead of the wording 'information to the public' that was used in the French, Italian, Spanish and other versions [123]. While the debate on the merits and dangers of DTC advertising continues in Europe, it is claimed that in the US, Schering-Plough's anti-allergy treatment Claritin has had more advertising dollars lavished on it than Coca-Cola [124]. DTC advertising in the US has been rising as a percentage of sales, over a period when direct-to-professional (or physician) (DTP) promotion has remained relatively constant. Still, in most therapeutic areas, ten times more is still spent marketing to professionals than to consumers [122], as the physician is still seen as the primary marketing target for prescription drugs (Figure 10.1).

Some evidence suggested that DTC spending rose another ten per cent in 2001, but there was a reduction in patient contacts with physicians arising from DTC advertising, perhaps indicating that the US public is becoming inured to DTC advertising in the media and new approaches may be needed [126] (Table 10.1).

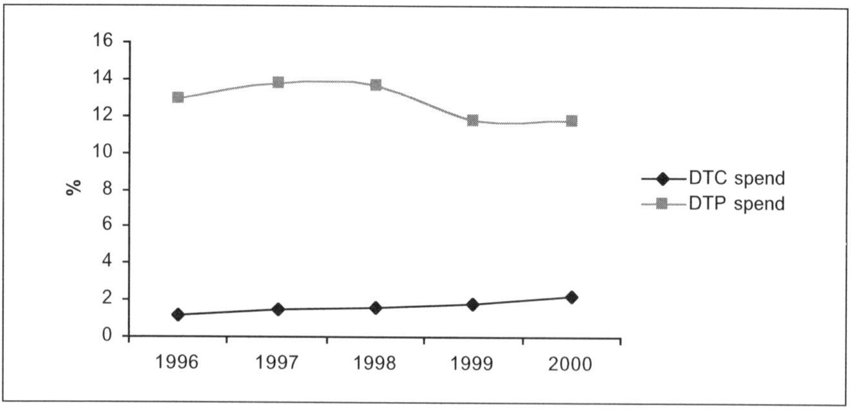

Figure 10.1 Pharmaceutical sales and marketing spend as a percentage of sales in the US

Source: [125]

TABLE 10.1

The ten most promoted DTC drugs in the US (2000)

Drug	Class	DTC spending ($m)
Vioxx	Anti-inflammatory	161
Prilosec	Anti-ulcer	108
Claritin	Antihistamine	100
Paxil	Antidepressant	92
Zocor	Antihyperlipidemic	91
Viagra	Erectile dysfunction	90
Celebrex	Anti-inflammatory	79
Flonase	Anti-inflammatory	78
Allegra	Antihistamine	67
Meridia	Weight reduction	65
Total		1451

Source: [125]

DTC advertising – a double-edged sword

It is claimed that one in eight Americans has asked for and received a specific prescription from their physician in response to seeing a drug advert on television [127], and 71 per cent of patients who requested a specific drug were prescribed that product [118]. However, the rise of DTC advertising has not pleased everyone, and some have serious doubts as to whether it actually helps consumers in its present form. Among physicians, DTC advertising is controversial, with some appreciating an informed patient and others being uncomfortable with lay-persons dictating therapeutic options. In a 2001 survey, over half of a sample of physicians in the US thought that prescription drug adverts did not help their patients [128], while over 70 per cent of consumers feel they learned little or nothing about the condition featured in an advertisement [127].

The Consumers Association in the UK is against any relaxation of European DTC advertising regulations, stating that it would drive up healthcare costs to a level that Britain's health service might not be able afford [129]. Indeed, a report from the National Institute of Healthcare Management Research and Education Foundation found that almost half of the $20.8 billion rise in US pharmaceutical expenditure between 1999 and 2000 was accounted for by the 25 most advertised (and, perhaps unsurprisingly, expensive) drugs [3]. Both the US Congress and the FDA are due to review the effects of DTC advertising on treatment outcomes, consumer use and prescription pricing [130].

E-DTC strategy

The Internet offers a range of innovative options for communicating product messages to health consumers. Firstly, it offers a rapid, cheap way of conveying information and can be a useful complementary tool when used in conjunction with television and print media. For example, a television spot can direct viewers to a product website for further information, or a DTC campaign for asthma or obesity can offer online diaries, reminder services or patient communities, in order to promote compliance.

San Francisco-based Genentech and ad agency Far Riley Call/Bozell promoted the breast cancer drug Herceptin using patient support groups and a direct-to-patient channel. Herceptin is a targeted, monoclonal antibody that improves survival in a specific group of breast cancer patients. The advertising agency, with input from the cancer community, produced educational material to be issued to patients at different stages of the diagnosis and treatment process. The 'Finding Your Way' programme consists of booklets that walk patients in simple, easy to follow steps through the disease and treatment [131].

TABLE 10.2

Ratio of US DTC and DTP spending for five drug classes

Class of drug	DTP spending (per cent of sales)	DTC spending (per cent of sales)	Ratio
Antidepressants	14.4	0.5	29
Proton-pump inhibitors	11.2	1.4	8
Antihyperlipidaemics	8.7	1.5	6
Nasal sprays	24.7	11.6	2
Antihistamines	12.4	6.1	2

Source: [125]

GlaxoSmithKline and Roche are sponsoring a global osteoporosis email information service for some non-US markets. The Osteoporosis Care Club (OCC) was developed by a medical communications agency that issues an email newsletter every two to three weeks which includes news and features about the disease. OCC updates are available to medical journalists and patient organizations from Europe, Canada, Australia and Brazil [132].

DTC spending is most effective for 'self-directed' treatments, be they prescribed or over-the-counter (OTC) medications, where physician involvement may not be required on a regular basis and where long-term compliance is important (Table 10.2). Once again, the Internet offers excellent opportunities to provide information and value-added services that encourage sustained product use.

According to FTC (Federal Trade Commission) statistics, drugs with a combined $20 billion in annual sales in the US will go off-patent by 2005. This is driving the growth of DTC advertising, as pharmaceutical companies attempt to build brand loyalty before patents expire and generic substitutes flood the market. However, payers, governments and managed care organizations push for the use of cheaper generics, and it is unlikely that loyalty-building campaigns will bear fruit. For example, on the day that the generic version of Prozac became available, Merck-Medco (a large pharmacy benefits management company) informed the 25,000 physicians who were the top Prozac prescribers and alerted online patients about the availability of a generic substitute and the potential cost savings. Eighty per cent of Merck-Medco customers who received the antidepressant Prozac by home delivery opted for the generic substitute in the week that it became available [133]. This huge generic switch would not have been

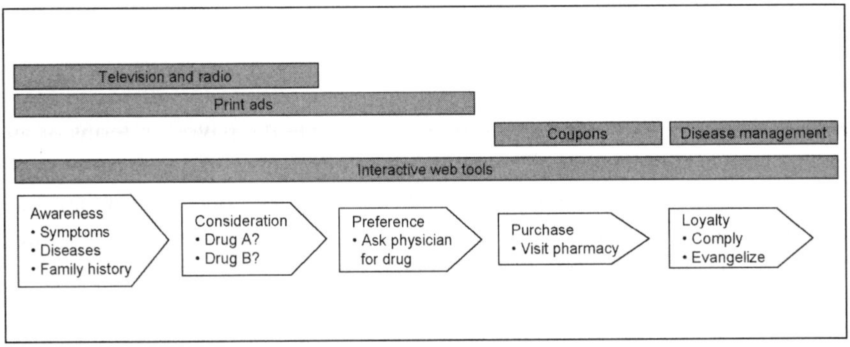

Figure 10.2 The DTC cycle

Source: Adapted from [128]

possible without digital technologies; the Internet to rapidly inform physicians and patients of the cheaper generic option, and a range of software tools to manage e-prescribing, orders and inventories to ensure a smooth transition.

DTC advertising, if permitted, is part of a complex marketing mix for the launch and continued promotion of a prescription drug (Figure 10.2). Within the DTC component of a campaign, marketers have to allocate resources between television, radio and print media, coupons and price reductions, relationship building (forming or aiding patient support groups or public awareness activities) and digital technologies (including email, websites, interactive tools and mobile Internet). Substantial research may be required to identify touch points such as embarrassment, fear or discomfort when it comes to discussing the condition with a physician. This provides some indication as to how to allocate resources. For example, in the case of a potentially embarrassing condition such as herpes, incontinence or erectile dysfunction, a pharmaceutical marketer may decide to support a health awareness-oriented campaign that sometimes involves public figures discussing the particular condition. The e-channel plays a vital role, as consumers can be offered a site where they can seek information and support anonymously and communicate with experts about their concerns.

Digital technologies offer an excellent, real-time solution for measuring the impact of DTC activities. Savvy marketers want to see real actions as the metric of success (or failure) of an advertising campaign. For example, a unique web address at the end of a television advert or magazine article can be used to measure the response to a particular 'call to action'. Within websites themselves, it is possible to track consumer information requests and measure demands for discount coupons or information leaflets.

A number of approaches exist to measure the ROI of DTC strategies, each having its strengths and drawbacks:

- Consumer tracking models are built to calculate the payoff in terms of an increase in awareness. The model depends on syndicated or custom research that provides the percentage of aware customers who are considering asking for or using a particular drug. Assumptions are generally imprecise, but this approach is relatively easy to implement and can be done without alerting competitors.
- Regression analysis compares sales before, during and after a DTC campaign. It can be a fairly robust indicator, but requires a longitudinal data set, usually over several years.
- Simulated test markets is a popular technique in consumer goods marketing, but presumes that DTC advertising is the main driver of sales, which is not the case with pharmaceuticals. It predicts sales levels based on varying advertising spends, but requires a deep understanding of market dynamics that is not generally currently available to the pharmaceutical industry.
- Test marketing involves testing different campaigns with focus groups and the general public. It is robust, but expensive and slow.

The Internet permits a range of new market research approaches as experiments can be conducted quickly. For example, a small panel of consumers can be convened from a web discussion or support group for a certain disease and the researcher can conduct online focus group discussions. Within the constraints of privacy and data protection legislation, data mining permits market researchers to set up an experimental hypothesis concerning predicted consumer behaviour.

Although the subject is beyond the scope of this book, we need to be aware of the OTC pharmaceutical market as a source of innovation in DTC advertising. Non-prescription drug marketing is much closer to that of consumer goods, as margins are low and competition is often intense. In many senses, the prescription drug marketing environment, in a context of price controls and consumer power, is indeed becoming a lot more similar to the OTC market; but the substantial difference remains the role of the physician as the main actor in the prescription decision.

The fact that DTC advertising is not permitted in many countries does not mean that the pharmaceutical industry does not communicate product messages to consumers in regions such as Europe. Companies often fund, or even establish, support groups for certain conditions and regularly receive regulatory approval for public awareness campaigns on certain diseases or the need for early diagnosis. In fact, a new pharmaceutical marketing science called 'enhanced DTC' exists that aims to explore options for promoting prescription products to consumers in countries where DTC advertising is prohibited. The Internet permits consumers in countries that ban DTC advertising to visit product websites in the USA and, despite warnings found on pharmaceutical sites, there is little to prevent the free global transfer of consumer-oriented information on prescription drugs (nor as we discuss later, prevent commerce in these products).

Conclusions – 'the take home messages'

> The ads make people really mad. People want drug companies to spend less money on that and to make sure drugs are affordable. – Maine State Senator Chellie Pingree (2000) [22]

At first glance, DTC advertising is a useful, if poorly understood, way of selling prescription drugs. However, it blurs our conventional distinction between patients and consumers, and antagonizes payers, and as such may well turn out to be a distinctly mixed blessing for the industry. Expansion into DTC advertising is an extension of push marketing activities and may serve to alienate consumers (and their physicians) who, after making a connection, however tenuous, between DTC advertising and rising drug prices, would prefer that the industry's money be spent on R&D rather than on commercial advertising.

The role of branding in prescription drug marketing remains controversial. On the one hand, the pharmaceutical industry has attained spectacular sales with little attention (relative to industries such as automobiles or beverages) on branding. Yet, on the other hand, tremendous effort is devoted to communicating the virtues of products (such as scientific attributes, patient convenience, safety) in a market where the difference between top-selling drugs in a certain category may be extremely small [134].

However useful branding becomes in both the physician and consumer marketing contexts, its importance will be largely mitigated by the inexorable economic reality of cost control, where product choice will be mandated and limited. In the case of prescription drugs, it is likely that all but the richest consumers (in Europe, at least) will continue to receive their healthcare from an insurer or provider (where the insurer may be the government). Formularies, generic substitution and practice guidelines are here to stay. Even if the consumer pays for care through defined-benefit insurance and has a choice of services, cost and cost-effectiveness are still going to be a key consideration.

In the short term, pharmaceutical companies will seek as many avenues as possible to commence a dialogue with consumers. Clearly, the first option is to offer information, diagnostic and disease management services (such as diaries, reminders, online communities) around their existing therapeutic offerings. It is possible that some adventurous pharmaceutical companies may, in an effort to own the customer, move beyond isolated disease management provision to become fully fledged service providers. We discuss the history of the pharmaceutical industry and disease management in Chapter 11, but here it should suffice to note that digital technologies allow a company to offer a range of disease or condition management services to consumers at a reasonable cost and without the complications of having to deal with a range of third parties.

As the technological landscape in healthcare changes, and here we are looking beyond 2010, the distinction between the product and the treatment process will blur, and pharmaceutical companies will have to capture an increasing portion of the value created by new technologies and information channels. Here we could see a recurrence of branding, where consumers will be offered packaged or complete solutions – a so-called one-stop shop for the diagnosis, treatment and long-term management of a condition. Similarly, in the context of pharmacogenomics, it is not difficult to imagine a world where affluent customers will pay premium prices for risk identification, early detection and pharmaco-prevention of diseases.

- Across the spectrum, from legal advertising to countries where DTC advertising is banned, pharmaceutical companies are looking for ways to enhance relationships with consumers. This needs to be attained without alienating physicians or attracting the attention of consumer groups concerned with the link between commercial drug promotion and drug prices.

- As compared with the depth of knowledge and level of success in physician promotion, the industry is still at an early stage in DTC strategies. We already see the initial DTC model of near-saturation print and TV advertising, and the use of prominent personalities to promote drugs, coming under increasing critical scrutiny.

- There is no simple answer to whether pharmaceutical companies should brand themselves or their particular product, each approach having particular virtues and dangers. In the near future, companies will seek to offer branded services, along with branded products, in order to provide the consumer, physician or payer with a complete solution. Digital technologies will make such offerings possible.

Consumer portals

Introduction

Digital technology permits a new class of information and assistance providers, so-called 'infomediaries', to aid consumers who are forced to manage more complicated healthcare transactions and choose between a bewildering range of therapeutic options. For instance, all the pharmaceutical companies covered in a 2001 US report now support or have product-focused or disease-specific websites, and the web share of DTC budgets is projected to rise from nine per cent in 2002 to 18 per cent by 2004 [128]. European pharmaceutical firms see consumer portals as a way of reaching consumers without breaching the strict laws banning DTC advertising. The Association of the British Pharmaceutical Industry (ABPI) does not currently lobby for US-style DTC advertising in Britain, but is advocating a relaxation of the regulations that limit what companies can tell consumers about their products. The industry is already pushing 'disease awareness' campaigns using unbranded health information, and the ABPI is looking at the Internet as a way for companies to reach consumers.

In Chapter 9, we explored physician-facing portals, as the interface between pharmaceutical companies and prescribers. Consumer health portals or websites offering a range of content, services, discussion areas, value-added services, e-commerce and links were one of the first major trends in the dotcom boom. The idea was simple and seductive; as health was a major consumer interest on the Internet, why not offer a one-stop shop to satisfy a range of health-related concerns, interests and needs, and make money from pharmaceutical and other health industry sponsorship? We have to some extent already described the reasons why this business model turned out to be a dismal failure. Notwithstanding the sad early history of health portals, now, more than ever, they are seen as an attractive way of increasing awareness about medical conditions and branded products. IMS and Cyber Dialogue data shows that during the first half of 2000, it cost pharmaceutical companies an estimated $54 per single specific drug request driven by the Internet, $152 per single specific drug request driven by television advertising and $318 per single specific drug request driven by print advertising [135].

Portals in the consumer marketing mix

Portals also help companies to understand their customers, as they provide an ideal forum for dialogue between consumers themselves, and between the company and consumers. Similarly, companies are starting to analyse and

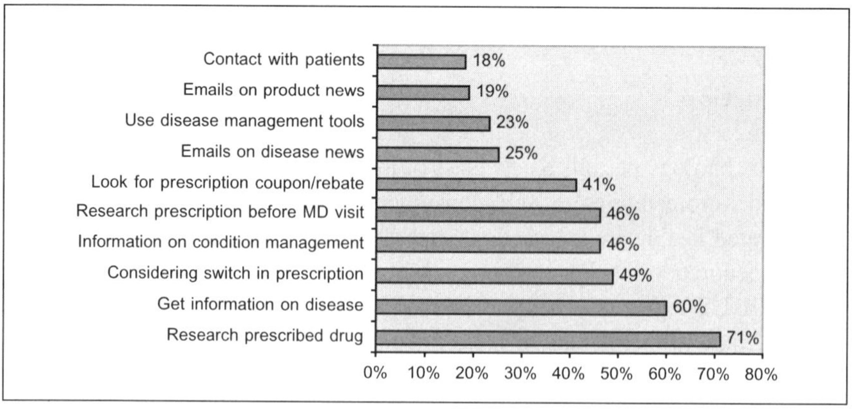

Figure 10.3 Reasons why consumers visit pharmaceutical websites (2000)

Source: [99]

mine web logs and data generated during web interactions. However, Internet marketing still makes up a tiny part of the industry's overall promotional spending, around 0.5 per cent in 2001. And until recently the vast majority of this was spent on relatively unsophisticated advertising such as banner ads and buying keywords on search engines. In a 1999 survey, 58 per cent of pharmaceutical respondents spent less than 25 per cent of online DTC budgets on website development and maintenance [99].

A 2000 US survey of 1023 respondents with Internet access revealed that almost half the sample thought it beneficial to check the Internet for health information before visiting a physician, and an almost equal number said they were likely to use the Internet to check information after the visit to the physician [136] (Figure 10.3).

Product and disease portals can be used to support a product at each stage of its lifecycle. During the pre-launch phase, a disease portal (whether owned by the company or an alliance partner) is invaluable for building awareness about the condition, recruiting patients for clinical trials and commencing a dialogue with support groups, especially if reimbursement or pricing negotiations are underway. When the product is launched, the linking of online and offline promotional efforts can be fruitful. For example, sales representatives can give physicians patient reminder cards or brochures that prominently feature the product website. As market share is built, the opportunity exists to use the e-channel to reinforce relationships, by offering value-added services and introducing disease management tools, such as interactive diaries, reminders or online advice. As the product reaches maturity, sustained relationships and compliance become a priority, and the website may offer a channel for longer term support and encouragement, especially in the case of chronic diseases [137].

Consumer protection

It is important to review the ongoing debate concerning the safety of consumer health information and the privacy of patient data on the Internet. During the early days of e-health, there were few real standards of accountability and ethical behaviour for healthcare on the Internet. E-health sites were left to draft their own codes of ethical behaviour, many of which merely gave the impression that their advice was safe, untainted by commercial relationships, or that the patient's privacy was respected [138].

In response, a number of initiatives sponsored by public and private sector organizations have been initiated to monitor and ultimately enforce standards for health information on the web. These efforts range from the World Health Organization's attempt to control the health domain name to a number of voluntary codes of conduct. The most well known of these, the Health On the Net (HON) foundation, was set up in 1996. It allows health webmasters to display the HON seal on their site, providing they adhere to an eight-point code of conduct designed to ensure that the user always knows the source and purpose of the information they are reading; although the HON seal does not guarantee the accuracy, validity or appropriateness of health content. Sites displaying the HON seal must ensure that all advice is provided by trained practitioners, the information supports and does not replace the relationship between a physician and his or her patient, patient privacy is respected, all sources of information are justifiable and attributed, it is clear who owns or is paying for the site, and adverts are clearly distinguishable as such [139]. An alternative to voluntary codes, in the US at least, is fee-based accreditation of sites. This would work in a similar way to fee-based accreditation of bricks-and-mortar healthcare providers, and as such exists in a well-defined legal framework – for instance US courts have held that the failure to comply with relevant accreditation standards can on its own signify medical malpractice [140].

Regulation of e-health safety by law is problematic, due to the inherent cross-border structure of the Internet. Additionally, the regulation of health information may conflict with US guarantees of free speech, although consumer protection law can be applied to sites that display obviously dangerous content. The US and EU have also taken different routes to enforce medical privacy on the Internet. The US HIPAA regulations allow the almost unlimited collection of data, but limit its disclosure outside processes such as consent to treatment or payment. However, this is also a key weakness of the HIPAA – it only applies to sites involved in these healthcare transactions, so e-health advice sites may not fall under it [140]. In the EU, data protection regulations limit the personal information that can be collected.

None of the regulatory methods discussed above is foolproof. For instance, a 2002 study of breast cancer advice sites found that none of the sites displaying the HON seal adhered to all eight points in the code of conduct. The study also found that the popularity of an advice site was not associated with the quality of its health content [141]. Even assuming that regulation, self-regulation or accreditation is 100 per cent effective, there will always be a large number of unregulated sites; a 2002 study found that, of the most popular health e-commerce sites, the majority sold products based on unproved health claims. The situation was especially serious for conditions such as weight loss, where there is great consumer interest but the underlying science is at an early stage [142]. However, as we reach the end of the first decade of intense Internet consumer health activity, we can reasonably assume that most Internet users are somewhat immune to information which lies at the dishonest end of the Internet spectrum and that Internet health warrants a form of protection not that dissimilar to the oversight provided by agencies such as the Federal Trade Commission (FTC) or national commercial fraud authorities. And it goes without saying that, if pharmaceutical companies are to build up constructive relationships with patients, pharmaceutical portals must be recognized as repositories of the best available scientific advice.

Consumer portal strategy

Some pharmaceutical companies have realized that the information that they generate while developing new drugs, including data on dosage, safety, indications, pharmaco-economics, physician and patient education and disease management, is indeed one of their products, and is valuable both to healthcare professionals and consumers [107]. Distributing it in a useful format to customers is no trivial task, but if tailored correctly, this information has the potential to greatly increase the perceived value of treatments for individual customers.

- Teva Marion Partners (TMP) launched Copaxone, a multiple sclerosis treatment, in 1997. Copaxone was competing with products from two established players, Biogen and Berlex. In addition to offline marketing, TMP decided to use the Internet to distinguish itself in the marketplace by offering an online resource for managing the disease. MSWatch.com was launched in July 1998 and had 26,000 users by 2001. It offers patients health management, access to nurse counsellors and peer support functions, and is used to raise consumer awareness, drive conversion and improve compliance. In addition, the site is used to collect demographic and disease data from patients in order to analyse the disease types that respond well to the drug and to better understand the customers [103, 143].

- mddatadirect.com is one of the first health infomediaries to offer real-time product information and links to service providers. The company's initial focus is on the cardiology market, but it intends to report on a broad range of medical devices in the future [144].
- Online clinical trial recruitment portals such as acurian.com link consumers to physicians conducting clinical trials. The aim is to boost recruitment by keeping interested consumers informed about innovations in therapeutics.
- US hospitals have found support groups for certain illnesses a great marketing tool, for instance many neurology patients have chosen Brigham and Women's Hospital in Boston after visiting their support site [2].
- Baxter Healthcare offers several educational websites for patients and clinicians, providing extensive information on diseases and treatment options. Baxter is working towards the private exchange of information between patients and clinicians via the Internet [105].
- Wyeth has developed VaccineWorld.com, a resource for healthcare professionals and consumers, where they can research vaccines as well as access immunization schedules. Physicians can use VaccineWorld to gather information, order products and learn about order status via the web [5].
- The American Diabetes Association (ADA) launched an email marketing campaign to add customers and donors and drive traffic to its website, diabetes.org. The ADA used a mass email service provider to help it to offer people with diabetes information to manage their illness. Email offerings include personalization features and advanced HTML formatting [145].

As healthcare organizations compete for increasingly informed consumers, it makes sense to consider what kind of information is being sought, and where these consumers are looking for this information. According to one 2000 study, the greatest number (28 per cent) look for condition-specific information, such as on cancer or heart disease. Prescription drugs (21 per cent) were another popular topic. As to where consumers got their information, the most popular sources were physicians and the Internet, each used by roughly 23 per cent of respondents [146]. The health consumer is increasingly seeking out individuals with similar concerns and conditions and forming online (and offline) communities, both to share information and provide support [147]. Product-focused or disease-specific websites will add most customer value for products that treat chronic diseases, have a high possibility of substitution and are relatively easy for the patient to understand.

Healthcare spending is skewed toward the elderly and the 'greying' of the population will necessitate changes in the marketing approach of pharmaceutical companies. The over 50s, who as a group are most interested in learning about prescription drugs, rely more on pharmacists, as well as on the print media. Pharmaceutical companies whose target demographics include a high proportion of the elderly have traditionally used media such as newspaper articles and direct mail [146]. However, we see growing evidence that as the baby-boomers age, many will have had access to the Internet during a substantial part of their working lives, and will use the Internet, and especially email, throughout their retirement.

Very few pharmaceutical companies measure the ROI on their online promotional efforts in a standardized or consistent way. As we have observed, the industry has, until recently, not had to monitor carefully promotional spending and many companies would be hard pressed to provide accurate ROI estimates for most marketing interventions. In the case of consumers', measuring ROI is difficult as it is generally the physician that selects the product. But it is important to seek metrics following compliance and retention in the case of online disease management programmes. Similarly, no DTC campaign involving the Internet should be designed without a range of metrics including online behaviour and response measurement (Figure 10.4).

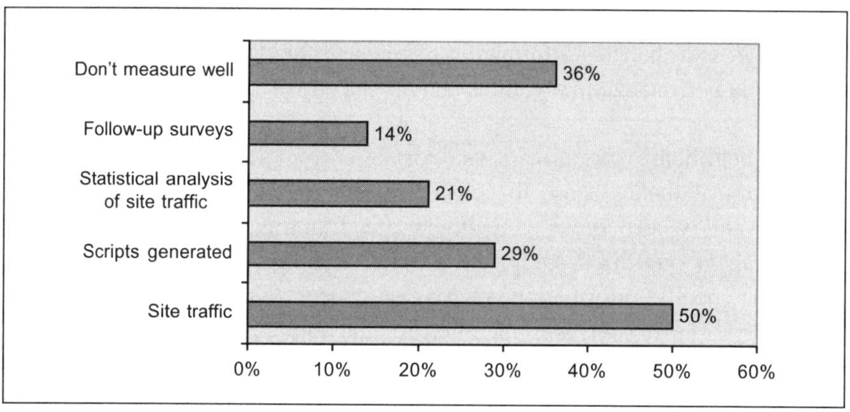

Figure 10.4 Methods used by pharmaceutical companies to measure ROI of online advertising (2001)

Note: Percentage of 14 pharma firms responding
Source: [128]

Conclusions – 'the take home messages'

The role of pharmaceutical company websites in consumer marketing remains a source of intense debate. Surveys show a wide variation in the level of consumer trust and confidence in pharmaceutical company websites (between 25 and 60 per cent of consumers claim to trust the information given on a pharmaceutical company website). It is vital to note that the number of consumers who trust pharmaceutical company sites (even when you accept the most conservative estimates) is far greater than for industries such as consumer goods or automobiles. Hence it is reasonable to operate from the premise that consumers do indeed use, and often trust, pharmaceutical company websites. While commercial websites (those of providers, pharmaceutical companies or insurers) are indeed used, it is not good practice to invest too much money and effort into turning these into sophisticated consumer portals. Visitors to these sites tend to have distinct, pressing needs in terms of product information or the disease or condition itself. These needs should be quickly and efficiently met, a goal that can often be well attained using fairly rudimentary website architecture. Patients and their families who are interested in sophisticated disease management tools and creating support groups and communities are best served by specialized portals, often created and managed by commercial e-health companies with patient involvement and financial support from the industry. There is certainly room for improving consumer prescription drug promotion sites in those countries that permit DTC advertising. In 2001, Cyber Dialogue projected that DTC websites will eventually offer personalized product messages, support information, patient education and even monitoring tools that enable online communication between a patient and physician. The hope is that this can make consumers more comfortable with interacting with pharmaceutical companies [135] (Figure 10.5).

Portals offer a reasonably cheap and focused channel for communicating with consumers over a product's lifecycle. For example, patients who seek truly innovative drugs and are interested in participating in clinical research can be reached through specialized clinical trial portals. Pharmaceutical companies have the opportunity, using digital technologies, to explore making selected research data accessible to the wider public, thereby driving the early demand for a specific product. However, physicians are concerned that DTC approaches in the dissemination of difficult to interpret scientific data will encourage unnecessary or inappropriate use of drugs and medical technologies [136].

- Portals and web services permit the repositioning of products and the bundling of a drug with a value-added offering. This allows a company to differentiate a drug in a market filled with 'me-too' competition.

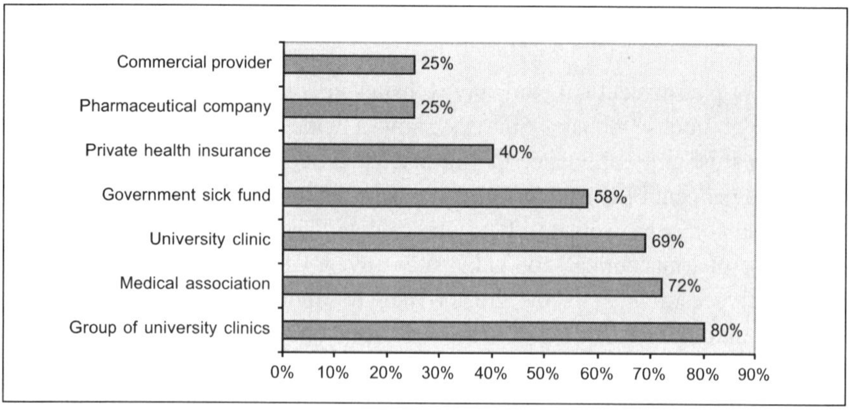

Figure 10.5 Trusted providers of healthcare information for German and Swedish consumers (2001)

Note: 1000 patients in Germany and Sweden
Source: [148]

- Consumers of the future will be even more interested in their health, as diagnostics allow them to find out what diseases they are especially susceptible to and what precautions or preventive treatments are available. As segmented or personalized medicine becomes a reality, consumer portals may have an essential role in guiding consumers towards the correct treatment option. The Internet may be the only efficient conduit for providing this information.
- A small but rapidly growing group of consumers will make the Internet their main health resource. Many consumers will be forced to use e-tools as the best way of managing health insurance benefits, providing a potential interface with providers of health products and services.
- Pharmaceutical marketers face a pressing challenge of identifying the most cost-effective way of deploying digital technologies to interact with consumers. Until fairly recently, vendors of e-health software and services have priced their offerings unrealistically high, thereby limiting the number of experiments and pilot projects.

Patient relationship management (PRM)

Introduction

The ultimate goal of the consumer facing marketing techniques that we have described is effective patient relationship management (PRM). PRM is designed to build and preserve the profitable customer relationships that offer competitive advantage in the long term. Although only 33 per cent of healthcare companies in a 2001 survey saw PRM as a current strategic priority, 83 per cent felt that it would be in the future [111]. In order to provide consumers with a personalized service, PRM requires segmentation, customer data analysis and interactive marketing. To meet these aims, PRM systems have to provide:

- Innovative service offerings
- Multiple channels of contact
- Systems to store and analyse customer data
- Impetus for reshaping business processes and employee attitudes [111].

As consumers are using digital technologies more frequently, the diversity of customer touch points is increasing (Figure 10.6). The advantages of using a PRM approach can be anticipated in the higher sales revenues due to the exploitation of selling opportunities, increased reach due to the diversity of channels and the opportunity to use premium pricing based on customer segmentation and product service bundling. Marketers can save money, through the more efficient use of CSCs and data mining to identify the best resource allocation options [111].

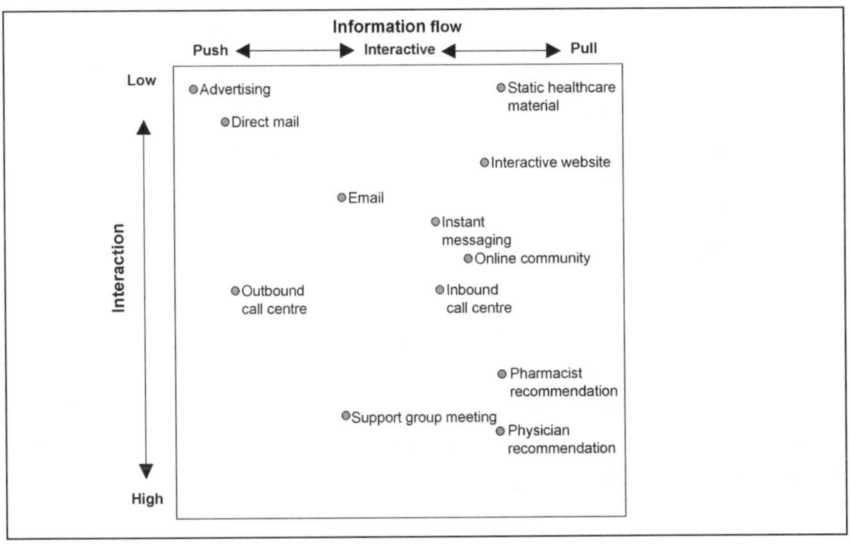

Figure 10.6 Consumer touch points

Source: Adapted from ZS Associates

PRM strategy

PRM can best be regarded as consumer or patient-focused CRM. The differences between PRM and CRM tend to be in the resource allocation to various communication channels. For example, DTC advertising will, where permissible, be conducted using the mass media, such as television, whereas physician promotion uses personal contact and specialized journals (Figure 10.7).

Although many companies are still at an early stage in both CRM and PRM planning and implementation, it is useful to highlight the important steps in PRM development:

- Good customer segmentation is the foundation of good PRM. After identifying and segmenting customers on the basis of their needs, it is possible to decide what services should be offered to each segment. The importance of segmentation and personalization is likely to increase as we approach the age of truly personalized healthcare. We describe some of the services that can be offered to various segments in the disease management and telemedicine sections in Chapter 11.
- PRM allows a company to offer innovative services to differentiate its product from similar competitive offerings.
- As consumers become more important healthcare decision-makers, it is inevitable that marketing spend will shift towards them at the expense of other, more established targets such as physicians. There are also likely to be large investments in the IT systems necessary to support PRM.
- It is highly unlikely that any one company will have the capabilities necessary to design, build and deliver healthcare services for multiple customer segments. Alliances and partnerships will become more common, with IT houses, content providers, advertising agencies, health insurers, health providers and even other pharmaceutical companies.
- It will be vital to establish PRM platforms and processes within the company, such as a central customer database and incentives to enter customer data. Many pharmaceutical companies have never devoted substantial resources to consumer communication, as they correctly saw physicians and payers as the key decision-makers in the health purchasing process.

The final and most difficult hurdle in PRM implementation is convincing customers that the offering is of value and creating demand among patients,

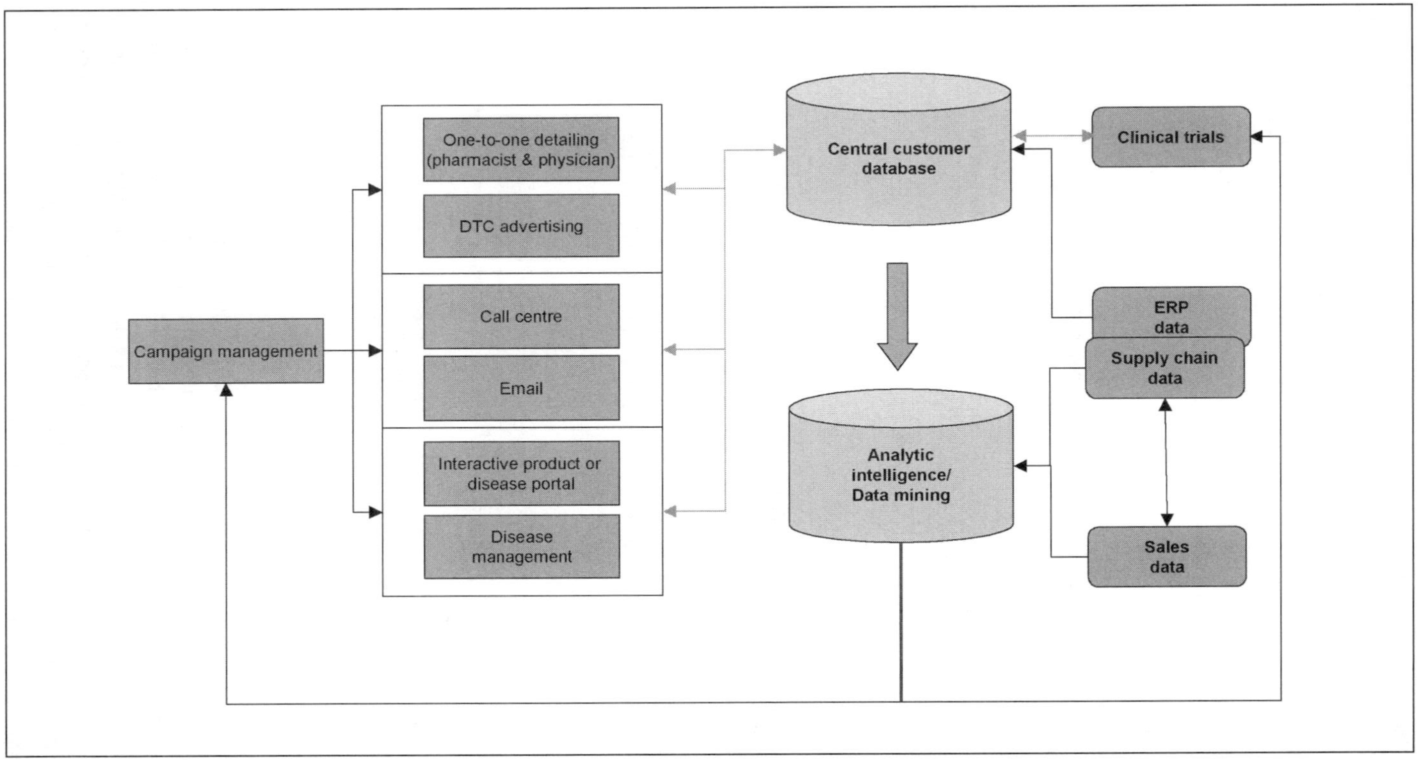

Figure 10.7 An idealized PRM schematic

TABLE 10.3

Consumer PRM solutions

Sponsor – Brand	Site focus	Features	PRM solution
Roche – Xenical	Weight loss programs for obese individuals	■ Personalised weight loss coaching and information ■ Prescription compliance and site update emails	Micromass Raport Server
Solvay Pharmaceuticals – Creon	Daily support for people with Cystic Fibrosis (CF)	■ Daily diary with chart to track symptoms ■ Personal messages ■ Information for managing CF	Dendrite, Protocol Driven Healthcare
Teva Neuroscience – Copaxone	Support for patients with Multiple Sclerosis and their caregivers	■ Personal diary ■ Patient–provider communications ■ Patient discussion forums ■ News and educational content	Softwatch SRS
GlaxoSmithKline – Nicorette CQ	Smoking cessation program	■ Personalised tools and content to support all phases of smoking cessation	Micromass Raport Server

Source: [112]

their physicians and payers for a range of value-added services. At a time when healthcare budgets are squeezed, people will certainly want more for less from the pharmaceutical industry and, today, most PRM solutions are limited in scope, focusing very much on the disease or condition management. Current PRM solutions are designed to either support 'lifestyle programmes' such as smoking cessation and weight reduction or for chronic diseases (Table 10.3). Patient-centric approaches are valuable in these cases, where:

- The patient has a greater degree of control over the purchase of a product or service (partially reimbursed or non-reimbursed drugs and OTC medicines).
- The relationship is long term (ranging from a smoking cessation programme over a few months to life-long dialysis).
- The product should be provided with continuous support and encouragement (including smoking cessation and weight reduction).
- The service makes a great difference to quality of life (such as asthma and diabetes treatments).
- Monitoring is valuable (asthma peak flow records and blood glucose monitoring in diabetes).
- Only intermittent medical supervision is required (asthma or hypertension control).
- There is a high level of competition and a possibility of substitution with another product or service.

A range of software tools exists to manage PRM interactions and these can be customized to provide interactive features to attract and retain users. The experience thus far has been that user retention rates have been low, this failure being attributable to the complexity of some of the offerings (which frustrated patients seeking a rapid service) and the fact that many of the services on offer were not really needed. Once again, PRM solutions were initially extremely expensive and this impacted negatively on ROI and gave interactive digital solutions for PRM a bad reputation among pharmaceutical marketers.

Conclusions – 'the take home messages'

We have described an inexorable change in the pharmaceutical marketing environment that is forcing companies to be more open and interactive in their relationships with consumers. The industry is only now starting to seek ways to convince customers and establish relationships using evidence-based approaches and comparative cost-effectiveness. Currently, most pharmaceutical companies concentrate on delivering products that can best be described as 'point solutions'. If they are to continue to charge high prices for their products in a highly competitive marketplace, they will have to bundle them with services that offer additional value to the consumer or payer. This is likely to mean a move away from single point solution products marketed to the entire patient population, and towards personalized services that offer value to the consumer throughout the lifecycle of their condition. This is an enormous challenge for the industry, requiring a far deeper understanding of customer segments and a competency to design and offer products and services to these segments. PRM systems allow companies to differentiate their products and services and build relationships that are sustainable.

- Companies cannot afford the luxury of building sophisticated, but unusable, PRM solutions. As margin pressures intensify, so marketing budgets will be devoted to building cheaper Internet-based tools for communicating with patients or consumers. As in the case of CRM, PRM will be about more efficient, rapid customer service, as a source of competitive differentiation.
- PRM is an incremental process and huge one-off global implementations are doomed to failure.
- As in the case of CRM, analysis of customer data is gaining in importance as marketers seek to match information, promotion and service offerings with customer segments.

PART V

Digital Strategies: Health Service Delivery

CHAPTER 11

Digital strategies in health service delivery

The Internet has already begun to accelerate a transition, driven by economic, technological and social forces, in the provision of health services. Early US e-health ventures such as WebMD were premised on the commercial opportunities offered by the Internet to better manage the huge amounts of documentation and complex reimbursement transactions that characterize health service delivery. Similarly, hospital managers, regulatory agencies, health professionals and patient groups speak (often prematurely) of the role of digital technology in disseminating evidence-based treatment guidelines, speeding up medical care delivery and reducing dangerous errors.

We already see a spectrum of digital technology penetration in healthcare. It is reasonable to observe that this penetration has been patchy in terms of both levels of sophistication and geographical diffusion. The manifold reasons for the wide differences in digital technology penetration are largely in the realm of health economics, medical practice patterns and politics, rather than a purely IT implementation challenge. A good example is France's *carte vitale* project where the vast majority of the population have, for a number of years, been equipped with a personal smart card permitting rapid reimbursement by the national social health insurance system. The application of the smart card system has been substantially hampered by the refusal of physicians to install and use the system in their practices, for mainly economic reasons. It is only recently that a combination of legal sanctions and financial incentives has resulted in physicians (and pharmacists) accelerating this project. Leading-edge health technology projects are mainly implemented in resource-rich hospitals where it is possible to manage a range of teething problems and where speed of implementation is not a major issue. Hospital physicians need to demonstrate enthusiasm for these projects and be interested in innovation, and hence many e-hospital projects are piloted in academic medical centres. Similarly, buy-in is required from insurers, technology providers and other partners in the management of large health facilities.

Digital technology best practice in a US Hospital

All patient and outpatient data at Brigham and Women's Hospital in Boston (including imaging studies, prescriptions, laboratory results and medical records) is stored in a central electronic archive that can be accessed by any authorized physician using the Internet.

- Clinical orders for procedures and drugs are managed electronically – all examination rooms are equipped with computers that can be used to order prescriptions and access reference material.
- Reports are dictated by physicians and transcribed by typists or voice recognition software into the archiving system.
- The Internet is used to check insurance coverage details (automated billing has not yet been implemented due to the difficulty in interfacing with insurers' proprietary systems).
- Patients have formed communities using the hospital's online support groups.
- Patients can use email to book appointments.

Clinical effectiveness is increased as e-prescriptions and e-diagnostic records have cut the number of serious medical errors by more than half. Estimated efficiency savings are $5–10 million annually, as the e-ordering system highlights both potentially costly errors and cheaper treatment options such as generic drugs. Prescribing errors were reduced by 86 per cent over a four-year period. Insurance claim rejections have fallen from 11 to 5 per cent. File sharing of data such as X-rays in order to get a second opinion has almost removed the need for a paper file transport system, saving $9,000–20,000 per year per physician. These savings are viewed against costs of about $2 million in 1993 to computerize the clinical order entry system, and about $500,000 per annum to maintain the system (the hospital admits about 50,000 patients and treats 500,000 outpatients per year, and has about $600 million in annual revenue) [2,149].

A range of data protection solutions is already available to ensure that medical confidentiality should not be a barrier to implementing e-based medical record management and other digital communication technologies in the hospital setting.

Many physicians are cognizant and supportive of the use of e-tools to store and manage patient records and facilitate professional communications. Throughout the world, we find innovative projects to establish networks connecting hospitals to family physicians in the surrounding area in order to facilitate referrals, communication and patient follow-up. However, financial constraints, system incompatibilities and inertia (resistance to changing the existing paper-based system) remain considerable barriers (Figure 11.1).

Despite these significant challenges, recent developments have driven digital solutions to near the top of the healthcare delivery agenda:

- Increasing proof from pioneers such as the Brigham and Women's Hospital that IT systems increase safety, improve patient outcomes and save money.
- Safety and budget concerns forcing payers to take action, particularly in Europe where the UK's NHS is committed to e-prescribing and universal electronic medical records by 2005.
- In the US, with its more fragmented payment system, pressure is coming from a coalition of payers known as the Leapfrog Group, who pay for healthcare of over 31 million Americans. Leapfrog publishes online

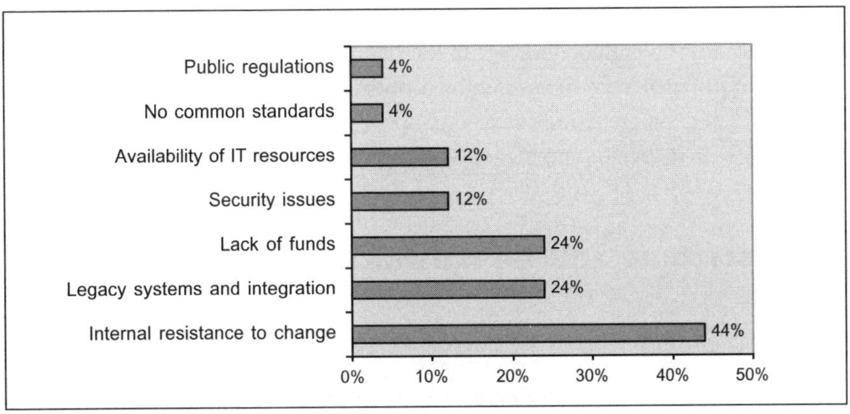

Figure 11.1 Barriers to expanding Internet use in 25 European hospitals (2001)

Source: [82]

rankings of hospitals based on whether they have computerized order entry systems. Federal HIPAA legislation (discussed in Chapter 2) and new health concerns (since 11 September, 2002) are also playing a part [149].

Pharmaceutical companies are well positioned to explore and exploit opportunities to play a more important role in digital health service delivery and the industry is supporting research to eliminate regulatory barriers to the incorporation of e-health services and technologies in healthcare [150]. As therapeutic complexity increases and cost containment becomes a pressing concern, physicians will become ever-more dependent on prescription guidelines and formularies, and products will increasingly be bundled with support services to create complete solutions. Pharmaceutical companies will seek to provide this support through digital technologies, some of which will be delivered by a new incarnation of the sales representative, who will become more of a sales 'engineer', providing technical advice and solutions.

It is not in the realm of fantasy to imagine a world where much of the routine diagnosis and treatment is done by digital 'agents' powered by artificial intelligence. Overall there will be a shift away from care provided by clinics and hospitals and towards a greater emphasis on prevention and monitoring in the home. This will be facilitated by predictive diagnostic technologies (telling people what they are susceptible to) and the widespread adoption of disease management and telemedicine programmes (allowing the prevention and management of conditions without visiting a hospital or clinic).

- For pharmaceutical companies, the most immediate opportunity is to play a more important role in the provision of information (scientific, patient-education or health economic) in the health service delivery process. To be a desired partner in areas such as e-prescribing, telemedicine and medical record management requires good market understanding and developing a range of internal competencies in digital technologies.

E-prescribing and e-pharmacies

Introduction

E-prescribing is the paperless management of the prescription process where a physician enters the medication name, dosage and patient instruction using a PC or PDA and this information is automatically transferred to the pharmacist. E-pharmacies take electronic orders (e-prescriptions directly from physicians or transmitted via the patient) and deliver the drug to the patient or provider. E-pharmacy sales are becoming increasingly common in the US (a country where the filling of prescriptions using mail order is already well accepted).

The benefits of e-prescribing include:

- The easy storage of a patient's medication records, permitting rapid prescribing for chronic conditions.
- Increased safety due to automated flagging of incorrect dosages and potential drug interactions, and hence reduced litigation due to medical errors.
- Automatic compliance with a restricted formulary.
- The ability to track easily medication histories to improve patient management, conduct pharmaco-economic research and post-approval surveillance (phase IV trials).

Computerized prescribing is still far from being universally adopted by physicians, as many practices still do not have e-prescribing systems installed and many pharmacies are not set up to receive and manage electronically transmitted prescriptions [151]. Some of the world's largest companies are attempting to 'wire' healthcare delivery and enable e-prescriptions. For example, Amicore was created by Pfizer, IBM and Microsoft to promote physician adoption of technology in small group practices [152]. Allscripts and Compaq have a competing joint venture. E-prescribing is also being pushed by various governments as part of their electronic healthcare initiatives. For instance, in April 2002, US Health Secretary Tommy Thompson endorsed an alliance between supermarket pharmacist Giant and Internet health companies InstantDX and NDCHealth to Internet-enable prescription entry and automate fulfillment in Giant's 154 superstores. It is hoped that 34,000 other pharmacy chains and independent pharmacists will join the scheme [153].

Regulatory constraints

Internet pharmaceutical sales have highlighted the complex and often incompatible regulations concerning medical products and their commerce at a local and international level. Additionally, pharmaceutical sales on the Internet are subject to abuse by unscrupulous vendors providing dangerous or counterfeit drugs and lacking the oversight concerning drug interactions, potential allergies and correct administration provided by physicians and pharmacists [154].

In the US, legal problems arising from online consultations for prescribing medications have forced the e-pharmacy sector to embark on self-regulation and develop codes of practice. For instance, the US Association of Boards of Pharmacies has established a voluntary certification process to accredit e-pharmacies [19]. The Internet encourages cross-state and cross-border trade in pharmaceuticals, where it is relatively easy to order a drug that is not available in a certain country for mail order delivery. Consumers have been quick to take advantage of e-pharmacies to order so-called ‘lifestyle drugs’ and seek prescription medications at lower prices from offshore vendors.

In the US, resistance to e-prescribing varies between state pharmacy boards. For instance, the Florida board is proposing that prescriptions can be filled only if prescribed by a physician with whom the patient has an existing relationship – and this would prevent many e-prescriptions being filled [155]. Many states also object to cross-border prescribing, particularly of lifestyle drugs – the state of California sued a Los Angeles pharmacist for filling Internet prescriptions [156].

Most EU countries still do not allow the distribution of drugs by mail and patients are often not reimbursed, even if they manage to obtain their drugs at a far lower price via e-pharmacies. This extreme reticence concerning e-pharmacy is reflected in the fact that, by 2001, only 0.4 per cent of Europeans with Internet access had bought a prescription or OTC drug online, and only 0.6 per cent intended to make a future purchase [82]. European professional pharmacist associations have been at the forefront of opposition to e-pharmacies, but the e-pharmacy movement has scored some notable legal victories, especially in Germany, and many believe that it is time for a radical change in the retail distribution of pharmaceuticals in Europe. The implications of the Internet for the small neighbourhood pharmacist are still unclear, as they do provide an important service in terms of convenience and patient advice. Certainly, the German pharmacists’ federation (ABDA) is incensed by the German Health Ministry’s proposals to legalize postal delivery of prescription medicines, claiming it could compromise patient safety and would ‘destroy today’s pharmacy system’. The Health Ministry counters that mail order would increase competition and reduce costs. Whatever the outcome, the Dutch e-pharmacy DocMorris.com has already signed supply agreements with a number of Germany’s public sector health insurers, using a loophole in German law [157].

Conclusions – ‘the take home messages’

The Internet is indeed playing a role in the wholesale and retail distribution of pharmaceutical products:

- Pharmaceutical and medical device companies have established exchanges such as GHX and GHXRx to facilitate easier ordering and inventory management in healthcare facilities.
- Pharmaceutical wholesalers are seeking ways directly to supply physicians and their patients, using e-prescribing to bypass traditional pharmacies.
- Managed care and large PBM organizations such as Merck-Medco are actively promoting the use of handheld devices for electronic prescribing [151].
- A number of companies have been established to provide handheld or mobile prescribing systems to physicians. Some of these companies are relying on pharmaceutical company sponsorship for the devices and are attempting to bundle prescribing and scientific information with the service to make it attractive to users.

E-prescribing and online pharmacies provide good examples of the direct impact of digital technologies on healthcare delivery. The role of pharmaceutical companies will be largely determined by the changing dynamics of retail pharmaceutical distribution and the relative power of the prescribing decision-makers.

- Pharmaceutical companies have to extract more value from the consumer-facing component of the value chain. We foresee radical changes in relationships with wholesalers and retail distributors as the industry faces relentless pressure on margins. The ultimate goal is to build sustainable partnerships with prescribers and consumers in order to sell more products and reduce the cost of these sales.
- As a defensive measure in the face of increasing demands for price controls, many of the major pharmaceutical companies are offering discount cards to US senior citizens. The PrescriptionRx card, launched in April 2002 by Abbot, AstraZeneca, Aventis, Bristol-Myers Squibb, GlaxoSmithKline, Johnson & Johnson and Novartis, allows low-income Medicare patients 20–40 per cent discounts on more than 150 drugs used to treat common conditions. The companies estimate that up to 11 million senior citizens could benefit [158]. Treading its own path is Pfizer, who launched a competing card the same month. Called the Share Card Program, it allows low-income senior citizens any Pfizer prescription for $15 a month. The company estimates that the programme will cost about $300 million per year [159]. The management of discount cards relies heavily on IT systems, especially those of the large pharmacy chains.

- In order to sell to and deal directly with the end-user, patient or consumer, the industry will be increasingly dependent on digital technologies that will force marketers to develop speedy, quality service as a vital competency.

Managed care and health insurance

Introduction

> If online prescribing could eventually generate, say, 80 percent formulary compliance across the managed care industry, then companies could no longer expect to easily circumvent formulary decisions by brute force of marketing effort, direct-to-consumer advertising, or the deployment of thousands of sales representatives. – [160]

Managed care, irrespective of whether it is in the private or public sector, is an approach to promoting the efficiency of health service delivery through a strong focus on cost containment, the designation of preferred providers and institutions, the application of gatekeeping and the stratification and management of risk. Many managed care organizations (MCOs) devote resources to disease management, prevention and health promotion. MCOs, government and consumer groups have, over the past decade, become obsessively concerned with the contribution of drug prices to rising healthcare costs. For an MCO, pharmaceutical benefits are seen as eminently more 'controllable' than hospital expenses, investments in diagnostic technologies or salaries. IT permits drug expenses to be followed on a near real-time basis and e-prescribing permits the application of restricted formularies. However, physicians often resist attempts to introduce evidence-based or generic prescribing. The reasons for this include the very personal nature of each therapeutic decision and resentment at having to deal with scrutiny from the patient's insurers (that may include 'callbacks' – notices from an MCO requesting that the physician use a different and cheaper procedure or drug to the one they prescribed). MCO drug cost-containment activities are also unpopular with consumers, who resent limitations on their healthcare access and feel aggrieved when an MCO blocks a treatment.

The explosion of the managed care movement in the US has occurred at the same time as the pharmaceutical industry's growth and profitability have come under the spotlight. Employers and their health insurers, worried by rising healthcare costs, have increasingly turned to MCOs in an effort to control those costs.

European governments seek to control drug prices through modalities that include the setting of reference prices, price controls, profit restrictions, generic substitution and the promotion of generic prescribing [161].

E-managed care

Digital technologies have the potential to greatly increase the compliance rate of physicians with strict formularies. Simple steps such as providing physicians with updated formularies on PDAs, allowing price comparisons, are effective. A greater emphasis on evidence-based or cost-effective treatment makes it less likely that physicians would indeed attempt to circumvent formularies [160]. The situation is certainly more complicated than a simple matter of ignoring prescribing rules. Pharmaceutical marketers are not averse to seeking ways of encouraging physicians to prescribe a certain drug, using intense promotion, opinion-leader management, free samples and participation in clinical studies as incentives. MCOs themselves may be sometimes ambivalent to the introduction of evidence-based medicine, especially when a strong case can be made for a more expensive therapeutic option. However, the overall picture is one of the growing use of IT solutions to facilitate transactions in managed care.

- MedUnite, an e-health connectivity company, launched an online system to offer eligibility and benefits checks, claims submission and status checks, referrals and authorizations. The goal of MedUnite is to provide solutions to physicians to better manage administrative problems in the hope that this will help to improve the damaged relationships between physicians and MCOs [162].
- MCOs are introducing technologies to encourage patients to manage costs and help plans to deliver better service. Humana featured an online 'alternative drug option' to encourage members to switch their prescription to a cheaper brand or generic within the same therapeutic class. Beneficiaries could also view estimated drug co-payments. Partners National Health Plans of North Carolina encouraged patients to use a web-based application called Planlinx that alerted members and employees to multi-tiered drug plans and other cost-effective treatment options and preventive care programmes [163].
- The day the generic version of Prozac became available, Merck-Medco informed the 25,000 physicians who were the top Prozac prescribers and alerted online patients about the availability of a generic substitute and the potential cost savings. Eighty per cent of Merck-Medco customers who

received Prozac by home delivery opted for the generic substitute in the week that it became available [133].

- To promote formulary compliance, MCOs need to provide bundled tools to aid prescribers. RxFiles won FDA approval for software designed to accurately match medication dosages to individual patient characteristics. The intelligent dosing system (IDS) is a set of three software applications designed to be used on PDAs or computers. A dosing calculator, a programme to safely switch patients from brand names to generics and a prescribing training simulator to introduce new drugs are provided. The company claimed that its IDS product provides accuracy, or the exact dose needed, at a 90–97 per cent precision level [164].

Health insurance

A wide spectrum of health insurance coverage systems exists across the industrialized world, both in the public and private domains, and we exclusively focus on the impact and future implications of digital technologies, as the pharmaceutical industry increasingly interacts with health insurers. In the US, the cost of employer-sponsored healthcare is a source of concern for companies that cannot pass on the full costs to employees, if they wish to use health insurance benefits as a way of attracting and retaining talent. As a result, a vigorous market exists for services to increase the efficiency of health insurance, and employees are being incentivized to reduce their health expenses.

The health insurance claims' process has generally been extremely 'paper-intensive'. Insurers in the US process about 5 billion claims annually and it is estimated that up to one-quarter of accounts receivable are on hold at any one time due to incomplete data or incompatible systems.

The Internet has radically transformed the approach of health insurers to claims, previously managed with proprietary applications. In the US, systems developed by EDI (electronic data interchange) vendors allow submission to multiple insurers (for example Envoy, a subsidiary of Quintiles, built connections to approximately 900 different insurers before it was acquired by WebMD). However, the cost of writing the necessary code, and therefore the cost to physicians of subscribing to a service such as Envoy, was high, and this was reflected in the uptake of these services [2]. In the US, only about 47 per cent of physician claims were submitted electronically in 2000; as compared with nearly 80 per cent of hospital claims [162]. In Germany, where patients can have more than one 'primary' physician, it is not uncommon for insurers to receive claims from several physicians for the identical treatment of the same patient [82].

Some insurers are taking action. Seven of the largest US health insurers (Aetna, Anthem, Wellpoint, Oxford, Cigna, HealthNet and Pacifi-Care) formed a joint venture in 2000, called MedUnite, to automate the insurance claims' process. MedUnite now connects 130,000 physician offices using XML-based, HIPAA-compliant data requests. Physicians can check the patient's coverage with hundreds of payers, Medicaid and Medicare. Despite a one-time $150 registration fee, savings are substantial, the typical MedUnite query costing 44 cents, as compared with around $5 for manual checks. MedUnite hopes to add transactions such as electronic payments and claim status checks in the future [165].

Employers, keen to increase individual responsibility as part of a strategy to contain health costs, are encouraging the movement from 'defined-benefit' to 'defined-contribution' health plans that allow employees to allocate their insurance contributions to the coverage areas that they feel they need. Employees are also given incentives not to spend their health insurance allowances. An example of such a tailored scheme is Pittsburgh-based Highmark's web-based insurance scheme, which allows customers to custom tailor their benefits online. However, by early 2002, only 20,000 of the 2.5 million existing Highmark members had enrolled. The company blamed the disappointing results on poorly trained sales representatives and employee discomfort with buying benefits online, and as a result it has stepped up its internal training and identified client companies appropriate for the online service [166]. UK employers are promoting a similar type of scheme, the health 'cash plan'. Rather than being provided with comprehensive healthcare coverage, the insured person is covered by a cash payout up to a certain level, depending on their health problem. These systems give consumers choice and allow portability between employers, and can be seen as a shift towards consumer-oriented healthcare.

The chief worry of sceptics is the equity of these choice-based systems, as it is a move away from shared-risk, shared-benefit comprehensive insurance (whether provided by the state or the private sector), and allows providers to cherry-pick the lowest risk customers. These schemes obviously demand far greater consumer participation (in selecting the desired level of coverage) than traditional schemes. This will lead to a growing market for services that help consumers to make the right choices, whether provided by government, insurers, providers or third parties. The service and the information given will have to be personalized for each consumer by age, sex, medical history, family history, risk factors (such as smoking or obesity) and the results of any diagnostic tests. The Internet is the only channel that can deliver this service in a cost-effective manner. If such services can be made effective, it would also incentivize small companies and individuals, who otherwise would be discouraged by the price or complexity, to buy cover. The key to success of such services may be obtaining the cooperation of insurance companies, who are likely to object to the inevitable commoditization of their products.

Conclusions – 'the take home messages'

MCOs and insurers face a similar challenge to any party that wishes to use digital technologies to change physician behaviour. Decisions to change processes such as prescribing are driven by a web of concerns including economic implications, convenience, patient acceptance, time and, perhaps most importantly, the value in terms of improving patient care. The inexorable introduction of digital technologies to better manage healthcare delivery will undoubtedly increase the transparency of pharmaceutical pricing. While insurers and governments may be fully aware that drug costs constitute only a small part of the entire healthcare cost burden, the pharmaceutical industry, in the short term at least, will remain a target of scrutiny and criticism concerning profits and pricing policy.

- The Internet provides a real-time link between the pharmaceutical industry and MCOs, government and insurers. As future medicines will be more sophisticated (and expensive), all communication channels will be vital when it comes to making a case concerning reimbursement and prescribing.
- Changes in the pharmaceutical supply chain and the rise of segmented medicine are forcing companies to deal directly with healthcare organizations, be they insurers, MCOs or hospitals. The inevitable differentiating factor between companies will be not only their products, but also the quality of their service.

Disease management

Introduction

Disease management is the ongoing management over a 'disease lifecycle' of mainly chronic conditions such as asthma, diabetes and hypertension. The goal of disease management is to offer continual rather than episodic care, thereby maximizing the quality of life and, through monitoring, prevention and early intervention, minimizing healthcare expenditure. Potential savings are considerable: specialists estimate that more than half of hospital admissions and sick days linked to asthma and about half of those linked to diabetes could be avoided by better monitoring and care [167].

The popularity of disease management has waxed and waned over the last few years. In the 1980s, a number of large US-based pharmaceutical companies invested heavily in disease management. Their logic was premised on the potential profitability of developing long-term relationships with chronic disease patients as the exclusive supplier of drugs and services. Companies saw disease management as one possible way of reacting to the nascent threat of price controls and as a means of diversification (or integration) along the pharmaceutical value chain. With few exceptions (perhaps Merck's entry into PBM via Medco), pharmaceutical companies' flirtation with disease management was a financial disaster. The reasons for this failure included the need to deal with a range of often intransigent partners including MCOs, government, nurses and physicians, the expense of setting up programmes, poor patient acceptance and the lack of experience among the executives managing these ventures. Recently, we have seen an upsurge of interest in disease management, but digital technologies allow pharmaceutical companies to avoid some of the pitfalls that were associated with their earlier activities in this area. Indeed, e-disease management is becoming popular, and many major pharmaceutical companies are experimenting with online disease management programmes to promote compliance and gather customer information. Digital technologies permit direct communication between the disease management provider and the patient, thereby eliminating the expensive logistics of having to deal with a range of parties, such as MCOs, insurers and government intermediaries. Similarly, the costs of monitoring patients (through either direct communication or biomonitoring), managing patient data and contacting patients are reduced. Indeed, new communications technologies can be used at each of the four key stages of disease management (Figure 11.2).

As remote patient monitoring of baseline parameters, such as blood glucose, becomes a standard procedure and as implantable monitoring devices for cardiac conditions are increasingly accepted, we can expect disease management to become a part of mainstream patient management. However, as with many health interventions, we are at an early stage when it comes to the measurement of ROI. Better patient monitoring, appropriate therapy and improved compliance certainly reduce the number of expensive emergency room or casualty visits and hospital stays. Disease management does, however, result in a different range of claims from health insurers – for technologies, educational and health promotion material and, sometimes, expensive drugs to maintain functional status. However, a 2002 study suggested that healthcare

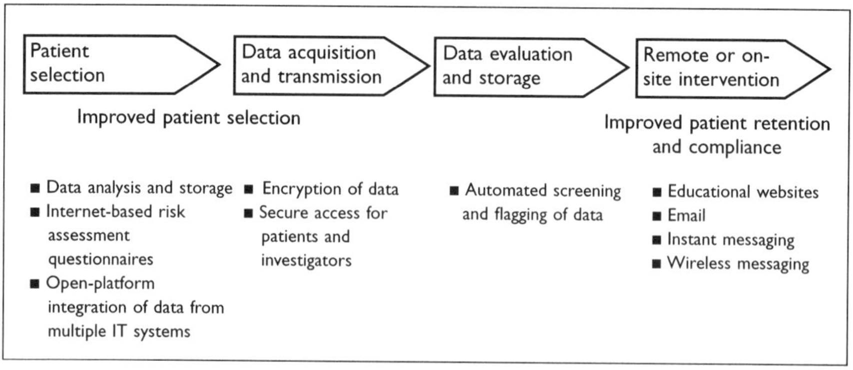

Figure 11.2 The four stages of disease management

Source: Based on [167]

cost savings for certain groups of patients, for example asthma sufferers in Germany, could be in the region of 10–30 per cent [167].

Disease management programmes are designed to coordinate care, encourage compliance and give early warning of any deterioration in the patient's condition. An ideal disease management programme has three elements [167]:

1. *Education and support*. For instance, the average patient with severe heart disease is hospitalized with pulmonary oedema (fluid on the lungs) about three times per year. In a disease management programme, the patient is taught about the disease and the positive impact of good diet, compliance with medication guidelines and weight monitoring. However, education on its own is rarely enough to ensure compliance. The patient may also be encouraged to join an online support group, and would be able to email specific questions to a medical professional, who would also contact the patient regularly.
2. *Monitoring*. As part of the above process, the patient records weight and blood pressure daily, inputting the information to a secure website that automatically warns the patient's carer if key thresholds are breached.
3. *Coordination between physicians, providers and insurers/payers*. If and when the patient needs additional treatment, the disease management system automatically arranges an appointment and bills the patient's insurer.

Disease management programmes require the constant updating of patient records that are held in a central database. The bigger and more comprehensive the database, the more effective the system is likely to be, as insurers or payers are interested in ensuring that patients do not receive unnecessary care (such as the same test being done twice) and data mining can be used to develop the optimal disease management protocols.

The German government is promoting disease management by compensating insurers for the costs of running programmes, a development that is designed to see German companies become world leaders in this field. In countries such as the US where employees often switch insurers when they switch jobs, the incentives for insurers to invest in disease management programmes are far less, as the benefits of investing may not accrue to the insurer that set up the programme. However, most MCOs have introduced elements of disease management in an attempt to contain the costs related to caring for chronic disease patients.

E-disease management strategy

Although the Internet promises to reduce the overheads of disease management programmes, two other critical success factors remain [167]:

1. Disease management programmes must target patients for whom there is the greatest potential saving in terms of reduced healthcare costs. Only patients who are likely to benefit should be included; some may have conditions too mild to be at risk of complications, or too severe to respond to disease management, while others may not be interested in or able to manage the technologies. Perhaps only five to ten per cent of a given patient population may qualify for a disease management intervention.
2. Disease management programmes must increase patient compliance and retention. The Internet permits a combination of education, monitoring, regular communication and motivation.

Companies are developing disease management and adverse reaction sites through which physicians can receive up-to-date information. In addition, physicians will be able to record adverse reactions in a format required by the FDA [11].

- Pfizer is involved in a disease management trial with the US government. Pfizer Health Solution's online disease management system InformaCare delivers individualized treatment recommendations to patients, as well as evidence-based clinical guidance, over the Internet. Thirty-three Maine hospitals began using InformaCare in 2001 to assess the effectiveness of disease management for chronically ill Medicare patients [168].

- Education alone is not enough; disease management needs to be interactive. Participants in a six-month weight loss programme were either given access to an Internet education course or an Internet education and behaviour therapy course, which included procedures such as a sequence of 24 weekly behavioural lessons by email, and weekly online submission of monitoring diaries and associated feedback. Participants in the behavioural course were more likely to meet their five per cent weight loss goal (45 per cent versus 22 per cent) [170]. Another study found that participants in a back pain Internet chat room moderated by a physician showed reduced symptoms and required less medical treatment than their peers [171].
- Online disease management can be just as effective as the face-to-face variety even in situations where patient compliance is notoriously poor. In one study, patients with schizophrenia were either given personalized computer intervention sessions (combining information from the patient's medical record with general information about schizophrenia), sessions with a psychiatric nurse or a combination of the two. The computer-based education was just as effective as the sessions with a nurse [172].
- Online dieting and smoking cessation programmes continue to expand. These websites offer meetings, shopping lists and tailored counselling letters among their e-services. Online weight loss service eDiets.com claimed that more than 300,000 people joined its programme within a few months of its inception [173].

Conclusions – 'the take home messages'

Pharmaceutical companies will find disease management attractive and worth funding where it conforms to certain criteria:

- A disease management programme will increase demand for a product and promote compliance.
- A disease management programme is offered as part of a higher value service package 'bundle' to customers (be they payers, physicians or individual consumers). This is particularly applicable to innovative and expensive new drugs that may require information, drug delivery and post-marketing offerings from the pharmaceutical company.

- A defensive manoeuvre where pharmaceutical companies will need to contribute to health promotion as an 'entrance ticket' to sell products or demand a certain price.
- The rise of segmented and personalized medicine will place a greater focus on prevention. Disease management approaches will have to be part of the overall service provided with drugs that will be used for long-term prevention.

Despite its chequered history, disease management is once again becoming an important strategic tool for pharmaceutical marketing. Digital technologies that permit direct contact with patients, carers and parties that can influence compliance substantially enhance the attractiveness of disease management.

Pharmaceutical companies in the USA have been forced back into disease management as the only option for remaining on state formularies. Companies are starting to guarantee improved outcomes and lower health expenditures if patients use their drugs. In order to promote compliance and ensure monitoring, the pharmaceutical industry has introduced sophisticated disease management programmes. The best-known example is the public–private collaboration between Florida's Agency for Health Care Administration (FAHCA) and Pfizer. Florida attempted to implement a restrictive Medicaid drug formulary, forcing manufacturers to offer deep discounts. Pfizer offered to supply disease management services for four chronic conditions (asthma, diabetes, heart failure and hypertension) to Florida's Medicaid patients. Services include community care management provided by 60 Pfizer-funded nurses using Pfizer disease management software. The payoff for Pfizer? As part of the deal, all Pfizer drugs are on the state formulary at no discount, so a physician never has to check the status of a Pfizer drug – and the FAHCA reported a 15 per cent rise in Pfizer Medicaid sales between Q2 2001 and Q3 2001. All other drugs went through a price and clinical review. To make the list, other drug makers had to offer rebates of at least 6 per cent, and several blockbuster drugs did not make the cut. Florida expects to save around $200 million over the next year from these rebates. Early reports claimed that the programme had run into difficulties, with as few as 4000 patients enrolled by March 2002. However, as of May 2002, Pfizer and the FAHCA claimed that ten hospitals and 8000 chronically ill patients were enrolled in the programme, with a further 4000 patients expected to follow. According to Pfizer, around 50,000 patients had been reached with educational material. Pfizer guaranteed that the programme would deliver $33 million of savings in healthcare costs over two years. However, experts suggest that it may be extremely difficult to quantify what savings are actually achieved [174, 175].

The electronic medical record (EMR)

Introduction

The electronic medical record (EMR) is a collection of data concerning a patient in a digital or electronic format. In theory at least, this permits rapid, secure, global and continuous access to patient data. The efficient management of the patient record reduces medical errors and EMRs give physicians access to all the information necessary to provide the best possible patient care. This includes information on current medication, medical history, known allergies, imaging studies and the results of diagnostic tests. The record can be made available to all providers and, where appropriate, payers, subject to strict privacy regulations. EMRs were a source of interest since the earliest days of the digital revolution, and the widespread availability of the Internet and broadband networks has made their benefits even more tangible, as the possibilities for access anywhere in the world (for example when someone becomes ill on holiday), remote diagnostics and the automatic identification of possible dangerous drug interactions become real options. Patient information (ranging from personal identification data to parts of the EMR) can be carried on smart cards that can be read by authorized health professionals. Smart cards are credit card sized and patient data is stored on magnetic strips or chips. The data can be read and modified (according to access privileges) using a specialized reader. They can carry information critical to emergency treatment, such as details of any allergies or medications being taken, and can also be used to determine the level of health insurance coverage the consumer has. Smart cards can either carry all the relevant information in their own memory, or act as a key to obtain information stored on a central database.

Acceptance of the EMR

EMRs are, for a number of technological, economic and medical practice-based reasons, not in widespread use. In 2000, only five per cent of US doctors were using EMRs [2], as physicians see no benefit in taking handwritten notes during a consultation and then typing them into a computer. Other issues include the resource constraints of the healthcare industry, as transferring all paper records into electronic format is no small task. Standardization is also a major issue, as there is no point in a provider transferring all records into an EMR system if all the laboratories, pharmacies or payers that are involved in patient care do not use the same system.

The EMR has important public health implications, as it permits the establishment of an accurate (and anonymous) database for epidemiological research. One of the consequences of the concern with bioterrorism, which arose in late 2001 in the USA, was a call for a national EMR system. Having a national health data network could provide an early warning of disease outbreaks and hence improve treatment. Various US government advisory groups also started working on ways to create a national health data network and the Department of Health and Human Services (HHS) issued privacy guidelines for EMRs and stipulated that health plans must comply with the rules by 2003. Experts say that these specifications should encourage EMR use, despite patient fears that data sharing threatens privacy.

The UK's National Health Service (NHS) has taken a number of steps to get closer to its ambitious goal of transferring all paper health records to an advanced, countrywide electronic system by 2005. The government decided to increase the overall NHS budget and devote nearly £1 billion ($1.5 billion) for four years until 2005 to create electronic patient record systems for all hospitals and provide 24-hour emergency access to health records. The NHS said it plans to have all general practitioners connected to its NHSnet system by the end of 2002 and electronic prescribing in place by 2004. The NHS wants all staff members to have Internet access and email by March 2003 [176]. In the Netherlands, 80 per cent of care providers use electronic patient records, encouraged by the government, which subsidizes 60 per cent of all computer costs as long as healthcare providers use an accredited system [82]. The adoption of smart cards is being encouraged by the EU with the aim of ensuring that all citizens have access to a health smart card to enable secure and confidential access to networked patient information by 2003 [177]. Efforts are also underway to develop national digital health networks in several less-developed countries, for example in Africa, with World Bank support.

Privacy is the primary concern of consumers, who understandably view their medical record as their personal, confidential property and have justifiable fears that their personal data may be used without their permission. Many consumer groups see EMRs as less secure than paper records locked away in a filing cabinet in their physician's office or a hospital basement. Although it can be argued that Internet-based records can be made secure (using identification technologies and encryption), the ease with which electronic data can be transferred causes persistent concern. In the US, HIPAA regulations are designed to allay some privacy fears by requiring consumer permission before sensitive parts of EMRs are released, and by requiring secure transmission technologies. The EU's data protection directive (in effect since October 1998) requires all member countries to enact legislation allowing consumers to access their medical records.

In some European countries, the widespread application of smart card technology is leading the way to larger EMR projects. A number of technology and telecommunication companies have already established pilot EMR networks with small numbers of physicians and hospitals. A pan-European physician-controlled EMR project (Privantis SA) is currently underway.

- Almost all French citizens have received a *carte vitale* – a smart card designed to reduce the mountains of paperwork associated with healthcare delivery. The card looks like a credit card and stores the patient's health insurance information and some medical data on a microchip. Using these cards, doctors and pharmacists can access the patient's details automatically, permitting direct reimbursement of some healthcare costs.
- The Austrian National Insurance Association (ANIA) issued electronic health insurance cards to citizens during 2002. Doctors who have contracts with the country's social health insurance are authorized to read the cards using equipment supplied and financed by the government. The health ministry in neighbouring Germany is carefully watching Austria's initiative in preparation for an e-prescribing system. German Health Minister Ulla Schmidt said that if Austria's initiative delivers the expected savings, then a German card would be tested in a 12-month pilot project [178].
- Kaiser Permenante, the largest non-profit HMO (health maintenance organization) in the US, is spending $1.5 billion over the next four years so that its 10,000 physicians can convert paper medical records into electronic ones. The system is designed by IBM and will allow physicians from different offices to share patient data [149].

Conclusions – 'the take home messages'

The EMR presents a range of exciting opportunities across the pharmaceutical value chain. For drug development, a standardized, accessible medical record would facilitate patient recruitment to, and management of, clinical trials, and post-marketing surveillance. Personalized therapeutics is facilitated by the ability to transfer and analyse medical data in a digital format. Health insurers also benefit as administration costs are reduced and better risk analysis can be achieved. Pharmaceutical and insurance companies are prepared to support

EMR initiatives in order to gain access to aggregated, anonymized data, as this would be better than many currently available information sources.

Physicians remain somewhat ambivalent about the benefits of EMRs. They see the benefits of standardized, accessible, secure patient records, but are also cautious about the time and cost implications of new technologies and are aware that the EMR opens their practice patterns (such as clinical record management) to scrutiny, with consequent medico-legal implications. Once again, as with a number of the digital technologies we have reviewed, adoption will be driven by payers, insurers and governments.

- The EMR permits high levels of specificity and consequent safety in drug prescribing. For example, linking the EMR to an e-prescribing system will flag any potential risk factors or allergies and facilitate appropriate dosing. As genetic tests for therapeutic choice and the identification of susceptibility to adverse drug reactions enter clinical use, this should increase EMR penetration in medical practice. The EMR will, in the future, be part of a basic standard of care, and the lack of an EMR system could expose health professionals to malpractice litigation.
- The protection of personal information will remain a sensitive public policy issue and patients will have to be given access to and, to some extent, control of the EMR. The transparency that the EMR brings to the physician–patient relationship is undoubtedly an ethical and deontological challenge for the medical profession.
- Further into the future, as and when clinically relevant genetic profiling becomes universally available, consumers will certainly want to control access to their medical records and legislation will be required to prevent discrimination at the hands of insurers and employers. It is not inconceivable that in the age of personalized medicine, consumers could interact directly with pharmaceutical companies when purchasing customized prevention 'cocktails', based on their risk factors for certain conditions. The economic implications of these new models, especially for social and private health insurers, will have to be explored.
- The EMR will reshape the provision of health promotion information, as it will be possible to develop tailored messages based on risks, current conditions and the medications being taken. For example, a pharmaceutical company could support links between a patient-accessed EMR and information sources, product advice, interactive tools (diaries or reminders) and support groups.

Evidence-based medicine (EBM)

Introduction

The rigorous application of research comparing the outcomes of alternative therapeutic interventions, that is, evidence-based medicine (EBM), is of great interest to health policy-makers seeking to ensure that patients receive appropriate and cost-effective care. The basic building blocks of EBM, the randomized controlled clinical study and the systematic review of medical literature, have indeed been in use for some time, but it is only recently that health economic, social and political factors have caused health authorities to critically assess the efficacy and cost-effectiveness of drugs and interventions.

EBM applications in healthcare can be manifold, ranging from daily clinical practice to the national policy level:

- Persuasion and peer pressure to adjust professional practices within the medical community.
- Development of guidelines and protocols for hospitals to manage resource allocation and improve the quality of care.
- Development of guidelines and protocols to improve national medical practice standards, quality assurance, and as a basis for developing reimbursement prices for units of service.
- Definition of positive and negative lists of publicly financed or publicly provided services.
- Assessment of new medical technologies proposed by pharmaceutical and medical device companies [179].

The impact of EBM

At a public policy level, EBM is often used to compare systematically the relative effectiveness of various interventions in preventing certain conditions or negative health outcomes. The data available to help make decisions as to costs versus benefits of a certain diagnostic test or treatment is often limited and the best policy is not purely a question of pharmaco-economics, but is also influenced by society's perceptions concerning the importance of the condition. This is reflected in the mismatch between the effectiveness of various interventions and the amount of resources devoted towards them. In the US, most of the healthcare system is designed to treat conditions, and only about three per cent of health expenditure is devoted to prevention. Primary prevention is generally a cost-effective option (as compared with treating advanced diseases), but the situation has been complicated by the increasing availability of expensive screening procedures, many of unproved, long-term cost benefit to society [180].

Wide differences exist, at local, regional, national and international levels, in the way that certain diseases are treated. The choice of therapy is determined by a complex web of economic, social and scientific factors and sometimes doctors do not offer the best treatment because the latest and most reliable information is not available to them. The Kanter Family Foundation joined forces with the Agency for Healthcare Research and Quality (part of the US Department of Health and Human Services) to create a national database on EBM for doctors and patients to use when deciding on treatment, based on previous outcomes for similar conditions. While, in the US, several initiatives are under way to create a national database to help guide evidence-based patient care, so far none has proved very successful in terms of acceptance by the medical profession [181].

Informing consumers of the best treatment options and aiding them to make better healthcare choices is an important component of an evidence-based health system. The availability of health information on the Internet, media coverage, advisory services such as NHS Direct in the UK and the financial responsibility being placed on consumers for their healthcare are driving an increased interest in the choices available concerning personal health. Consumers do need decision support and, in the USA, where illness places a heavy financial burden on individuals and their families, we see a burgeoning industry providing web-based quality rankings of healthcare providers and detailed summaries of treatment options. Support, information and interactive tools can be made available to patients before, during and after medical consultations, and are adapted from decision support systems (expert systems) by physicians [182]. For consumers, the aim of such support systems is not to make a definitive diagnosis or propose treatment, but to answer questions, allay fears and alert individuals about dangers and risks. The main challenge in developing evidence-based tools is that little is known about how consumers interact with these tools or act upon the information that these tools provide [177]. EBM presents serious challenges to current resource allocation policy, especially in countries with limited health budgets. For example, the best treatment option may also be the most expensive, and it may be impossible to offer everyone the same standard of care.

Despite the constraints we have discussed, EBM is indeed starting to impact on the healthcare systems:

- A multi-site, randomized controlled trial conducted in 2000 studied the effect of two point-of-care decision support systems on the decision-making process of medical students, residents and faculty. Not surprisingly, the utility of the system increased with the inexperience of the user. Extrapolating these results to patients, systems of this kind could have the greatest positive effect on consumers who are incentivized to seek quality healthcare [177].
- One decision support system that is being adapted and tested for consumers is HouseCall (Applied Medical Informatics), an informatics system derived from an existing physician knowledge-base called Iliad. HouseCall generates a diagnosis based on the user's symptoms and medical history, allows a personal medical history to be recorded and offers easy to read information on a variety of medical topics. Focus group evaluations have shown that the program is easy to use and that consumers like using technology at home to investigate health issues and participate in solving their medical problems [177].
- Even in very basic forms, decision support systems can be of considerable benefit. A 2002 study showed that the PDA drug reference guide ePro-cratesRx helped 50 per cent of doctors to reduce medication errors by one or two a week [149].
- With 18 HIV drugs on the market, physicians have to select the optimum 'cocktail' of drugs for their AIDS patients from more than 2000 possible combinations. And physicians must repeat the exercise for each patient, because individual factors such as medical history, other ailments and resistance to medications must be factored into the equation. TherapyEdge developed a web-based product that employs artificial intelligence to analyse patient data and suggest a list of potential therapies based on their projected likelihood of success. It also can be used as a safety net, enabling physicians to make sure that they have not mistakenly prescribed drugs that, given a patient's medical history and condition, could have potentially disastrous side effects. The software also alerts physicians to important new medical developments. If a drug were to withdrawn from the market, the physician would not only receive notice of the withdrawal, but also a list of patients taking that drug. The software also alerts physicians when a patient's laboratory results deviate from established ranges. However, one drawback is that entering patient data is labour-intensive [183].
- The American Heart Association (AHA) and healthcare information technology company Nexcura have launched an online cardiovascular

decision support tool for doctors and patients on the AHA's heart.org website. Nexcura handled the technology development, with the AHA coordinating and approving content for the effort. The coronary artery disease tool is called the Heart Profiler, and was partly funded by the AHA's pharmaceutical round table, which comprises Bristol-Myers Squibb, Wyeth, AstraZeneca, Novartis, Merck, Pfizer, GSK and Takeda [184].

Evidence-based systems should be thoroughly tested to ensure that they are better than current practice. For example, a study of a computer-based decision support system for the management of hypertension reported in the *British Medical Journal* did not show significant improvements over current clinical practice [185].

Conclusions – 'the take home messages'

Although it is not the panacea that will solve all the problems in healthcare, EBM will be an important feature of healthcare in the digital age [179]. The introduction of EBM will result in new approaches to healthcare financing. For example, the HIV EBM website (previously discussed) only charges about $50 monthly for a two-physician practice, plus a small per-patient processing fee. The primary revenue source will be customized reports, based on the data it accumulates about patients and their response to treatment, to pharmaceutical and managed care companies and the government. It anticipates charging $100,000 or more annually for the reports, which will be based on aggregated, anonymized data, so as not to infringe on the privacy of individual patients [183].

The combination of EBM, advanced disease genetics and pharmacogenomics, biomonitoring and medical artificial intelligence has the potential, in the longer term, to transform the practice of medicine. Many routine diagnostic and patient monitoring tasks will take place in the patient's home and the role of physicians will inevitably change.

- For the pharmaceutical industry, EBM presents exciting opportunities, especially if pharmaco-economic evidence shows that an innovative, yet expensive therapy is indeed the best and most cost-effective option for a certain condition. On the other hand, the rigorous application of EBM will result in many 'me-too' drugs in a therapeutic class being removed from formularies and force physicians to standardize approaches, sometimes at the expense of a 'fashionable' treatment.

- It is difficult to decide on the extent to which a pharmaceutical company should support or sponsor the provision of EBM tools and technologies to physicians and consumers. Every pharmaceutical marketer would like to see his or her company represented on the physician 'desktop' as a trusted partner in medical innovation. However, the price may be too high and we have seen that physicians are fickle in their loyalties and increasingly constrained in the latitude of their prescribing. For consumers, it is too early to opine on the profitability of bundling an EBM service with a drug, but this will be worthy of serious consideration as personalized medicine becomes a reality.

Telemedicine

Introduction

During September 2001, the scientific and popular media reported that a surgeon in New York successfully removed the diseased gall bladder of a 68-year-old woman in Strasbourg, France. The world's first transoceanic operation (involving data transfer over a 14,000 km circuit) took about an hour using a robotic surgical system (Computer Motion Inc.) and a fibre-optic network operated by France Telecom. Professor Jacques Marescaux, who headed the surgical team, said of this breakthrough event: 'Until now, we could share voice and data [over a network] but not gesture – the important part of real surgery. Now, there is no limit to what we can do with telemedicine.'

Telemedicine is the provision of health services and the exchange of health information over barriers such as distance and time. The ability to monitor, diagnose, inform and treat remotely can save lives and may, in certain cases, reduce the cost of treatment and improve the quality of care.

Telemedicine can be used for the monitoring and treatment of chronically ill patients. The goal is to reduce costs and increase the quality of life for patients by minimizing their time in hospital and maximizing the effectiveness of their treatment. Patients transmit key health indicators to their physician from their own home or another convenient location, and the physician recommends treatment accordingly. Data can be fed automatically to the physician, using monitoring devices, some of which can now be implanted, and there may be no need for patients manually to enter the data. The availability of wireless systems is revolutionizing telemedicine as it is now possible to use telephones, PDAs and other mobile devices in a range of settings, from acute care (a sudden deterioration in a parameter recorded with

TABLE 11.1

What patients with Internet access would like to do online (2002)	
Ask questions where no visit is necessary	77%
Fix appointments	71%
Get repeat prescriptions	71%
Receive results of medical tests	70%

Source: Harris Interactive

an implantable cardiac monitor generates an alert on a cardiologist's pager) to chronic disease management (an SMS is sent to a teenager reminding her to take her asthma medication).

A simple form of telemedicine is the patient call centre. In the UK, NHS Direct aims to triage callers into those who need to visit the accident and emergency department in a hospital, those with less serious ailments who should visit a physician, and those who require reassurance and advice or should self-medicate. However, the implementation of telemedicine in routine health services is being hampered by a lack of scientific evidence concerning its clinical utility and cost-effectiveness [186]. The UK government has committed itself to the application of telemedicine within the NHS as part of its modernization of the health service [187], provided cost-effectiveness is proved. It is interesting to note that while the safety of the NHS Direct system has been fairly well proved, it does not save the NHS any money; and a 2000 study of 32 paediatric call centres in the US found that all were losing money [186].

The market for telemedicine certainly exists; according to a 2002 report, 90 per cent of online adults in the US would like to be able to communicate with their physicians electronically, and 37 per cent of them would pay an average of $10 per month or $7 per email for the privilege [188] (Table 11.1).

Telemedicine applications

A large number of companies are developing and offering innovative telemedicine solutions:

- MyDoc.com, an Indianapolis-based subsidiary of Roche Diagnostics, is offering 24-hour online diagnosis and treatment from a physician in 15–20 minutes. The service uses software commonly used by nursing call centres.

Patients fill in questions about their symptoms; the physician then reviews the software-generated assessment and advises or prescribes medications or refers the patient as necessary. The service is targeted at busy professionals and their employers, and costs from $20 to $40 per visit, depending on the frequency of use. However, as there is no existing physician–patient relationship, several state pharmacy boards may prevent prescriptions being filled (see the earlier section on e-pharmacies). And the American Medical Association (AMA) remains unconvinced about such services: AMA policy states that patient care should be based on an established physician–patient relationship, taking a history and a physical examination [189].

- Medem, the for-profit Internet company backed by the AMA, has launched a competing service allowing physicians to charge existing patients for online 'visits'. Patients typically pay $20–30 by credit card (most insurers don't cover Internet consultations) for email consultations using a secure messaging system. Medem charges the physician $2.50 per consultation, but only if they bill the patient – a physician might not charge for a simple question. The service meets 'eRisk' guidelines for online medicine that have been endorsed by 33 malpractice carriers and the AMA. Medem's messenger service is used by about 8000 physicians, and already allows patients to request appointments and prescription refills online [190].

- LifeMasters developed an online diabetes management tool for Roche Diagnostics. LifeMasters integrated its diabetes assistant program as part of a consumer-driven strategy to web-enable Roche's blood glucose monitor. Patients can upload data from a Roche glucose meter into the program and longitudinally track their glucose and weight levels. The system provides feedback and offers management tools [191].

- Data Critical, a vendor of wireless devices, provides a system that can monitor blood pressure, oxygen saturation and electrocardiograms. If any parameters cross a critical threshold, an alert is sent out. By 2000, 330 systems had been installed in US hospitals, mostly in intensive care and cardiac wards. Data Critical has partnerships with several medical device manufacturers, including Agilent, Siemens and GE Medical Systems [2].

- HealthFrontier's ecg@home product is an FDA-approved Internet-enabled ECG monitoring device. The company describes its product as a pocket-sized gadget with built-in electrodes into which users place their thumbs to obtain a reading. The data is then sent to HealthFrontier via the Internet, a wireless device, email or a built-in telephone adapter. If the reading is outside set parameters, the firm will forward the ECG to the patient's physician for review. Other web-enabled or web-based ECG products cleared for patient use include MicroMedical's PocketView, a handheld tool which reads and transmits heart readings for physician review, and Medtronic's CareLink Monitor which monitors implanted cardiac devices and reports the results to physicians via a secure website [178].

- The Cleveland Clinic offers online second opinions for 150 diseases through e-Cleveland Clinic. Consultations will cost $750 each and can be accessed from clevelandclinic.com. Online patients select their original diagnosis, answer general medical and disease-specific questions, and then go through a checklist to provide the information that e-Cleveland Clinic physicians need, such as ECG results and X-rays. The patient then sends the previously completed test results to the Cleveland Clinic via an overnight service. An e-Cleveland Clinic doctor then analyses the data and an opinion is provided to the patient online, and is also sent by mail with the materials that the patient sent to the clinic. Nurses then call the patient to facilitate any required follow-up or answer questions about the second opinion [169].

Telemedicine in space

NASA is developing technologies to permit earth-bound physicians to diagnose and treat astronauts on the International Space Station, orbiting 250 miles above earth. Until now, NASA has relied on exhaustive pre-flight health examinations and preventive medicine to ensure that an astronaut doesn't get seriously ill. Increasing the amount of time spent in space raises the chances that a serious health problem could occur. The NASA telemedicine project plans to incorporate Internet standards, interfaces and protocols. A distributed medical network would enable physicians to use standard web browsers and Internet protocols to communicate with astronauts. Standard technologies would enable physicians from different countries to use these ubiquitous technologies to access and share medical information. NASA also wants to use on-board devices to provide physicians with important clinical data and ensure that physicians have only the data they need instead of massive amounts of unnecessary information. The idea is to automate the lowest level of decision-making and assessment. Examples of the automated technology are handheld readers that can be used to scan an astronaut's body to monitor tissue and blood chemistry. NASA also hopes that its efforts will have a ripple effect on earth. Lightweight, non-invasive devices that can diagnose medical problems could give patients unprecedented access to care [192].

Conclusions – 'the take home messages'

For telemedicine to be widely implemented, it will be necessary to prove both clinical and cost-effectiveness. A study by Lehoux et al. found that specialities relying on either thorough physical examination or specialized investigations (such as cardiology) are unlikely to restructure their work routines to accommodate telemedicine, whereas specialities that primarily use images or numerical data (especially radiology and dermatology) tend to perceive telemedicine as more useful [193]. Not surprisingly, the perceived usefulness of telemedicine increased the further the patient was from the clinic. A 2000 UK study compared the effectiveness and cost of conventional and telemedicine delivery of dermatology consultations to 204 patients. It found that real-time teledermatology was clinically feasible; no major differences in outcome existed between the two approaches. Teledermatology was only cost effective if the patient would have had to travel at least 39 km for a hospital appointment [187]. Other studies have proved the cost-effectiveness of home videophone use for patients with various chronic conditions (congestive heart failure, cancer, diabetes, anxiety) and of teleradiology (used extensively in the US to free smaller hospitals from having a full-time specialist radiology staff) [186].

The main barriers to the implementation of telemedicine are organizational and legal rather than technological. Physicians tend to believe that only objective data can be safely viewed from a distance and remote interpretation of subjective data is inappropriate [193]. The confusion regarding the legal status of an online doctor–patient relationship and the liabilities of practising online have prevented many physicians offering Internet services to their patients. As we have discussed, EBM, complex new therapies and cost containment will be among the drivers behind the adoption of telemedicine.

- For a pharmaceutical company, telemedicine facilitates drug development, as patient monitoring in clinical trials can be done from a central unit. Similarly, post-marketing surveillance can be improved when the option of real-time monitoring exists.

- The extent to which the pharmaceutical industry should directly support telemedicine is largely determined by where prescribing and therapeutic choices will fit into this new care model. In the case of highly specialized products or those required for critical care interventions, it would be good for a pharmaceutical company to be involved at the 'point of care' and to be close to the data interchanges that are part of patient management.

PART VI

Managing Digital Strategies

CHAPTER

12 Digital technology management in the pharmaceutical industry

The speed and transparency that are the hallmark of digital technologies make the competitive challenges faced by today's pharmaceutical companies all the more acute. The management of patent expiration, new product introductions, price scrutiny and mandated formularies become all the more urgent when the Internet permits changes in the market environment at almost the blink of an eye. Similarly, as communication with stakeholders through digital channels becomes almost instantaneous, pharmaceutical executives no longer have the luxury of spending considerable time in carefully planning and designing their interactions with consumers, physicians, insurers, hospitals and payers. The industry is indeed cognizant of the 'mindset change' that succeeding in a connected world requires. Market leaders are restructuring their human resource functions and are investing in workforce management programmes that promote high-performance teams, improve cross-functional training and facilitate worker empowerment. Companies are having to focus on promoting creativity and flexibility, previously not regarded as the most important skills required for career advancement in the pharmaceutical industry [85] (Figure 12.1).

The pharmaceutical industry's digital transformation journey is best characterized as being 'suspiciously enthusiastic'. Most senior managers see the benefits of investing in the e-marketing channel, but are unconvinced whether their organization is in a position to properly implement these programmes or whether any acceptable ROI will be generated. Managing digital technologies requires an awareness of the unique context of global pharmaceuticals, and especially the pivotal role of country affiliates or market companies, that often operate with a high level of independence. Similarly, we need to be aware of what some claim is the 'silo mentality' of pharmaceuticals, where collaboration between groups such as marketing and R&D may be extremely limited.

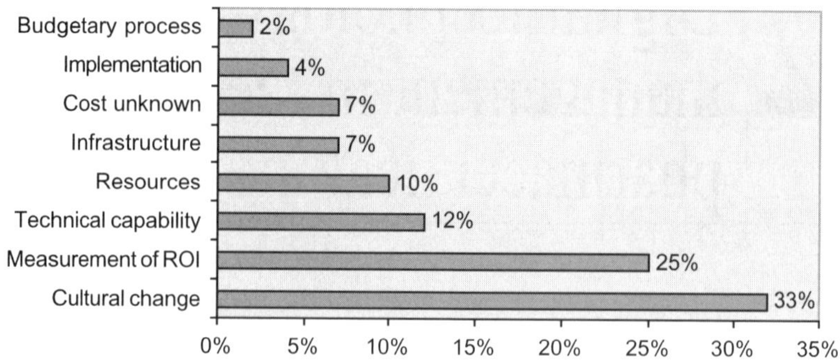

Figure 12.1 Top barriers to effective e-implementation (2001 survey of 101 pharma executives)

Source: [7]

In this section, we explore the management challenge of 'e-pharmaceuticals' from the perspective of organizations, processes and core technologies. We aim to identify the lessons from early experience in this area and elucidate some of the best 'techniques' for success.

Managing digital organizations

Introduction

Until fairly recently, major pharmaceutical companies tended to develop and control their digital initiatives from centralized, stand-alone e-business divisions. However, many companies are now splitting up these groups and reintegrating their e-business experts into key departments such as marketing in an attempt to move digital technologies into the mainstream business activities. For example, in 2002, GlaxoSmithKline closed its stand-alone e-business division and shifted more budget responsibility for the e-channel to the marketing and sales departments and Aventis and Johnson & Johnson have also dismantled their e-business groups [194]. As pharmaceutical companies reach a certain level of digital 'maturity', there is a growing realization that leveraging the opportunities that the Internet offers requires an understanding of digital technologies combined with a deep knowledge of the relevant business area. For example, R&D skills are at least as essential as e-skills when implementing e-R&D, and e-marketing success certainly has more to do with marketing skills than IT skills. The guiding idea behind the integration of 'e' into existing departments is the hope that digital business will become 'business as usual'. Another advantage of this integration is the reduced need to duplicate efforts and waste resources. As a result of this integration, an e-marketing campaign can simply be regarded as part of the accepted marketing mix, rather than a stand-alone initiative.

The Internet revolution has challenged existing IT management structures. Historically, many companies had separate IT groups supporting each business unit or department. As e-pharmaceuticals often require the integration of the work flow of many departments, the structure of IT management within organizations needs to be adapted. The prevailing consensus is that IT management should be increasingly centralized as a support function and focus on providing the infrastructure and tools for line managers to facilitate e-pharma. As we have previously mentioned, digital technologies, or at least their proper use, force cross-company communication and interchange. For example, a television DTC advertising campaign requires the monitoring of websites, analysis of CSC interactions, data mining and multichannel ROI calculations.

In the nascent world of digital technologies, it has been almost impossible to specify baseline standards, let alone design fully integrated processes. The profusion of vendors and an early reluctance to develop collaborative standards resulted in a mixture of sophisticated software and hardware; a veritable 'tower of Babel' in terms of systems integration. The early phases of e-R&D and drug development rely on computational power, but clinical trials and regulatory submission preparation are more e-business oriented. It is difficult for organizations to form groups to manage a seamless digital process, without a radical reconsideration of people, skills and vision required.

This new digital context has moved IT departments from the background into full partnerships with business units. Many pharmaceutical companies now employ a cross-functional team approach, bringing together scientists, supply chain experts, marketers and IT professionals to create new solutions at each stage of the value chain.

For example, in order to match digital resources to real needs, Bristol-Myers Squibb assigned an IT counterpart to each business unit manager within the company. A VP of IT works in R&D to ensure that the unit's IT needs are met. This model is particularly useful in the biotechnology and pharmaceutical industry, because of the large number of alliances, acquisitions and divestitures [5].

Leadership in digital strategy

The early history of pharmaceutical digital strategy is characterized by a variety of motivations behind senior management's support for e-business. We have already discussed the various defensive strategies taken by an industry that originally feared that the Internet would result in new and potentially dangerous intermediaries controlling its relationship with its key customers, the physicians. Lest it be forgotten, following the dotcom crash, it is important to note that many senior pharmaceutical managers were indeed enthusiastic about what they believed would be an e-health revolution. One IT VP wryly recounts that his CEO became a believer in the Internet the day after he attended a barbecue at the palatial home of Bill Gates. The speed with which the pharmaceutical industry embraced the Internet says more about the internal dynamics of companies than the implications of digital technologies for health and healthcare. A number of important organizational lessons have already been learnt about leadership in emerging technologies. Some pharmaceutical companies believed that the way to benefit from the Internet was to hire an expert from an industry that was further advanced in digital strategy. With an e-guru and a small team (and a small budget) it would be possible to convince business unit heads and country managers to experiment with e-business, especially for sales and marketing. Another popular strategy was for the leadership to invest heavily in pilot or demonstration projects in certain countries. Here the hope was that the success of a single e-detailing or e-CRM initiative would inspire similar projects. A pilot project would also identify pitfalls, good vendors and best practices for widespread diffusion. The e-guru and successful pilot project approaches have not been very successful, as they floundered on the difficult and complex internal politics of companies and often antagonized important stakeholders. For example, managers were quick to point out that a successful e-marketing campaign in one country was unlikely to work in the particular regulatory, medical practice and social context of their own country. Similarly, managers who held marketing budgets were not prepared to experiment with the Internet, claiming that despite the fanfare of the e-health revolution, current non-digital channels were working well (Figure 12.2.).

Roles in pharmaceutical digital strategy

The Internet is certainly far from being the most important marketing channel for the pharmaceutical industry. To date, many pharmaceutical executives have had very limited exposure to digital technologies, a situation that can be

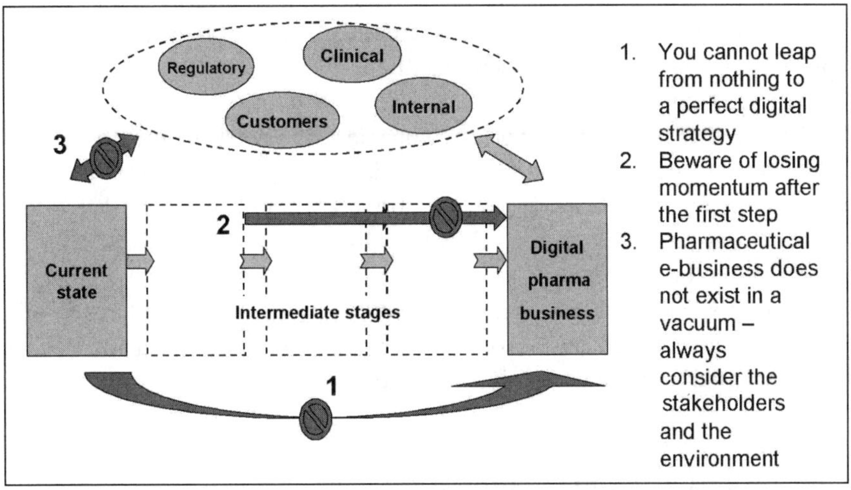

Figure 12.2 Some common pitfalls in digital strategy implementation

Source: J. Van Gorp, personal communication

expected in an industry characterized by its justifiably cautious approach to any innovation which may impact on the relationship with its most important customers – physicians. Our thesis remains that economics and technological transition are indeed forcing companies increasingly to use the Internet and new technologies. What skills are required to aid pharmaceutical companies as they move into this digital world?

We have already seen that the combination of IT and operational (be it R&D or sales and marketing) competencies is necessary to manage digital technologies. However, these competencies, while necessary, are not sufficient. It is important to find people who are willing to experiment, a possibility that exists when the Internet is used as a marketing channel. For example, it is fairly easy to change aspects of a website or e-detailing campaigns and measure the impact of such an intervention on a defined target audience. The willingness to experiment and develop innovative offerings has been difficult to nurture in the resource-rich world of pharmaceuticals. It has been relatively easy to leave the mechanics of marketing to consultants and technology providers. The result has been that very little knowledge about e-marketing is actually retained within many large pharmaceutical companies. It will be necessary to look outside pharmaceuticals to recruit people from sectors where margin pressure is acute and marketing experiments are essential for survival. Similarly, many pharmaceutical marketers have not been trained to follow the rigorous design and evaluation processes essential for the design of sustainable and scalable applications, a standard practice in consumer goods marketing, where maximum value has to be extracted from limited marketing spend.

To succeed in a digital world, companies will need to instil a culture, especially in sales and marketing, where data is 'respected'. Today, it is not uncommon for companies to spend substantial amounts for market information from providers such as IMS, and this data is often looked at very superficially or ignored. In a resource-constrained future, it will not be possible to spend freely on aggregated data and companies will have to rely on new sources such as customer information generated via e-CRM or Internet-based marketing experiments for decision support.

Conclusions – 'the take home messages'

The role of scale in the pharmaceutical value chain is a source of growing critical debate. Senior management face the trade-offs between the savings associated with centralized administration, accounting and technology functions, the inertia of huge organizations and the need to provide innovators with the freedom to operate. Companies grapple with the best way to structure the value chain and GlaxoSmithKline, for example, split its late-stage research unit into competing centres of excellence, each with a specific disease focus [32]. The strength of large pharmaceutical and biotechnology companies lies in their ability to develop and sell products globally, irrespective of whether those products were discovered internally or in-licensed. As technologies such as web applications and e-CRM will inevitably become standardized (or at least easier to integrate), a strong case can be made for returning to a more centralized operational model.

- Core IT functions (such as central databases for e-R&D and CRM and communication capabilities for e-detailing) should be managed by a specific group. This group must develop robust, scalable tools for business units across the value chain. For example, a standard e-detailing application should be available for customization to local marketing needs or an 'out of the box' website application with analytic tools should be made available.
- Knowledgeable leadership is required to enforce the standardization of digital technologies across pharmaceutical companies.
- Companies must recruit people who are willing (and trained) to use the Internet, in terms of its flexibility, potential for targeting and speed of response, for experiments, especially in sales and marketing.

Managing digital processes

Introduction

We are still at an early stage when it comes to the refinement of best practice, and even in defining cross-industry standards, for the management of digital processes in the pharmaceutical industry. In the heady dotcom era, a cornucopia of providers, solutions and systems was on offer and very little time was spent on developing rigorous evaluation processes or even matching technologies to specific needs. The resultant spending on a range of quickly redundant offerings sullied the reputation of digital technology, at the very time when it was important to prove its value, especially in pharmaceutical sales and marketing. The pharmaceutical industry is under pressure to extract maximum value from sales and marketing investments and digital technologies will undoubtedly play an important role. The financial markets, once almost exclusively concerned with research and development and the drug pipeline, are asking whether companies have the resources, strategic orientation and skills to sell products aggressively. When we consider government, insurer and payer cost-containment pressures, recent high-profile drug withdrawals, the failures to obtain regulatory approval and the constant criticism of the industry on many fronts, we can begin to discern why focusing on customers (especially physicians), and extracting maximum value from these customers, is becoming a vital concern for most companies.

Therefore, we explore the management of digital processes from a mainly sales and marketing perspective, in the belief that this is where immediate investment should be focused. The first priority is developing an understanding of the implications of the Internet in particular, as one of the factors behind the transition in the way that the pharmaceutical industry perceives its customers. Digital technology presents the first practical opportunity (from a cost and implementation perspective) to establish close and sustainable relationships with all customers, be they consumers or physicians, as it is possible to meet information and service needs on a personalized basis. This demands innovative thinking about customer segmentation, partnerships and alliances and ROI.

Segmentation

Market segmentation is the tool of choice for identifying target customer groups and developing the best possible offerings to market to these target groups. This has been defined as:

> a process of splitting customers, or potential customers, within a market into different groups, or segments, within which customers have the same, or similar requirements satisfied by a distinct marketing mix. [195]

Segmentation is a rational and more precise approach to adjust the product message to the requirements of the target market and has an immediate, positive impact on a product campaign [196]. The process of market segmentation builds consensus and a unity of purpose among all stakeholders in pharmaceutical marketing and allows a company to be more sensitive and responsive to customers. Problems encountered with prevailing segmentation approaches include:

- Incomplete sets of variables
- A clustering approach that does not highlight useful differences across a common set of variables
- Difficulties with the identification of target segments [197].

A wide range of segmentation methodologies exists, but in the current complex marketing environment, there is growing interest in multi-axial approaches to segmentation, especially when these include more subjective indicators such as attitude and life-stage [198].

The Internet is a superb tool for communicating with individuals. A print advertisement can never be changed to meet the immediate needs of a single reader; yet it is possible to deliver specific content to a specific person using a website. Clearly, an immediate, personalized interaction with every web user is an unattainable goal, but the Internet is a better, as opposed to perfect, channel for a one-to-one interaction between a pharmaceutical company and a physician or consumer. The Internet also allows real-time segmentation of web users. Through questionnaires, click-stream analysis and simple screening questions, it is possible to customize a web page for an individual. While online segmentation and the resulting attempts at customization may still be somewhat crude (one need only recall some of the personal book recommendations from a site such as Amazon.com), visitors to some of the better pharmaceutical websites can have their questions reasonably well answered. Once individuals and their information needs are better identified, web application servers are powerful tools for delivering the appropriate content and customizing the user experience. Here we need to look outside pharmaceuticals, at sectors such as financial services, in order to see the high quality of web interaction that customers can now expect. Within the constraints of privacy legislation, it is possible to rapidly analyse the behaviour of online visitors and improve the offerings on a website. The Internet represents a paradigm for a personalized interaction between a pharmaceutical company and an individual (physician, consumer or payer). The Internet forces us to think about the individual customer and, while it is impossible to deal with every individual, there is considerable virtue in thinking about smaller groups of customers. For the purposes of a working definition, let us describe these smaller groups, subgroups within 'conventional' market segments having distinctive needs and purchasing behaviour, as 'micro-segments'. The idea that it is possible to segment target customers into smaller groups is by no means alien to pharmaceutical sales representatives. As part of a research project into pharmaceutical segmentation, we interviewed a number of experienced sales force members of global pharmaceutical companies. The interviews were open-ended discussions focusing on developing a description of target physicians. A predominant theme was dissatisfaction with existing market segmentations, especially the approach whereby physicians are crudely divided into categories such as 'dynamic innovators' or 'old conservatives'. Irrespective of the often considerable resources devoted to existing market segmentation approaches, as well as their large sample sizes and their analytic rigour, sales representatives wanted to see an approach to segmentation that better reflected their view of the world. A simple qualitative, thematic analysis of the interviews indicates that experienced pharmaceutical sales representatives believe that there are about 12–18 subgroups (or micro-segments) of physicians. More specifically, while the subgroups may have a lot in common with each other, each is distinguished by a need, attribute or outlook that is particularly important for selling to a particular physician who falls into that subgroup.

A good way of elucidating the rationale behind a segmentation focused on small groups or micro-segments (Internet-driven segmentation) is to juxtapose it against current approaches to pharmaceutical market segmentation (Table 12.1). A more fine-grained segmentation maintains the richness of the interaction between the partners in the healthcare transaction – some sales representatives, for example, considered that physicians who were deeply concerned with how a product was reimbursed, or whether the product was affordable by all patients, constituted an important micro-segment. In addition, some felt that changes in 'attitude' ought to be better reflected; opinion-leaders, scientific trends and sales representatives may, for example, influence an individual physician and a more 'flexible' approach to segmentation allows a company to modify the marketing approach for target groups over time [199].

The ability to deal with a larger number of micro-segments also, to some extent, 'liberates' marketers from having to use statistical techniques to

TABLE 12.1

Comparison of segmentation 'approaches'

	Current market segmentation	Internet-driven segmentation
Approach	Segments are aggregations based on similarities	Segments can be based on differences that have marketing implications
Customer response	Data has to be actively gathered	Large volume of online behaviour data
Features	Similarities are important	Differences are important
Subgroups	Collapsed into larger groups	Subgroups maintained
Context	Moderately influenced by the environment	Highly context dependent in terms of health economic, regulatory and practice environment
Segment attributes	General attributes are described	Specific attribute suitable for specific intervention identified
Flexibility	Fairly rigid	Segments change over time

produce a few comprehensive segments. This permits a focus on single encounters with customers, the meanings of these encounters and their implications for marketing to the individual. This phenomenological approach is driven by the idea that, somewhere within even a single interaction with a customer, there lies a decision point, often emotional, about a product or a brand [200]. This approach is suitable for the healthcare environment, characterized as it is by complex patterns of influence and interactions. From a pharmaceutical marketing perspective, letting the data 'speak for itself' does lead to some interesting and useful insights about traditional targets. For example, in a series of interviews about a specialized hospital product, sales representatives easily disaggregated 'opinion-leaders' into smaller groups, each requiring somewhat different marketing approaches (Table 12.2).

While the groups clearly share many similarities, it is possible to identify particular interventions that may be suitable (or inappropriate) to build product and company interest and loyalty, thereby improving an opinion-leader 'development' strategy [201]. The role of physicians not tradi-

TABLE 12.2

'Micro-segmentation' of opinion-leaders into four groups
1. Traditional opinion-leaders who are susceptible to launch messages, support pre-marketing efforts and clinical trials and generally accept what they are told about the product
2. Physicians who are opinion-leaders but feel excluded from the product as they may not have suitable patients or may not have participated in the clinical trials
3. Physicians who, while not regarded as opinion-leaders, influence a large number of their peers through various channels (publications, specific expertise, responsibility in a specific area)
4. Physicians who are opinion-leaders and are sympathetic to the product, but are not in a position to prescribe the product for economic or resource reasons and require considerable support from the company

tionally regarded as opinion-leaders, yet exerting substantial influence amongst their peers, is highlighted. The in-depth qualitative approach to what are fairly discrete encounters also promotes a product-specific segmentation, which encourages more focus on the design of a marketing or launch campaign. Fine-grained segmentation has immediate benefits. It allows more experienced sales representatives to share market understanding with less experienced colleagues and for the fine-tuning and rapid evaluation of marketing interventions aimed at small groups. This opens the door to a culture of experimentation and innovation.

We have discussed the potential of consumer-facing activities such as disease management and web-based information provision, and alerted the reader to the fact that these transactions require a range of partnerships and offerings. For example, in the case of a chronic disease such as diabetes, a pharmaceutical company seeking to participate in patient care as a provider of information and interactive tools would have to provide simple educational or self-help material, online communication tools and perhaps interactive tools (diaries or reminder systems). The identification of the needs of the stakeholders (in this case, physicians, patients and nurses) is based on a simple micro-segmentation of each group and the weighting of the most important interaction between these groups. Marketing strategists need to carefully seek out these interactions, as the company may well be able to provide information or e-tools to facilitate or enhance this interaction (Figure 12.3).

Digital technologies offer pharmaceutical companies new opportunities to cost effectively enter into partnerships with patients and their carers. This strategy does require careful consideration (which includes segmentation and the analysis of relationships) of the stakeholders. For example, it would be

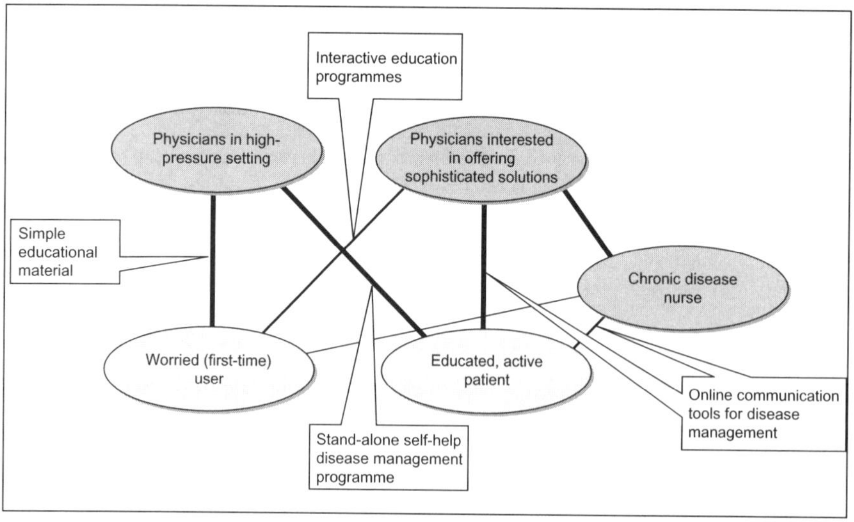

Figure 12.3 Model of the interaction between different patient and carer segments with proposals for support materials and interactive tools

counterproductive to provide e-tools to patients, if their physicians are not interested in or are opposed to the role of the Internet in disease management.

Alliance management

Digital technologies, by providing near-instant communication and interaction, facilitate partnerships between all the stakeholders in healthcare. For a pharmaceutical company, generally used to arms-length interactions (with consumers, in particular), the speed, intensity and transparency of these new interactions is a challenge, both in terms of logistics and organizational mindset.

The dotcom era and the new skills and technologies required to market over the Internet put pharmaceutical companies under some pressure to develop a range of relationships, alliances and partnerships with start-ups or specialist providers. Whereas pharmaceutical research executives had extensive experience in business development, licensing, collaborative agreements and the assessment of opportunities presented by small biotechnology companies, the same could not be said of marketers, who were involved mainly in buying services from, and outsourcing work to, consultancies or advertising agencies. The dotcom hype of the late 1990s resulted in many pharmaceutical companies entering into alliances with portals that would fail to deliver much traffic or overpaying for website development or e-marketing advice. The failure of poorly planned e-business campaigns, combined with the dotcom crash, severely damaged the reputation of digital technologies and has, to some extent, resulted in a pervasive air of scepticism as to the potential of the Internet in pharmaceutical marketing. Venture capital arms established to invest in health e-business have not been very successful in identifying and developing opportunities and some are being integrated into existing R&D business development structures. Pharmaceutical marketers are certainly not alone in having to develop new approaches to the evaluation and exploitation of new opportunities in digital technology. Other players in the healthcare value chain have had to take the decision to partner (or not) in areas as diverse as proteomics (for example, Myriad, Hitachi and Oracle), personalized medicine (for example, the AstraZeneca and Orchid joint venture) and B2B exchanges (GHX, the joint venture between J&J, GE Medical Systems, Baxter International, Abbott Labs, Siemens and Medtronic and a range of other suppliers) (Figure 12.4).

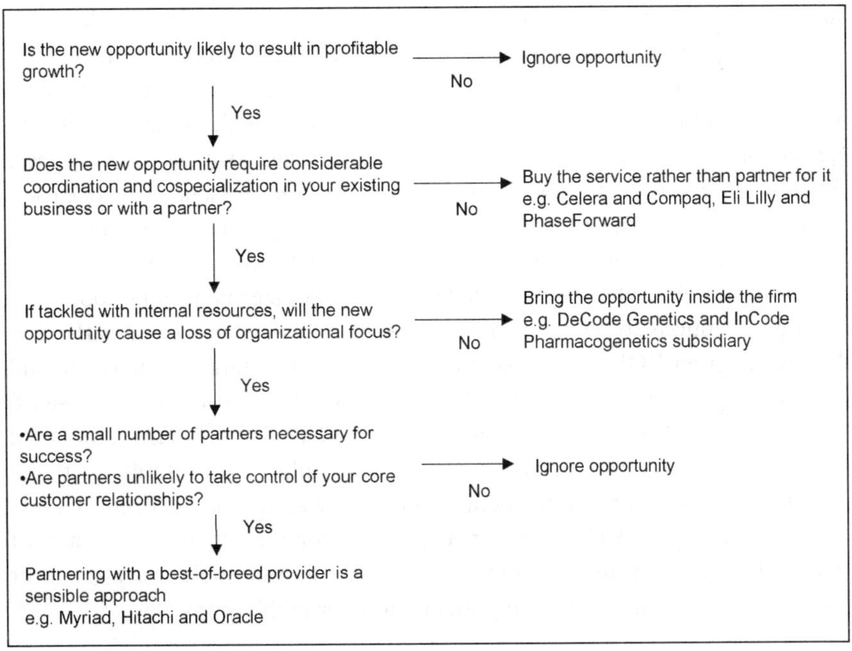

Figure 12.4 When is partnering with a best-of-breed provider a sensible approach to growth opportunities?

Source: Based on [202]

Return on investment

The return on investment (ROI) of digital technologies in the pharmaceutical industry remains a source of controversy. A perennial complaint of e-business experts concerns the double standards that are applied to new technologies. While most senior executives would be hard pressed to provide objective ROI data on traditional marketing interventions such as journal advertisements and conference travel, they demand extensive ROI exercises for activities such as e-detailing. The interest in ROI of digital technologies is certainly substantial, when compared to the amount of money being spent in this area by the pharmaceutical industry (well under five per cent of marketing budgets in 2002). Ironically, e-business does provide excellent opportunities for the evaluation of ROI, as clear end points are often attainable and measurable. Also, the scalable and flexible nature of Internet-based medical marketing permits the design of small experiments that can include control groups. Precise quantification of the impact on sales remains a function of the availability of individual (or small group) prescribing data and is constrained (in the EU, at least) by the reimbursement structure, privacy legislation, the role of wholesalers and distributors and the controlling influence of some of the information providers.

The building of an ROI 'model' is a vital component of any e-marketing project. While some of the projections will naturally be speculative, the process of disaggregating the steps leading to an increase in sales alerts marketers to the measurable stages and permits a simulation of a range of possible outcomes. Where it is possible to promote a specific therapy, ROI simulation is a lot easier; but marketers often have to consider carefully the impact of promoting awareness about a disease or condition on the sales of competitive products.

Using the example given in Table 12.3, a marketer expecting about 200 extra prescriptions to be generated by a website campaign every quarter can then develop an ROI model based on the known building, maintenance and promotion costs of the website and the revenue generated by the extra sales. ROI modelling may indeed be simplistic, in that other media, promotional activities and physician detailing substantially influence prescribing, but it does introduce an element of rigour into resource allocation decision-making.

An approach to ROI should not only be confined to the often almost impossible task of quantifying payback at an individual physician or consumer level. A number of important and measurable steps exist:

- Metrics of activity such as online behaviour and participation and demands for information or services.

TABLE 12.3

ROI model for a disease website

	Number
Total number of expected visitors/quarter	10,000
Assume that 60% are patients or carers	6,000
Assume that 50% of patients are identified by themselves or their carers (based on the criteria provided on the website) as eligible to receive the product	3,000
Assume that 80% of eligible patients or their carers seek more information	2,400
Assume that 50% of patients discuss the product with their physician	1,200
Assume that 50% are eligible (based on their physician's opinion) to receive the product	600
Assume that 30% of the eligible patients are prescribed the product	200
'Conversion rate' 5 2%	

- Changes in attitudes and perceptions measured through online questionnaires and user surveys.
- Changes in activities such as patient visits to physicians or physician demands for sales representative visits.

The most neglected aspect of the ROI debate surrounding digital technologies in the pharmaceutical industry concerns the longer term impact on sales. We believe that the Internet, and especially the opportunities that it provides for standardized, targeted communication with all the healthcare stakeholders, will play an important role in the reduction of cost of sales. While the future role (and size) of the pharmaceutical industry sales force is still unclear, digital technologies, be they new communication tools or e-CRM, will promote more value-laden customer interactions, and reduce training and administration costs (Figure 12.5).

The ROI debate has also to some extent deflected marketers from the full consideration of the application of digital technologies to increase sales. In a competitive marketing environment, customer loyalty will be won through service excellence. As marketing budgets are inevitably cut and incentive programmes come under tight regulatory control, physician relationships will

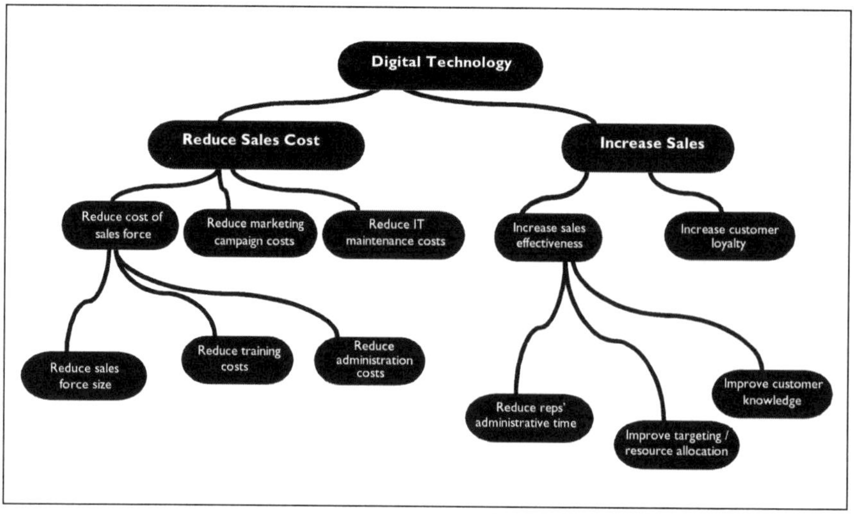

Figure 12.5 Modelling ROI for digital technology based on reduced cost of sales and increased sales

Source: [96]

inevitably have to be transformed, from what some have described as 'reward-driven' to 'service-driven'.

Conclusions – the take home messages

As pharmaceutical companies attempt to evaluate their early forays into e-business, it is unlikely that they will be in a position to devote considerable resources to segmentation exercises designed for e-marketing. Paradoxically, we believe that more resources should be devoted to customer understanding, when the immediacy and intensity of the communication leave little margin for error. For example, physicians will not be keen to revisit a product website following a disappointing interaction and are highly unlikely to recommend a disease management website to their patients, if they have little confidence that a patient would benefit from the website. The Internet is a channel for rapid interaction, requiring new approaches to customer response, management and real-time analytics. For market segmentation, the Internet is a laboratory, where predictive approaches and various offerings can be tested through observing interactions with websites, customer feedback and sales. As most 'conventional' segmentation relies on post hoc analysis of extensive surveys, it is often difficult to predict future behaviours, especially in a rapidly changing market environment. As pharmaceutical companies increasingly use tools such as e-detailing and CRM, segmentation methodologies will have to become more rapid and deliver a more individualized view of the market.

The pharmaceutical industry is being forced into considering far more individualized or segmented approaches to the way it does business. The era of 'shotgun' therapeutics is drawing to a close as more data on individual risk, predisposition to side effects and treatment efficacy becomes available. Consumers are no longer blindly accepting treatment with drugs that are effective for only a small proportion of patients, as some companies are actively exploring marketing specific treatments to small groups, identified using genetic testing [36]. Narrower therapeutic indications and the consequent demise of the 'blockbuster' model of drug profitability represent a disconcerting challenge for pharmaceutical sales and marketing organizations. A case can undoubtedly be made for devoting more resources to focus on customers in order to extract the maximum value from small target groups. This will certainly require an innovative approach to segmentation.

The optimal management of digital processes is achieved through a series of incremental improvements (Figure 12.6). The first step lies in the domain of optimizing operational effectiveness by using existing resources to better understand the 'digital customer'. This requires the linking and integration of available data sources. Differentiation through analytical insight, the next step, is the development of a deeper, more fine-grained and accurate customer view and using this actually to influence and change sales and marketing activities. The final step is the building of collaboration, based on this differentiated, analytical approach to customers, across the value chain (within a company) and through partnerships and alliances. While aspects of this model are more likely to be in the realm of aspiration (as opposed to action) for

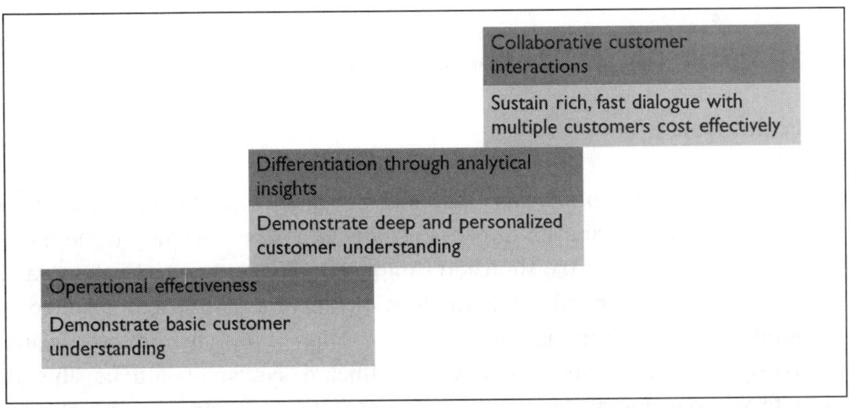

Figure 12.6 Incremental improvements in digital technology strategy

Source: [96]

many companies, the schema does alert us to the importance of rigour in managing customer information and the need to better segment all potential customers and seek partnerships to reach these customers.

- Wherever possible, the processes of project design and technology specification in e-marketing should be codified and standardized. The aim is to have a toolkit of best practice and disseminate this across a global pharmaceutical company. In the case of segmentation for e-marketing, a standardized process would include:

  1. Identifying target groups on the basis of real points of leverage for marketing or influencing health behaviour.
  2. Developing the best possible offerings for segments in terms of content, interactive tools and value-added services.
  3. Design and delivery of targeted and tailored marketing messages, interactivity, value-added services and information for consumers and physicians.
  4. Identifying these segments online and using the insights gained through market research and collective knowledge about customers.
  5. Reaching these segments through multiple e-channels.

- Pharmaceutical managers are indeed aware that digital technologies should not be viewed purely as an IT issue, but rather as an important communications and marketing channel. In order to clarify the role of digital technologies in the pharmaceutical marketing mix, managers need to set up multiple small 'experiments'.

Managing digital technologies

Introduction

The Internet revolution patently illustrates the disjuncture between the speed of digital innovation and its impact on daily life. The tendency to be overoptimistic in estimating the short-term implications of a new technology (and some claim overpessimistic in predictions of longer term impacts) resulted in misguided confidence in the potential of the Internet to transform healthcare.

Today, no industrialized country healthcare system would be able to operate without digital data transfer, for activities ranging from reimbursement to the monitoring of sophisticated diagnostic equipment. Yet the majority (albeit a decreasing number) of consumers have no pressing need to use the Internet to seek health information or conduct healthcare transactions. It is difficult to predict accurately which technologies or 'killer applications' will indeed cause huge numbers of physicians and consumers to participate in an e-health revolution. What we do see, however, is a range of technologies which, combined with the inevitable changes in the way that healthcare will be financed and delivered, are indeed becoming incrementally important. We explore a number of these new technologies, especially as their evolution impacts on digital strategy development in the pharmaceutical industry.

Core technologies

The Internet

The majority of the digital strategies described in this book have been driven by the emergence of the Internet and wireless networks as worldwide standards for transferring data. The explosive growth in the Internet has been well documented and looks set to continue – there were approximately 530 million Internet users worldwide in 2001; this number is expected to double by 2005. In 2002, the Internet enabled $823 billion of B2B transactions, and conservative estimates expect this to reach $2.4 trillion by 2004. As more and more IT applications migrate from proprietary closed standards to the open standards used across the global Internet, the importance of digital strategies to the health business can only be expected to increase [203, 204].

Wireless networks and mobile devices

New generation mobile networks are designed to allow broadband access for rapid data transfer. By 2006 3G networks should be rolled out across the globe; however high infrastructure costs may limit coverage. Pharmaceutical companies have identified two areas where wireless and mobile devices have the most potential. In the case of SFA, a strong case can be made for providing tools that allow a salesperson in the field to be able to access databases and share important information in real time. Similarly, for personnel who travel extensively, mobile email access and diary management tools are extremely useful. The near doubling of the sales force size in the US over the past few years has forced managers to seek real-time capacity to monitor field activities and ensure that representatives use their time better (by offering tools for reporting and visit scheduling to be used during 'down time'). Companies are investing resources to track relationships with individual physicians, especially during critical periods such as drug launches and it is hoped that mobile devices will encourage representatives to report more regularly and accurately. Most CRM providers are offering mobile technologies and some smaller companies are exploring the implementation of wireless CRM as a core system connected directly to a customer data warehouse. Mobile applications are an integral part of all modular CRM offerings and as communication technologies become robust, widespread and cheaper, the use of handheld devices may well replace 'traditional' approaches such as daily sales data transfer using laptop computers.

Clinical trial management (CTM) using mobile devices, such as wireless PDAs, has attracted considerable interest, with a number of vendors offering solutions. Few companies have implemented wireless CTM, as they are still migrating from paper-based to web-based systems. Remote data capture has a number of promising applications in areas such as patient diaries (the patient records symptoms, progress or adverse effects on a device such as a mobile telephone or a wireless PDA) or environments where access to desktop computers is limited. The availability of real-time data has the potential to shorten the drug development process. To date, pharmaceutical companies are mainly engaged in small pilot projects in the wireless and mobile arena. Security is an important concern, as many pharmaceutical manufacturers have still to establish intruder-proof networking environments.

Languages and standards

> Once the human genome had been sequenced it was like the starting gun had been fired. All of a sudden, this massive amount of data began pouring into these databases. What everybody realized is that the complexity of understanding the data, making use of the data – that was really the challenge. – Jeff Augen, Director of Strategy for Life Sciences at IBM

Standard-setting collaborations among competitors are common in the electronics and computer industries, but were rare in life sciences until fairly recently. As a result, it is extremely difficult to compare the reams of data being generated by private companies and public initiatives such as the Human Genome Project. In response, companies have begun to mount joint computational projects, often with government researchers [205, 206]. For example, XML-tagging standards are being developed to permit the exchange of biological data held in non-compatible databases. The World

Wide Web Consortium (W3C) first published eXtensible Markup Language (XML) as a data-tagging standard in 1996. XML was initially intended to be a more sophisticated version of HTML tagging (instead of merely describing how to display a piece of data, XML data tags also describe what the data represents). Led by the Biotechnology Industry Association, a coalition of biotechnology companies and research organizations is currently developing a worldwide XML standard for storing and retrieving biological information including genetic, genomic and proteomic data. This specification will be available free to any company or scientist that wishes to use it to help organize and mine information. The project has been dubbed the Interoperable Informatics Infrastructure Consortium, or I3C. Other consortia are setting electronic standards for storing and transferring clinical trial (see Chapter 5 on e-clinical trials) and healthcare product transaction data (see Chapter 6 on supply chain).

Artificial intelligence, real-time software and P2P

Artificial intelligence (AI) is an automated analytical system that replaces or supersedes human thinking. AI technology utilizes a wide range of techniques and algorithms mostly based on variations of probability theory. AI technologies can be categorized into three types: logic-related, search-based and generalization. Logic-related AI systems evaluate a range of possibilities and reason the most likely answer using a process of deduction and induction based upon a set of clues. Logic-related systems are useful for well-defined problems. An example of a search-based system is IBM's Deep Blue chess computer, which uses enormous processing power to examine all possible moves and chooses the best one. Search-based systems are good for problems where there are a limited number of possible answers. Generalization AI uses approaches such as neural networks and clustering to draw conclusions from incomplete data and respond appropriately to new situations. AI can also be used for rules-based analytics, segmentation and personalization, topics covered later in this section.

Real-time software is highly complex enterprise software based on mathematical modelling. Many of these products do not require large investments to deploy; instead they make existing IT networks run more efficiently. Real-time software works on the same basis as a spreadsheet; if data in one cell is updated, the values in all linked cells are instantly recalculated. If deployed on an enterprise-wide scale, this means that any new information (such as a new order) percolates instantly through the company's IT systems and that of its partners. Building integrated systems to do this is expensive, as interfaces between applications have to be specially coded. One solution to the problem of data integration is an 'information bus' where all relevant systems publish key information in an open format such as XML to defined electronic addresses. Other systems can subscribe to these fields and be updated automatically.

The benefits of real-time software implementations include more effective management insight into the state of the business, supply chain optimization and better customer service. GE calculated that its real-time efforts saved it $1.6 billion in 2001 [70]. For pharmaceutical companies that often have a diversity of management information, accounting and sales force management systems spread across the world, real-time software offers the opportunity to consider linking operations with minimal disruption. Real-time software also opens the way for true build-to-order and stock-to-order systems. Manufacturers could theoretically discern the product needs of pharmacies, hospitals or even individual consumers instantaneously, as their requests are passed instantly up the value chain. Some commentators believe that this could ultimately lead to 'batches of one' for individual consumers, a concept discussed in Chapter 6.

P2P (peer to peer) applications permit the structured exchange of data through a variety of systems. There are three main classes of P2P; file-sharing, collaboration and distributed computing. File-sharing applications, such as music and video file-swapping services, link users' storage capacity in a controlled manner. P2P collaboration systems share functionality across systems. An example of this is instant messaging that allows real-time communication across a diversity of systems. GlaxoSmithKline uses the Groove P2P solution to link its scientists with researchers at biotechnology companies and universities across the world (it has purchased 10,000 licences), allowing them to share the same virtual workspace and edit the same documents without using a company server. Distributed computing technology harnesses the unused processing cycles of networked PCs and applies them to solving large, computationally intensive problems, including sequence analysis and fragment assembly, target identification, biological modelling and virtual compound screening. The average corporate PC sits idle more than 90 per cent of the time, even while running common software applications. Several thousand desktop PCs networked together should theoretically give supercomputer power. The most famous example of distributed computing is the SETI (search for extra terrestrial intelligence) project, a screensaver application that is activated when a participating computer is idle, and allows it to analyse packets of data from the Arecibo radio telescope in Puerto Rico. The idea is to use the vast global computing power of thousands of connected machines to look for repetitive signals that might be a sign of extraterrestrial life. The best-known medical application of distributed computing is the FightAIDS@home joint venture between Entropia and the Scripps Research Institute, which uses unused PC processor power in the same way as the SETI project to model the evolution of drug resistance and design anti-HIV drugs. Interestingly, Entropia reserves the right to 'occasionally' run commercial tasks on PCs that are added to the FightAIDS@home grid.

The pharmaceutical industry is an ideal user of distributed computing, providing performance and security concerns can be met. Entropia, has pilot installations of its technology at Bristol-Myers Squibb and Novartis. The pilots are designed to test the computing power, scalability, manageability and return on investment of distributed computing technology and demonstrate how an existing network of PCs can be transformed into a high-performance computing engine to accelerate drug discovery.

Digital R&D technologies

Bioinformatics

Digital technologies can streamline the processes and reduce the costs of drug development. Grouped under the umbrella term of 'bioinformatics', these technologies all involve the use of computers to store, organize, generate, retrieve, analyse and share genomic, biological and chemical data for drug discovery. And their usage is spawning an entirely new branch of IT.

Although pharmaceutical companies do not provide precise data on their investments in research and development informatics, the amounts are substantial. In 2001, Merck announced it was paying $620 million to acquire Rosetta Inpharmatics, a genomics and technology informatics company. In 2001, Pfizer announced it had spent more than $100 million to create an 'integrated system of high-speed discovery technologies'. Pradip Banderjee, a senior partner with Accenture, a technology consulting company, estimated that, in 2001, the pharmaceutical industry spent more than $4 billion on bioinformatics, excluding hardware costs [31]. Bioinformatics offers the only viable approach for drug companies to deal with the gigabytes of data they produce and receive every day. PhRMA Association (the Pharmaceutical Research and Manufacturers of America) predicts that, by 2003, scientists will have discovered more than 10,000 potential targets for drug development, resulting in what some call 'target glut'. And that number will only get larger thanks to the 30,000 genes and an exponentially greater number of proteins being identified and analysed.

Drug companies also employ a variety of 'cheminformatics' software; tools that can predict the activity of a particular compound by studying its molecular structure. For instance, scientists can use molecular modelling software (tools that rely on interactive 3-D visualization or mathematical algorithms) to discover and design safe and effective compounds. Chemical databases allow researchers to store and retrieve compounds and related data. Robotics makes it possible for chemists to readily synthesize hundreds of thousands of chemical compound variations from a library of simpler molecules. High-throughput screening technology allows researchers to screen thousands of compounds at once, rather than just 10 or 20. Technology may help at the drug testing stage too. Virtual patient software can simulate patient physiology, targets and therapies in order to predict experimental outcomes before companies commit major resources to laboratory research and clinical trials [31].

Biocomputing and nanotechnology

Over the past years, there has been much media coverage of two related and potentially breakthrough technologies: biocomputing (also known as DNA computing) and nanotechnology. Biocomputing is the use of DNA to solve complex computational problems. It is not surprising that DNA is an ideal system for solving certain types of problem, as it has evolved over millennia to become a hugely powerful system for storing and 'playing' genetic information. Biocomputing first came to prominence in 1994, when Leonard Adleman used a recombinant DNA system to solve the 'travelling salesman' problem. The potential advantages of biocomputing over conventional electronic computing are huge: DNA can store data at billions of times the density of conventional electronic media, and can perform billions of calculations in parallel in a very small physical space with minimal energy input. However, many fundamental problems remain before a versatile biocomputing architecture is developed, and biocomputing is unlikely to have wide commercial application in the foreseeable future.

Biocomputing can also be thought of as a sub-discipline of nanotechnology, the manipulation of single atoms or molecules with great precision by tiny machines. As well as hugely powerful computers, nanotechnology raises the prospect of self-replicating machines that can do anything from synthesize organic material to clean polluted land to destroy cancers in the body. Despite its undoubted potential, most believe that powerful nanotechnology applications will not be available for a number of decades.

Data warehouses and data mining

Data warehouses are large databases accessible throughout an organization. Their purpose is to allow users to manage, share and analyse large volumes of data. Data warehousing technology is extensively used across the pharmaceutical and biotechnology sectors, particularly in the early discovery stages of the drug development process and in clinical trials [62]. For example, laboratory information management systems (LIMS) are dependent on good data warehousing. LIMS are used for a number of 'book-keeping' and knowledge-sharing tasks, such as tracking DNA samples as they are sequenced, stored and analysed by scores of different scientists. Other processes that rely on data warehouses include bioinformatics, pharmacokinetics and clinical trial data management. Companies are adopting a strategy of deploying more warehouses rather than adding new users and functions to existing warehouses. This means that the average number of new users for each warehouse is static at around 300 users and that scalability is not a major challenge. The evolution of different warehousing architectures at various points in the discovery pipeline may limit the degree of functional integration that is possible or indeed desirable across the drug discovery process [62].

Data mining is the extraction of implicit, previously unknown and potentially useful information from data, by elucidating patterns and trends from complex data. Data mining is commonly used in data-intensive industries such as consumer product marketing, financial services and travel. For example, Harrah's Entertainment, the world's second largest casino operator, has collected detailed behavioural data on members of its club programme since 1997, and can now accurately predict how profitable a customer will be after only one or two visits [70]. The application of data mining in life sciences and healthcare has up until now been limited. However, it is increasingly used in e-R&D applications to interpret high-throughput screening data. Data mining for e-R&D should not be confused with bioinformatics, which is more typically focused on sequence analysis and pattern matching [207]. In a 2001 survey, about two-thirds of pharmaceutical respondents highlighted problems with aggregating and then applying data to meaningful business problems. Far fewer healthcare providers and insurers, who deal mainly with financial and transactional data, reported problems in these areas [79].

Supply chain and marketing technologies

ERP and CRM

Enterprise resource planning (ERP) software is sophisticated cross-company or cross-enterprise software designed to link different functions (such as manufacturing, finance, distribution and human resources). This is achieved by setting up a central database or tightly integrating existing databases. The aim of ERP is to improve efficiency and permit management to better monitor, control and plan all activities. Most major pharmaceutical companies have spent large amounts on implementing ERP since the early 1990s. Major ERP providers include SAP, Oracle and PeopleSoft and a huge management consulting and technology integration industry has developed around the installation of ERP.

While ERP focuses mainly on the 'back-end' activities of a company, CRM systems are designed to enable pharmaceutical companies to extract maximum ROI from investments in sales and marketing. CRM systems aim to integrate various channels such as SFA, CSCs, e-detailing and promotional activities, thereby providing more efficient service and permitting better customer analysis. CRM solutions are being used to manage all customer touch points, whether at the level of the patient, physician, pharmacist, insurer or payer or via the web, telephone, email or direct sales force contact. CRM data is being warehoused and analysed for more focused marketing. Most CRM initiatives are based initially on improvements to the SFA system in order to make the sales force more effective.

Analytics

Prescription pharmaceutical sales and marketing, as compared with industries such as consumer goods, is not highly data intensive. The main reason for this is that, to date, most of the sales and marketing activities of a pharmaceutical company have not been 'transactional', in the sense that the actual distribution and sales (with exceptions in areas such as specialized products and medical devices) are handled by wholesalers, pharmacists and healthcare providers. Also pharmaceuticals have traditionally been a fairly low-volume, high-margin industry where the end-user (the patient or consumer) or payer is often not the target customer (this is usually the prescribing physician). Pharmaceutical marketing is, on the other hand, very 'relationship intensive'. It is based on close contact between sales representatives and physicians and between the company and biomedical researchers and medical opinion-leaders. These factors have strongly influenced the approach of pharmaceutical companies to analytics – the development of powerful new ways to evaluate customer behaviour and more effectively target their sales messages to the right customer at the right time.

As profit margins come under increasing pressure and companies face a relative drought in new product development, and as new channels such as the Internet challenge older marketing paradigms, the industry is seeking new ways to extract the maximum value from every customer interaction. In this context, we see a growing interest in analytics as a source of competitive advantage, particularly as CRM systems and the web make new forms of customer data available. The Internet offers a real-time laboratory for analytics; for example, customer behaviour on a company website can be examined almost immediately and small modifications tested and compared. Similarly,

SFA data can be transferred, warehoused and automatically analysed using web tools. The benefits of analytical marketing approach include:

- The ability to measure quickly the impact of marketing activities and calculate ROI.
- The opportunity to balance and allocate resources better between various marketing channels.
- The opportunity to link user experience more tightly to the available offerings.

All analytic processes require the meticulous cleaning of data and its preparation. Internally generated data, be it from the sales force or customer Internet interactions, is usually far cheaper than buying in external data (which is often not fine-grained enough for good analytics). In the case of web analytics, data preparation involves the cleaning and delimitation of web logs, ascertaining the relevant fields and linkage with other data sources. Analytics is an iterative process, where results have to be tested against real experience in the market.

It is important to differentiate between strategic intelligence approaches (such as market and competitive intelligence gathering) and analytics. Strategic or business intelligence activities tend to be sporadic, often driven by a specific challenge, whereas analytics is a continuous process using data mining and sophisticated tools such as decision trees and clustering, and increasingly tends to be automated. Analytics permits marketers to test segmentation and see if online behaviour supports pre-existing segmentation models. Similarly, marketers may be able more rapidly to spot opportunities for reaching certain segments and be in a better position to predict customer needs and hence the 'payoff' of a certain intervention.

The barriers to introducing a strong analytics approach in pharmaceutical marketing are manifold and include the often poor communication between line marketing and market research and e-business departments. The industry is also at an early stage when it comes to the development of analytic tools specifically designed for the highly qualitative, personal selling context of pharmaceuticals and is hampered by the relative paucity of dynamic, real-time, quantitative data that feeds analytics in other industries.

Personalization

Terms such as personalization, targeting and tailoring describe a series of increasingly sophisticated offerings for the online visitor (Table 12.4). The design of these offerings, their delivery and the analysis of the results of

TABLE 12.4

Working definitions of online marketing actions

Personalization	Changing web pages and web offerings based on online visitor behaviour
Targeting	Selection of content and interactive tools for specific groups
Tailoring	Rewriting information with a specific marketing message
Source: [208]	

an e-marketing campaign require forms of customer segmentation, however rudimentary.

Personalization and customization are both ways of adapting marketing content to the needs and interests of individuals in the hope that a website will become 'sticky' (it will be used often and for longer periods and the user will respond positively to various calls to action). Customization generally requires that users manually set a series of preferences. Websites are personalized by analysing online behaviour (for example what content a user accesses or searches for). The user's profile is inferred from this data, and the site is specifically tailored; but personalization is an inexact science and few sites implement it very well.

Several types of customer data can be captured from web users including data supplied by the user's browser (IP address, referring site), click-stream data (pages viewed and for how long, what is being searched for), data from cookies (that allow the identification of repeat visitors) and transaction or registration data supplied directly by the user.

There are four main methods of analysing this data in order to group users and tailor website content [209]:

1. *Clustering*. This statistical technique targets groups of people who behave in similar ways. Click-stream data on how users navigate around a site is used to categorize them into narrow groups. Depending on which groups they fall into, users are then steered towards specific content or merchandise.

2. *Profiling systems or rules-based personalization*. Individual users are analysed and grouped depending on specific, flagged areas of the website they access and the keywords they search for. Generally, only certain key areas of the site are flagged and monitored, such as search bars and certain links. If someone is searching for reviews of organic food shops and

gardening supplies, this indicates an interest in a 'green' lifestyle, and the user is guided in the direction of related content. Or if the user is linked from a site in Brazil, they can be offered the opportunity to view the site in Portuguese.

3. *Collaborative filtering*. Algorithms compare data from users with similar tastes and guide them to merchandise and content previously chosen by members of this segment. The most famous example is Amazon.com's recommendation service. Because these algorithms are comparison based, the more people who use the engine, the smarter it gets. But recommendations can become inappropriate when people use it only occasionally or are buying for people whose interests differ from their own. This technique works fairly well in narrow markets with well-defined personal tastes (such as books and CDs), but its usefulness in other situations is questionable.
4. *Artificial intelligence* (natural language processing, expert systems, neural networks). This is the most sophisticated type of personalization technology. AI systems learn from users' behaviour. They typically require minimal human intervention (in this respect, collaborative filtering is a type of AI). Many AI solutions were originally intended for credit card fraud detection or industrial process control. AI solutions have great potential in the area of customer care, such as the intelligent routing of email queries from users.

A range of sophisticated tools, such as web application servers, provides fairly robust and standardized systems for personalized marketing using the Internet. Marketers without an IT background can manage many of the newer applications.

Conclusions – 'the take home messages'

The application of newer digital technologies across the pharmaceutical value chain is indeed fairly patchy. R&D remains the main focus for innovation, especially when it comes to the management of the huge volumes of data generated by advances in areas such as genomics, proteomics and drug screening. The 'e-health revolution' has failed to deliver much of its promise in terms of either physician communication or consumer empowerment, and many managers remain sceptical as to the importance of the Internet in pharmaceutical sales and marketing. The intensely personal relationship between sales representatives and physicians seems impossible to emulate using the web or other communication channels and CRM systems are seen as a support tool, rather than a core marketing competency. On the other hand, we have ample evidence that digital technologies are indeed becoming pervasive, especially in the pharmaceutical supply chain and the reimbursement and insurance transaction. We have already reviewed the implications of technologies such as e-prescribing and mobile devices for pharmaceutical marketing and especially the new challenges in terms of promoting products through these new channels. The Internet offers exciting and potentially profitable opportunities to better identify and reach smaller customer groups, and this will become vital as segmented medicine, be it on the basis of pharmacogenomics or economics, becomes a reality.

Pharmaceutical companies will have to transform in terms of both organizational architecture and the skills required to best 'leverage' the opportunities provided by digital technologies.

- The barriers between various departments and groups will have to be broken down to ensure the better management, analysis and practical application of the data. In R&D, the data generated at each stage of the drug development process will need to be pooled and analysed. In sales and marketing, customer data will be generated from many channels (including the web and integrating SFA and CSCs); integrating this data is a vital task.

- Digital technologies offer the opportunity for more experimentation and consequent innovation, often for minimal investment, in pharmaceutical marketing. The development of standardized, rules-based marketing approaches and the commitment to intensive experimentation have been lacking in pharmaceuticals, where margin pressure has not, until recently, been a major issue.

PART VII

The Future

CHAPTER

13 The future of pharmaceutical digital strategy

Throughout our exploration of the interface between digital technologies and the pharmaceutical industry, we have attempted to adopt a very practical approach, sympathetic to the exigencies and constraints faced by strategists and line managers in their daily work. Wild swings of sentiment, which accompanied the Internet boom, bust and hopefully renaissance, have certainly characterized the short history of e-pharmaceuticals. In less than four years, we have seen almost a generation shift, as the first group of e-business leaders in most of the global pharmaceutical giants have moved on to new positions and many e-business units have been closed or folded into existing IT and marketing departments.

We wish, however, to share our confidence in the future success of 'e-pharma', based on the external drivers of digital technology uptake in the healthcare sector, the changes in the pharmaceutical business environment and the attributes of digital technology vital across the pharmaceutical value chain. Effective use of digital technologies is already critical for success in today's information-rich R&D environment. And we are certainly not alone in our belief that the Internet will move into mainstream pharmaceutical operations, especially in sales and marketing. While websites, CSCs, e-detailing and e-disease management will indeed become more important, it is impossible to predict the extent of their roles in pharmaceuticals in the near future. Pharmaceutical executives, cognisant of the limitations of the sales representative and current promotion options, are certainly open to considering innovative channels, especially for marketing to physicians (see Figure 9.1).

It is worth recapping those aspects of digital technology that make it a priority for consideration across the pharmaceutical value chain. The Internet is characterized by the immediacy, transparency and intensity of interactions. For a pharmaceutical company used to arms-length contact, especially with consumers, the Internet challenges all aspects of the management of customer relationships. Similarly, the speed with which news, both bad and good, flows via digital media has resulted in unprecedented scrutiny of the industry, at a scientific, business and even ethical level. At the same time, the demands of modern R&D require companies to segment both their products and their customers by successfully interpreting the vast amount of data produced by genomic, pharmacogenomic and market analysis. Thus we are faced with an unprecedented complexity and intensity of customer contact, which will continue and probably increase, for the foreseeable future. On their own, perhaps, digital technologies probably will not dramatically transform the global pharmaceutical industry; however, when we begin to factor in a range of 'environmental' transitions, the situation becomes somewhat more complex. Faced with uncertainty in R&D and marketing in terms of poor development pipelines and price control pressures and unsympathetic financial markets, pharmaceutical companies are forced to use digital technologies to sell more products and reduce the cost of sales.

- Digital technologies offer the only practical approach for selling products cost effectively to smaller customer segments. It will not be possible to develop service offerings, focus development and bundle products and services for smaller patient groups without the Internet.
- Only by combining genomic and digital technologies can companies better understand and predict the relationship between product use and medical outcomes (or pharmaco-economic outcomes) within patient groups. This level of understanding is vital to be able to price medicines or services at a level that is both profitable and acceptable to ever-more demanding payers.
- The Internet allows companies to promote a dialogue between themselves, physicians, patients, payers and providers. Pharmaceutical companies can actively shape and partner in a range of e-health initiatives to establish their place in future models of health service delivery.
- The Internet provides an opportunity to revisit the deployment of disease management as a marketing tool and use CRM at a consumer level.
- As the debate around drug pricing and access intensifies, pharmaceutical companies will have to actively manage their relationships with governments, payers, insurers and advocacy groups. Much of the communication will take place using the Internet.

The health information chain

Digital technologies have already inexorably transformed all aspects of the flow of health information. Pharmaceutical IT departments have been forced to move from their traditional focus on hardware and software procurement, distribution and maintenance to the management of information. We believe that the time has come for pharmaceutical managers to consider seriously the chain of health information and its application in daily business. The Internet permits a transparent link between drug discovery and pharmaceutical sales. A product consists not only of the active ingredient, but all the information, both scientific and branding, that has been 'attributed' to that particular drug over years of development. We have already discussed some of the strategic aspects of leveraging product information, but wish to re-emphasize the fact that despite the travails of the dotcom portal model, the health information chain (especially concerning consumers) is the key component of a range of digital communication channels that will become more important for pharmaceutical marketing. As pharmaceutical e-business matures, it is appropriate to seek cross-industry best practices. We believe that the health information chain should be an area of priority focus, especially to ensure a transparent, traceable chain of health product information for consumers.

Closing comment – the challenge of digital organizations

Digital technologies will undoubtedly be, in concert with financial pressures, a catalyst for organizational transformation in the global pharmaceutical giants. Interaction with customers, be they physicians or consumers, in real time and at a small group or individual level, demands skills in areas such as CRM and analytics that have not previously been regarded as important for career success in pharmaceuticals. Similarly, the forces that we have discussed will break down the artificial, and often 'political', barriers between the various functions across the pharmaceutical value chain. The importance of rigorous measurement, data management and evaluation, facilitated by digital technologies, is slowly being realized and we can expect a new generation of pharmaceutical marketers, oriented towards experimentation and innovation, to come to the fore. The digital technology debate has already largely moved from justifying investment (why should we spend anything on the e-channel?) to assessing return on investment (how do we extract the maximum value from a range of interventions?). The modest goal of integrating digital technology into the pharmaceutical value chain is well on the road to attainment; the next step is realizing the full potential of digital strategies.

References

1. Andersen & INSEAD, *The future of customer value and customer focus in the pharmaceutical industry*. 2002.
2. Red Herring, *Healthcare and the net*. Red Herring, 2000. October.
3. The National Institute for Health Care Management Research and Educational Foundation, *Pharmaceutical drug expenditures in 2000: the upward trend continues*. 2000.
4. IMS Health, *IMS method of payment report*. 2000.
5. L. Greenemeier, The internet as antidote. 2001, *Information Week*. 17/9/2001.
6. M. Adams, Forecast 2001: An E-healthcare Odyssey. *Pharmaceutical Executive*, 2000. December: pp. 12–20.
7. INSEAD & Cap Gemini Ernst & Young, *Vision & Reality: The quantum shuffle – the impact of e on the pharmaceutical and medical device industries*. 2001.
8. Gartner, 2001.
9. Economist Intelligence Unit, *Genentech reaps major benefit from innovation*. Management & Finance Research Report, 2000.
10. Anonymous, GSK shows the cost of IT mergers. *Computing*, 2001. June.
11. S. Konicki, Prescription for Change: IT. 2000, *Information Week*. pp. 129–38.
12. D. Pilling, Astrazeneca to farm out IT, *Financial Times*. 26/10/2000.
13. PR Newswire, *Merck & Co., Inc. Announces Plan to Invest Up to $100 Million in Capital in Emerging Businesses*. 1999, www.prnewswire.com.
14. M. Casey, Merck Maintains its Sterling Image. 2001, *Medical Industry Today*.
15. Business Wire, *E-Lilly Targets Strategic Investment Op fund; E-Lilly Funds E-business Ventures*. 2001, last accessed 18/1/2001, www.businesswire.com.
16. ePharm 5, The top medical practice stories in 2001 from ePharmaceuticals (TM), *ePharm 5*. 24/12/2001.
17. Institute of Medicine, *Crossing the quality chasm: a new health system for the 21st century*. 2001, Washington DC: National Academy Press.
18. F. Charatan, DrKoop.com criticised for mixing information with advertising. *British Medical Journal*, 1999. **319**: p. 727.

19. D.S. Bakhle, *The E-pharma Expedition*. 2000, last accessed 6/6/2000, www.pharmabiz.com.
20. IDC Executive Insight, *The convergence of biology and IT: market impacts of the bioscience era*. 2001, IDC.
21. Advest, *The pharmaceutical outsourcing industry*. 2001.
22. G. Harris, New script: drug firms, stymied in the lab, become marketing machines, *Wall Street Journal*. 7/6/2000.
23. PhRMA, *Pharmaceutical Research and Manufacturers Association Annual Survey*. 2000.
24. The National Institute for Healthcare Management, *Changing patterns of pharmaceutical innovation*. 2002.
25. eyeforpharma, *IBM and MDS Proteomics form alliance to speed drug development*. 2001, last accessed 30/1/2001, www.eyeforpharma.com.
26. P. Sherrid, *Bytes and bits meet biotech*. 2001, www.usnews.com.
27. IBM, *IBM unveils $100 million research initiative to build world's fastest supercomputer*. 1999, www.ibm.com.
28. S. Stewart, Putting the tech in biotech. 2001, *Industry Standard*. 26/3/2001.
29. M.M. Jones, Report says biochip market poised to reach $3.3b by 2004, *Genomeweb*. 10/4/2001.
30. J. Hibbard, Research Gains from IT Boom. 1998, *Information Week*. 14/9/1998. pp. 217–24.
31. S. Overby, Drug Companies on Speed. 2001, *CIO Magazine*. 15/10/2001.
32. Boston Consulting Group, *A revolution in R&D: how genomics and genetics are transforming the biopharmaceutical industry*. 2001.
33. R. Edmunds, Splicing a cost squeeze into the genomics revolution. *McKinsey Quarterly*, 2001. **2**: pp. 15–18.
34. Boston Consulting Group, *A revolution in R&D: the impact of genomics*. 2001.
35. D. Champion, Mastering the value chain – an interview with Mark Levin of Millennium Pharmaceuticals. *Harvard Business Review*, 2001. **79**(6): pp. 108–15.
36. D. Firn, Suitable cases for treatment, *Financial Times*. 12/7/2001.
37. Dow Jones News Service, Astrazeneca pays Orchid Bio for gene analysis, *Dow Jones News Service*. 29/6/2001.
38. G. Anand, Big drug companies try to delay 'personalised' medicine regimes, *Wall Street Journal*. 18/6/2001.
39. G. Naik, Rx4U: More drug firms are trying to get personal, *Wall Street Journal*. 25/3/2002.
40. L.M. Krieger, *Genetic testing leaps ahead of social implications*. 2001, last accessed 6/3/2001, www.siliconvalley.com.
41. M. Herper, Britain's big biotech bang. 2001, *Forbes*. 31/7/2001.
42. Genaissance Pharmaceuticals, *Press release*. 2001, last accessed 1/8/2001, www.genaissancepharmaceuticals.com.
43. V. Fuhrmans, DNA tests for drug responses planned, *Wall Street Journal*. 25/7/2001.
44. K. Lindpaintner, The impact of pharmacogenetics and pharmacogenomics on drug discovery. *Nature Reviews: Drug Discovery*, 2002. **1**: pp. 463–9.

45. M. Bhandari, A genetic revolution in health care. *McKinsey Quarterly*, 1999. **4**: pp. 58–67.
46. J. Enriquez and R.A. Goldberg, Transforming life, transforming business: the life-science revolution. 2000, *Harvard Business Review*. March–April. pp. 95–104.
47. The Motley Fool, *Motley Fool research guide to biotech investing*. 2000.
48. C.D. Hardison et al., Clinical Trials: Where Patient Care and Clinical Research Meet. *Clinical Trial Advances*, 2001.
49. L. Roner, *Survey reveals EDC use on the rise for clinical trials across the globe*. 2001, last accessed 20/9/2001, www.eyeforpharma.com.
50. Forrester Research, *Web clinical trials break through*. 2001.
51. Datamonitor, *Clinical trials: exploring wireless opportunities*. 2001.
52. P. Bleicher et al., Pharma–Physician E-hubs. *Pharmaceutical Executive*, 2000. **20**(10): pp. 86–96.
53. CDISC, *Top biopharmaceutical and technology companies unite to develop standards for clinical trial data*. 2002, last accessed 26/6/2002, www.cdisc.org.
54. ePharm 5, NIH employing web-enabled service to speed up Hepatitis C study, *ePharm 5*. 10/6/2002.
55. eyeforpharma, *CenterWatch launches wireless PDA access to clinical trials information*. 2001, last accessed 18/4/2001, www.eyeforpharma.com.
56. ePharm 5, Pharmco taps PDA diary firm for phase IV diabetes clinical trial, *ePharm 5*. 17/6/2002.
57. ePharm 5, Wearable monitor firm poised to fine-tune drug development, *ePharm 5*. 24/4/2002.
58. eyeforpharma, *Lilly selects Phase Forward as global platform for Web-based clinical trials*. 2001, last accessed 31/5/2001, www.eyeforpharma.com.
59. eyeforpharma, *DataLabs teams up with Microsoft*. 2001, last accessed 18/9/2001, www.eyeforpharma.com.
60. D. Rennie and H.S. Luft, Pharmacoeconomic analysis – making them transparent, making them credible. *Journal of the American Medical Association*, 2000. **283**(16): pp. 2158–60.
61. B. Hanley et al., Involving consumers in designing, conducting and interpreting randomised controlled trials: questionnaire survey. *British Medical Journal*, 2001. **322**: pp. 519–23.
62. eyeforpharma, *Silico Research finds prevelant use of warehousing in R&D*. 2001, last accessed 1/3/2001, www.eyeforpharma.com.
63. D. Scheraga, LIMS revolutionize operations throughout chemicals and pharmaceuticals. *Chemical Market Reporter*, 1999. **256**(4): p. 17.
64. R. Burcham, New pharma business model: Can you survive it? *Pharmaceutical Executive*, 2000. **11**(November): pp. 94–100.
65. K.G. Rivette and D. Kline, Discovering new value in intellectual property. *Harvard Business Review*, 2000. January–February.
66. NPS Pharmaceuticals, *Increasing competitive advantage in the pharmaceutical industry through strategic intellectual asset management*. 2000.
67. L.S. Tillett, Medical companies track e-learning, *Internet Week*. 20/8/2001.

68. D. Brown, Glaxo rolls out P2P solution. 2001, *Computer Weekly*. 12/4/2001.
69. eyeforpharma, *Eli Lilly deploys Plumtree Corporate Portal for employees*. 2001, last accessed 11/6/2001, www.eyeforpharma.com.
70. The Economist, How about you? A survey of the real-time economy. 2002, *The Economist*. 2/2/2002.
71. G. Dyer, GSK considers spinning off its research units, *Financial Times*. 24/1/2002.
72. A. Michaels and D. Pilling, Pfizer reorganises for $4.5 billion R&D push, *Financial Times*. 20/11/2000.
73. Deloitte & Touche, *A new edge for pharma: the ebusiness guide to managing innovation, risk and speed*. 2001.
74. M. Aitken et al., A license to cure. *McKinsey Quarterly*, 2000. **1**: pp. 80–9.
75. G. Hughes and M. O'Neill, The worldwide CRO scene in 2001. *European Pharmaceutical Contractor*, 2001. February: pp. 26–37.
76. PricewaterhouseCoopers, *High performing strategic alliances*. 2000.
77. T. Finn and D. McCamey, P&G's guide to successful partnerships. *Pharmaceutical Executive*, 2002. January.
78. T. Clarke, Biotech firms gain power at big pharma's expense, *Reuters News Service*. 28/6/2001.
79. Forrester Research, *Pharma's marketing collaboration opportunities*. 2001.
80. P. Kager and M. Mozeson, Supply chain: The forgotten factor. *Pharmaceutical Executive*, 2000. **6**(20): pp. 84–96.
81. Forrester Research, *The pharma apps prescription*. 2001.
82. Forrester Research, *Europe's eHealth cure: connectivity*. 2001.
83. Medical Broadcasting Company, *Online exchanges*. 2001.
84. Biopharmaweb, *ARC sees batch systems market to exceed $3 billion by 2005*. 2001, last accessed 10/4/2001, www.biopharmaweb.com.
85. Anonymous, Survival keys for manufacturing companies. 1998, *CMA Magazine*. p. 33.
86. ePharm 5, The top pharma/products and brands stories in 2001 from ePharmaceuticals (TM), *ePharm 5*. 27/12/2001.
87. eyeforpharma, *GlaxoSmithKline's procurement process: an e-success story in the making*. 2001, last accessed 24/5/2001, www.eyeforpharma.com.
88. P. DeJohn, Five Major Vendors Join E-commerce Ranks. *Hospital Materials Management*, 2000. **25**(5): pp. 2–10.
89. M. Casey, Drug wholesalers give GPOs a dose of competition, *Medical Industry Today*. 17/2/2000.
90. ePharm 5, Amerinet joins group pushing for healthcare commerce standards, *ePharm 5*. 9/4/2002.
91. J. Dalton, Device, med-surg manufacturers should prepare for 'heavy lifting'. *Health Industry Today*, 2000. **63**(10): pp. 1–18.
92. Cap Gemini Ernst & Young, *Death of a pharmaceutical salesperson?* 2000.
93. Andersen, *The value of eCommerce in the healthcare supply chain*. 2001.
94. Clarkston Group, *The value of wireless applications in the pharmaceutical industry*. 2001.

95. Forrester Research, *Pharma's detailing overhaul*. 2001.
96. Cap Gemini Ernst & Young & INSEAD, *Vision & reality 2002: Cracking the code – unlocking new value in customer relationships*. 2002.
97. R. Vanderveer, Pharmaceutical marketing is going to be very different, and very soon. *Medical Marketing & Media*, 2001. **36**: pp. 88–98.
98. D.W. Glascoff, Articles of Interest; The Internet and Pharmaceuticals. *Marketing Health Services*, 2000: p. 37.
99. Jupiter Media Metrix, *Pharmaceutical marketing online*. 2000.
100. eyeforpharma, *Physicians and the Internet: What pharma needs to know*. 2001, last accessed 23/8/2001, www.eyeforpharma.com.
101. J.K. Brody, Defining the benefits of online medical market research. *Marketing Health Services*, 2001. **21**(1): pp. 31–4.
102. ePharm 5, Aventis officially launches mydoconline.com, *ePharm 5*. 13/8/2001.
103. A. Evenhaim, Taking e-health relationship management into the next millennium. *Medical Marketing & Media*, 2001. **36**: pp. 104–12.
104. M.D. Coffee, Hedging your bets. *Pharmaceutical Executive*, 2001. Digital Pharma supplement: pp. 30–1.
105. Baxter Healthcare Corporation, *Baxter Healthcare Corporation Launches Three New Internet-Based Continuing Education Programs on Nutritional Therapies for Nurses and Pharmacists*. 2000, last accessed 4/12/2000, www.baxter.com.
106. E.P. Beyzarov, Growth hormone approved for rare genetic disorder. *Drug Topics*, 2000. July.
107. F. Hasnain, *Case Study: Glaxo Wellcome's lessons learnt in e-sales and marketing*. 2000, www.eyeforpharma.com.
108. ePharm 5, Study: more physicians using PDAs, participating in e-marketing, *ePharm 5*. 17/1/2002.
109. NUA Internet Surveys, *Jupiter Media Metrix: CRM spending growing in US*. 2002, last accessed 6/3/2002, www.nua.com.
110. Cap Gemini Ernst & Young, *Perspectives on life sciences*. 2001.
111. Cap Gemini Ernst & Young, *Patient relationship management*. 2001.
112. Medical Broadcasting Company, *e-CRM*. 2001.
113. Forrester Research, *Pharma Must Bridge The Sales And Marketing Chasm*. 2001.
114. Institute of Medicine, *To err is human: building a safer health system*. 2000, Washington DC: National Academy Press.
115. ePharm 5, U.S. says many web users of all incomes seek health info online, *ePharm 5*. 7/2/2002.
116. X. Chen and L. Siu, Impact of the media and the internet on oncology: survey of cancer patients and oncologists in Canada. *Journal of Clinical Oncology*, 2001. **19**(23): pp. 4291–7.
117. L. Lerer and N. Rowell, *On the e-health consumer*. INSEAD Working paper, 2000.
118. S. Shalo and J. Breitstein, Prevention: today's DTC arms critics. *Pharmaceutical Executive*, 2001. May: pp. 92–3.
119. P. Jenkins, Huntingdon debt transferred to secret backer, *Financial Times*. 9/1/2002.

120. D. Pilling, Victory for S Africa as drugs industry dons fig leaf, *Financial Times*. 18/4/2001.
121. M. Elliot, Global agenda: embracing the enemy is good for business. 2001, *Time*. 10/8/2001.
122. M. Aitken and F. Holt, A prescription for direct drug marketing. *McKinsey Quarterly*, 2000. **2**: pp. 82–91.
123. ePharm 5, Mistranslation muddies European DTC drug information proposal, *ePharm 5*. 30/1/2002.
124. The Economist, Pill pushers. 2001, *The Economist*. 19/4/2001.
125. M. Rosenthal et al., Promotion of prescription drugs to consumers. *New England Journal of Medicine*, 2002. **346**(7): pp. 498–595; Competitive Media Reporting.
126. DTC Marketer, 2001: DTC spending up. *DTC Marketer*, 2002. **5**(2).
127. S.J. Landers, Studies showing pharmaceutical ads piquing patients interest. 2001, *American Medical News*. 24/12/2001.
128. Forrester Research, *Pharma's DTC reorganization*. 2001.
129. S. Pfeifer, EC clears way for new drug ads, *Sunday Business*. 15/7/2001.
130. S. Skidmore, Consumer desire drives drug costs, *Florida Times Union*. 17/7/2001.
131. D. West, Direct to cancer medicine gets direct to patient campaign. *Pharmaceutical Executive*, 2000. **20**(4): pp. 138–42.
132. ePharm 5, Roche and GSK sponsor non-US osteoporosis information service, *ePharm 5*. 6/3/2002.
133. V. Griffith, Majority of Prozac users switch to generics, *Financial Times*. 21/8/2001.
134. T. Blackett and R. Robins, *Brand medicine – the role of brands in the pharmaceutical industry*. 2001, Basingstoke: Palgrave Macmillan and Interbrand Healthcare.
135. Cyber Dialogue, *Pharmaceutical e-Marketing Initiatives are Cost-effective Drivers of Direct-to-consumer Brand Conversion, Compliance and ROI*. 2001, last accessed 7/2/2001, www.businesswire.com.
136. G.L. Johnson and A. Ramaprasad, Patient–Physician Relationships in the Information Age. *Marketing Health Services*, 2000: p. 21.
137. J. Denlinger, The link between internet strategy and product lifecycle. *Product Management Today*, 2000. August: pp. 55–60.
138. K.A. Dyer, Ethical challenges of medicine and health on the internet: a review. *Journal of Medical Internet Research*, 2001. **3**(2): p. 23.
139. Health On the Net Foundation. 2002, last accessed 26/6/2002, www.hon.ch.
140. N. Terry, Regulating health information: a US perspective. *British Medical Journal*, 2002. **324**: pp. 602–5.
141. F. Meric et al., Breast cancer on the world wide web: cross sectional survey of quality of information and popularity of websites. *British Medical Journal*, 2002. **324**: pp. 577–81.
142. M.D. Slater and D.E. Zimmerman, Characteristics of health-related web sites identified by common internet portals. *JAMA*, 2002. **288**(3).
143. ePharm 5, Biogen offers MS treatment info., e-detailing on Salu neurohub, *ePharm 5*. 14/1/2002.

144. J. Dalton, Med-surg companies struggling to understand Internet strategy. *Health Industry Today*, 1999(11): pp. 1–18.
145. ePharm 5, Diabetes association e-mails to seek donors, deliver health info, *ePharm 5*. 6/3/2002.
146. A. Peres, Measurable quality is the bait for savvy consumers. *Managed Healthcare*, 2000. **10**(9): pp. 44–6.
147. J. Mack, *Frontiers of health services management*. 2000, Ann Arbor.
148. Boston Consulting Group, *Patients, physicians and the internet: myth, reality and implications*. 2001.
149. L. Landro, Health care goes digital, *Wall Street Journal*. 10/6/2002.
150. J. Bentivoglio, Unleash the Internet; Outdated laws and regulations are holding back advanced in e-health ventures. *Modern Healthcare*, 2000. November: p. 76.
151. D. Bellandi, Transformation in small doses. *Modern Healthcare*, 2000 (May Supplement): p. 48.
152. eyeforpharma, *Pfizer joins Microsoft, IBM to form Amicore and wire doc practices*. 2001, last accessed 27/12/2001, www.eyeforpharma.com.
153. ePharm 5, Thompson calls e-Rx effort 'a significant step', *ePharm 5*. 10/4/2002.
154. B. Janoff, Bill of Health. *Progressive Grocer*, 2000. **79**(3): pp. 76–8.
155. ePharm 5, Florida pharmacy board proposes rules to restrict web Rx ordering, *ePharm 5*. 14/6/2002.
156. ePharm 5, Calif. cites 2 druggists, store for $88.7 million over web Rx sales, *ePharm 5*. 30/5/2002.
157. ePharmaceuticals, *Government backs mail order drugs in Germany*. 2002, last accessed 3/4/2002, www.epdaily.com.
158. ePharmaceuticals, *Seven drug firms offer discount to low income medicare patients*. 2002, last accessed 26/6/2002, www.epdaily.com.
159. ePharmaceuticals, *Seniors line up for Pfizer drug savings*. 2002, last accessed 26/6/2002, www.epdaily.com.
160. W. Cooper, Drug Wars, Episode Two: The Health Plans Strike Back. *Pharmaceutical Executive*, 2000. **20**(5): pp. 110–14.
161. C. Huttin, Drug price divergence in Europe: regulatory aspects. *Health Affairs*, 1999. **18**(3): pp. 254–9.
162. M. Casey, MedUnite Hopes to Become the 'ATM System' for Healthcare Business, *Medical Industry Today*. 21/11/2000.
163. ePharm 5, The top health management stories in 2001 from ePharmaceuticals (TM), *ePharm 5*. 28/12/2001.
164. eyeforpharma, *Biotech firm develops FDA-approved dosing system for PDA or PC*. 2001, last accessed 19/10/2001, www.eyeforpharma.com.
165. M.K. McGee, MedUnite's protocol: less is more for easy data access. 2002, *Information Week*. 27/5/2002.
166. ePharm 5, Highmark's web-based insurance plan falls short of expectations, *ePharm 5*. 11/4/2002.
167. A. Adomeit, A. Baur, and R. Salfeld, A new model for disease management. *McKinsey Quarterly*, 2001. **4**.

168. L. Landro, Computer programs help physicians track chronically ill patients, *Wall Street Journal*. 4/1/2002.
169. ePharm 5, 'E-Cleveland clinic' to start providing second opinions via the web, *ePharm 5*. 30/1/2002.
170. D.F. Tate, R.R. Wing and R.A. Winett, Using internet technology to deliver a behavioral weight loss program. *JAMA*, 2001. **285**(9): pp. 1172–7.
171. ePharm 5, Study: email group discussions decrease back pain, doctor visits, *ePharm 5*. 10/4/2002.
172. R.B. Jones et al., Randomised trial of personalised computer based information for patients with schizophrenia. *British Medical Journal*, 2001. **322**: pp. 835–40.
173. ePharm 5, Top ehealth consumers stories in 2001 from ePharmaceuticals (TM), *ePharm 5*. 26/12/2001.
174. Pfizer, *Governor Bush declares Pfizer, Florida Agency for Health Care Administration's Medicaid program on target*. 2002, last accessed 9/5/2002, www.pfizer.com.
175. R. Gold, S. Hensley and J. James, Pfizer avoids pressure on prices by helping Florida on Medicaid, *Wall Street Journal*. 9/7/2001.
176. ePharm 5, Top policy and regulation stories in 2001 from ePharmaceuticals (TM). 31/12/2001.
177. G. Eysenbach, Consumer health informatics. *British Medical Journal*, 2000. **320**: pp. 1713–16.
178. ePharm 5, *Austria to issue e-health insurance cards: Germany is taking note*. *ePharm 5*. 21/2/2002.
179. T. Palu, Personal Communication.
180. S.H. Woolf, The need for perspective in evidence based medicine. *JAMA*, 1999. **282**(24): pp. 2358–65.
181. eyeforpharma, *WSJ survey shows lack of doctor access to latest treatment info*. 2001, last accessed 30/10/2001, www.eyeforpharma.com.
182. M. Holmes-Rovner et al., Patient choice modules for summaries of clinical effectiveness: a proposal. *British Medical Journal*, 2001. **322**: pp. 664–7.
183. D. Ranii, Web site uses artificial intelligence to give doctors advice, *The News & Observer*. 3/9/2001.
184. ePharm 5, Heart association and Nexcura launch online cardio decision tool, *ePharm 5*. 21/3/2002.
185. A.A. Montgomery et al., Evaluation of a computer based clinical decision support system and risk chart for management of hypertension in primary care: randomised controlled trial. *British Medical Journal*, 2000. **320**: pp. 686–90.
186. R. Wootton, Recent advances: telemedicine. *British Medical Journal*, 2001. **323**: pp. 557–60.
187. R. Wootton et al., Multicenter randomised control trial comparing real time teledermatology with conventional outpatient dermatological care: societal cost-benefit analysis. *British Medical Journal*, 2000. **320**: pp. 1252–6.
188. Harris Interactive, *Patient/physician online communication: many patients want it, would pay for it, and it would influence their choice of doctors and health plans*. 2002.

189. ePharmaceuticals, *An internet startup claims it is the first company to diagnose and treat common conditions, sight unseen*. 2002, last accessed 26/6/2002, www.epdaily.com.
190. A. Carrns, Medem to enable physicians to charge for online 'visits', *Wall Street Journal*. 17/6/2002.
191. ePharm 5, Roche Diagnostics integrating glucose monitor with online DM tool, *ePharm 5*. 20/3/2002.
192. G. Gillespie, Telemedicine takes aim at the final frontier. *Health Data Management*, 2002. January: p. 88.
193. P. Lehoux et al., The theory behind the use of telemedicine: how compatible with physician's clinical routines? *Social Science & Medicine*, 2002. **54**: pp. 889–904.
194. ePharm 5, Exclusive: GSK follows industry trend, redeploys e-biz expertise, *ePharm 5*. 11/2/2002.
195. M. McDonald and I. Dunbar, *Market segmentation*. 1998, London: Macmillan – now Palgrave Macmillan.
196. W. Smith, Product differentiation and market segmentation as alternative marketing strategies. *Journal of Marketing*, 1956. **21**(3–8 July): p. 5.
197. C. Kuenne and L. Choi, Segment based marketing: from dream to reality. *Pharmaceutical Executive*, 2000. October: pp. 54–68.
198. E. Hutt, R. LeBrun, and T. Mannhardt, Simplifying web segmentation. *McKinsey Quarterly*, 2001(3): pp. 12–18.
199. M. Jones, S. Greenfield and C. Bradley, Prescribing new drugs: qualitative study of influences on consultants and general practitioners. *British Medical Journal*, 2001. **323**: pp. 378–86.
200. B. Stern, C. Thompson, and E. Arnold, Narrative analysis of a marketing relationship: the consumer's perspective. *Psychology & Marketing*, 1998. **15**(3): pp. 195–214.
201. K. Knight and J. Ives, Opinion leader development: a neglected area. *International Journal of Medical Marketing*, 2001. **1**(2): pp. 142–7.
202. S. Rangan and R. Adner, *Profitable growth in internet-related business: strategy tales and truth*. INSEAD Working Paper, 2001.
203. ePharmaceuticals, *Worldwide B2B commerce will total $823.4 billion by the end of 2002, eMarketer found, and the strong growth will continue through 2004*. 2002, last accessed 3/11/2001, www.epdaily.com.
204. ePharmaceuticals, *Internet users will top 1 billion in 2005, wireless internet users will reach 48% in 2005*. 2002, last accessed 22/3/2002, www.epdaily.com.
205. K. Philipkoski, Making a language out of ATCG. 2001, *Wired*. 27/6/2001.
206. J. Gillis, Biotech industry developing worldwide standard for data, *Washington Post*. 23/5/2001.
207. Nature Biotechnology, Data mining. *Nature Biotechnology*, 2000. 18S: pp. IT35–6.
208. M. Kreuter, *Tailoring health messages*. 1999, Chicago: Lawrence Erlbaum Associates.
209. Andersen, *Fishtank: personalisation, a non-technical guide*. 2000.

Index

M

N

O

P